D1572272

Uniting Mountain & Plain

Uniting
MOUNTAIN & PLAIN

Cities, Law, and
Environmental
Change along
the Front Range

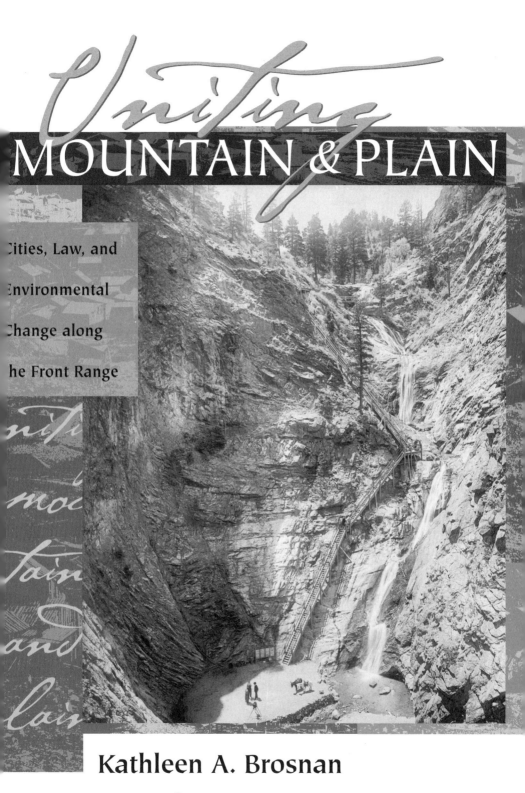

Kathleen A. Brosnan

University of New Mexico Press
Albuquerque

Library of Congress Cataloging-in-Publication Data

Brosnan, Kathleen A., 1960–
Uniting mountain and plain : cities, law, and environmental
change along the front range / Kathleen A. Brosnan. — 1st ed.
p.   cm.
Includes bibliographical references and index.
ISBN 0-8263-2352-9 (alk. paper)
1. Denver (Colo.)—History.
2. Colorado Springs (Colo.)—History.
3. Pueblo (Colo.)—History.
4. Denver (Colo.)—Eco-nomic conditions.
5. Colorado Springs (Colo.)—Economic conditions.
6. Pueblo (Colo.)—Economic conditions.
7. Denver (Colo.)—Environmental conditions.
8. Colorado Springs (Colo.)—Environmental conditions.
9. Pueblo (Colo.)—Environmental conditions.
10. City planning—Colorado—Case studies.
I. Title.

F784.D457B76 2002
978.8'83—dc21

2002007567

TO

MY FAMILY

AND

KATHLEEN NEILS CONZEN

CONTENTS

LIST OF ILLUSTRATIONS

Figures

Maps

ACKNOWLEDGMENTS

A S I contemplate the path that this project followed over the years, I am reminded of the many obligations I incurred. Like many first books, this one emerged from my dissertation. At the University of Chicago, I worked with outstanding professors who daily offered new intellectual challenges. I am particularly grateful to my dissertation committee. Kathleen Neils Conzen, the committee chair, has been a teacher, colleague, and friend. Her unfailingly critical eye and her constant encouragement made this project possible. Kathy is the mentor we all hope to find in graduate school and aspire to emulate in our careers. William Novak's ability to discern the larger themes underlying my work proved essential and his unbridled enthusiasm kept me going when my own lagged. I worked with Michael Conzen on the dissertation and on other projects that expanded my professional horizons, and through his intro-duction to historical geography, reexamined how I interpret the world.

The University of Chicago's Department of History attracts talented graduate students whose intellect is matched by their generosity. Gabi Arredondo, Andrew Cohen, Jonathan Keyes, Andrew Sandoval-Strauss, and many others supported me in my academic career. The heroic Drew Digby and Cathleen Cahill read large parts of the dissertation and manuscript. Diane Brady and David Goodwine in the history office always offered good cheer. With the support of Ted Steck and the Environmental Studies Committee, I was privileged to teach the first environmental history course at the University of Chicago. I thank my fellow Maroons.

The University of Chicago financially supported my graduate educa-tion and research with Century Scholarships, the Von Holst Prize, and the Harry Barnard Dissertation Fellowship, which his family generously sup-ports. Additionally, the American Historical Association's Littleton-Griswold Research Grant helped finance time in Colorado. Richard White, Jim Grossman, the Newberry Library, and the American Library Association invited me to work on other projects that deepened my under-standing of the West. I appreciate the kind assistance and amazing talents of the staff members at the Colorado Historical Society, the Colorado State Archives, the Denver Public Library, and the Regenstein Library at the University of Chicago. The University of Tennessee SARIF-EPPE fund supported the creation of a map by Wendi Lee Arms. My thanks to both.

My intellectual debts are numerous. I presented aspects of this book at various conferences and received insightful comments from Carol O'Connor, John Findlay, David Goldfield, James Connolly, and Ari Kelman. Among the many scholars whose work shaped my ideas are William Cronon, Timothy Mahoney, Donald Worster, Donald Pisani, William Robbins, Elliott West, Carl Abbott, Howard Lamar, and Tom Noel.

As a new professor, it is difficult to imagine better colleagues than I found at the University of Tennessee. Lorri Glover is a true and wonderful friend who always makes me laugh. She, J. B. Finger, and Steve Ash read the manuscript and guided this novice through the intricacies of publishing. Their suggestions strengthened the arguments and the writing, while I alone remain responsible for any flaws. Bruce Wheeler's commitment to the department and the American musical is awe inspiring. Palmira Brummett is a good friend with good advice. Tom Burman, Jeff Sahadeo, Todd Diacon, Vejas Liulevicius, Janis Appier, Kim Harrison, Penny Hamilton, Shirley Walker, and the other Volunteers make every day in the office fun.

I am grateful to the editors and the anonymous reader at the University of New Mexico for their support and criticisms. Durwood Ball took a chance on a first-time author. David Holtby, Evelyn Schlatter, and Floyce Alexander saw me through the completion of this project. And thanks to Katherine Osburn for the first word to the editors.

Many good friends grace my life. Special thanks to Kathy Schurr, the Brittons, the Quinlans, the Brismans, Patty Stewart, and Kay Cessna. I owe my greatest debt to my family—Joe and Colleen, Peter and Betsy, Tim and Barb, Mary Clare and Tom. They offered unstinting moral support when others might have questioned the changes I made in my life. They remain my inspiration. Words are insufficient to express my gratitude.

dreams - hang on this guy?

INTRODUCTION

Twenty-four-year-old Henry Porter left Atchison, Kansas, for Denver in 1862. Like many other talented young men, he saw opportunity in the frontier town along the front range of the Rocky Mountains. Recognizing the young city's role as the regional entrepôt, Porter hoped to make his fortune in freighting and merchandising there. He soon expanded into telegraphing and joined other residents in a local railroad when the Union Pacific left Denver off the transcontinental line and threatened their city's existence. Over the decades, he owned ranches and general stores in Colorado, New Mexico, and Arizona and orchards and residential lots in Los Angeles. Porter became vice-president of the Denver National Bank, directed the Trinidad National Bank, and had international dealings in Mexico and England. Among other charitable contributions, he donated one million dollars for the construction of a Denver hospital.[1] Porter's career illustrates the dynamic and innovative ways in which Denver's entrepreneurs seized control of the region's nascent economy following the discovery of gold in 1858. They diverged into new commercial activities and extended the city's influence over hinterlands throughout the West and across international borders. At the same time, these urban leaders remained committed to the welfare of their communities, sometimes sacrificing personal profit for a lasting social legacy.

Porter's Denver stood at the intersection of the Rocky Mountains and the Great Plains. Denver and its front range cohorts, Colorado Springs and Pueblo, became cities of nature. Their growth and survival depended on the extraction, processing, and marketing of the region's natural capital—precious metals, industrial ores, livestock, produce. More than this, residents viewed their cities as natural phenomena, destined to greatness by geography and joined in some unwritten birthright with the ecosystems from which this capital flowed. Denver, Colorado Springs, and Pueblo provide the geographical focus for this book, but their history contains implications that

what does that mean?

So China

1

*broader
Themes -
representent
Use*

transcend the region. Their struggles for control defined a new United
States in the latter half of the nineteenth century: cities' control over
diverse hinterlands; local entrepreneurial control over outside investment dollars; regulated societies' control over laissez-faire capitalism;
and humans' control over their physical world. These same tensions
shaped the transformation from a nation of disparate traditional agrarian communities to a modern urban industrial society.

This contested transformation in the Rocky Mountains and on the
adjacent plains was an urban story. Like Chicago three decades earlier,
Denver quickly emerged as a "nature's metropolis." It dominated key
financial, transportation, and communication functions that, in turn,
enabled its entrepreneurs to develop fledgling mining, agricultural,
and industrial hinterlands and to rapidly and permanently alter their
environments. Cities such as Denver became hubs of market activity
and places of cultural interactions; they belong at the center of our
understanding of the American West.[2] Yet, in emphasizing urban
primacy and the preeminence of a particular metropolis, it is important to recognize that the metropolis did not exist in an urban vacuum.
Hierarchical relations with other cities and towns defined Denver's
ascendancy as much as its control of resource-rich hinterlands.[3]
Colorado Springs and Pueblo, for example, sometimes competed with
Denver to control certain sectors of an increasingly integrated, specialized regional economy, but more frequently filled roles that complemented the primary entrepôt. Associates in the hinterlands, including
often transient mining towns and smaller, permanent agricultural
communities, performed more limited functions.[4]

Front-range entrepreneurs, like Porter, managed an urban system
on the periphery of a national and international economy that had
turned toward industrialism. On this western frontier, the extension of
an urban-based economy allowed for the assimilation of such marginal
areas. Before 1858, the Rocky Mountains remained loosely bound to
the country's expanding market economy. This sparsely populated
region was distant from the core geographically, economically, and
socially, but activities there involved more complexity than most nineteenth-century commentators acknowledged. On the adjacent plains,
the Cheyennes and Arapahos participated in commercial bison

*argument
for
urban
reading*

no environmentalism *no determinism* (handwritten annotation)

hunting for decades. Ute communities of the western slope bartered at Bent's Fort and in Taos, as did European and American traders. New Mexico established a few isolated agricultural settlements in the arid San Luis Valley.[5] The U.S. Army scattered forts throughout the region after 1848, but few Americans envisioned a basis for urban, agricultural, or industrial growth in the seemingly desolate landscape. Migrants to Oregon or California bypassed the barriers they saw in the "Great American Desert" of the plains and the high mountains just beyond.

Of course, a human geography existed in the region, defined by the ability of those who lived there to hunt, farm, trade, and otherwise sustain their communities. This natural, cultural, and historical geography resulted from actions by their ancestors and themselves. Environmental constraints influenced, but never dictated, its conception. Over the next four decades, following the discovery of gold, the physical environments of the region underwent more radical and rapid alterations than in a millennium of Native American inhabitation. Settlers by the tens of thousands flooded the area, bringing new cultural perceptions of how natural resources could sustain and promote different economies and societies. They manipulated the environment to conform to these perceptions and their material needs. Once barriers, the mountains became a source of precious metals, industrial ores, and reservoir water. The plains, long conceived as a desert, emerged as an endless grazing pasture or an irrigated farming factory feeding the region's growing population and worlds beyond.[7] *nice phrase* (handwritten annotation)

The concentrated capital that flowed through Denver and later through Colorado Springs and Pueblo proved essential to the realization of these new environmental visions. Entrepreneurs recruited investments, and in turn linked the region to the capital-rich cities of the eastern United States and Europe. Regional residents, however, determined how, when, and where the money was applied. Both the opportunities provided and the limitations imposed by nineteenth-century technology allowed local actors to control information about investment options, and consequently, to make their cities more than conduits for outside capital. These entrepreneurs developed their own vision of a regional empire, and sought to enhance its competitive

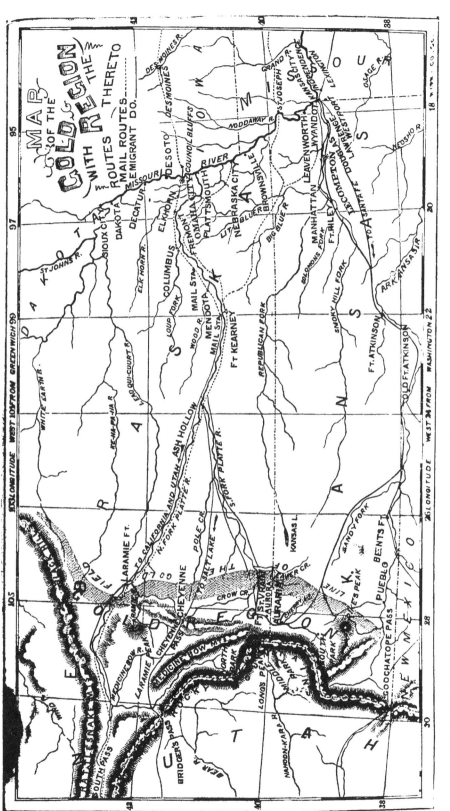

Map 1. The Gold Region. *Although not yet visible on this early 1859 map, Denver soon dominated these mines, and front range entrepreneurs eventually spread their influence across the Rockies and the Rio Grande valley. Map from Wm. N. Byers and Jno. H. Kellom, A Hand Book to the Gold Fields of Nebraska and Kansas (1859). Courtesy of the Denver Public Library.*

position within the larger economy, in part, by reorienting industries along a broadly defined north-south axis and investing throughout the western United States, Mexico, and Central and South America.[8]

Yet their vision left little room for perceived "outsiders." In a common nineteenth-century story, Americans treated longtime residents as outsiders, removing or marginalizing Native American and Hispano societies. Using racist assumptions about the superior productivity of American industry and the benefits of private property, Denverites justified the annexation of Indian and Hispano land, water, and other resources. Dominance over these "outsiders" also demonstrated that these new urban dwellers controlled their world. The timing and speed of these usurpations depended upon the ability of the cities to spread their economic influence over the more distant, but ever-shrinking hinterlands populated by these marginalized groups. As their clout grew, Denverites simply removed the human occupants and drew their lands into the city's regional network. A sense of region and its inherent linkages facilitated human and resource exploitation. Growth along the front range and in the adjacent hinterlands was interrelated. Urban members constituted interdependent units bound by economic and social interactions; a significant change for one unit necessitated adjustments by others. Denver, Colorado Springs, and Pueblo developed differently because of their residents' unique talents and because the cities performed distinct functions within the urban system.[9] As roles changed, due to internal tensions or external pressures, front-range entrepreneurs developed increasingly more remote and diverse hinterlands, redefined new resources as commodities, and reorganized populations and physical spaces to create fresh linkages between the region and distant markets. Key

The model offered here uses cities and urban systems to define the region because urbanization remained the central synthetic means, dynamic over space and time, through which modern life emerged on the periphery and the region became less peripheral. Integrating the realities of this particular place with the broader processes that shaped the nation as a whole provides an illustrative framework to explain changing economic roles, interdependent relations, and environmental conversions.[10] This model embraces many variables, but the most important in determining the hierarchical order of urban places was a city's capacity to control exchanges within the region and between the region and distant markets by dominating transportation, communications, and finance. Links with the new urbanites' places of origin and with centers of capital enhanced these exchanges. The order of urban settlement also influenced which city ascended. The West rarely involved a gradual, bottom-up urbanization process; instead, the highest-ranking member, in this case, Denver, consolidated its role at an early date and promoted other regional communities with vigor. At the same time, nineteenth-century cultures of technological advancement and institutional innovation, such as those in manufacturing, corporate structure, and American law, promoted rapid diversification and integration among cities. Finally, entrepreneurial skill in the utilization of an area's raw resources within these new cultures helped define the region's place within the broader society and economy.[11]

Nineteenth-century legal innovations expanded economic opportunities for those who controlled or enjoyed access to capital. The values of the marketplace charged the new American society and its law, guiding resource usage and making new enterprises feasible. For example, changes in corporate law allowed for more concentrated investments. In turn, this capital bought for regional smelters the new technology that gave once difficult-to-reduce ores value as commodities. The capitalist principles inherent in most laws, more than environmental limitations, structured the newcomers' relations with their physical world and cities' relations with their hinterlands.[12] The notion of an all-consuming market revolution has attracted scholars, yet stretching this paradigm too far diminishes its value as an explanatory tool and obscures the more complex nature of the society that emerged at the base of the Rocky Mountains. There, on the economic periphery, the law took myriad forms. Many legal institutions and judicial decisions reflected an instrumental approach that facilitated market exploitation. At the same time, however, self-governing community organizations and quasi-legal trade associations abounded. Tenets of localism and systems of self-imposed regulation persisted into the 1890s. The transition to a modern capitalist society in this region was contested, inconsistent, and incomplete. Miners, farmers, and even state court judges regularly *"by a scholar for scholars" not a holiday gift* *students*

turned to traditional legal principles that protected local economic interests and community welfare against outsiders with more dynamic property interests and concentrated capital.[13]

However, even in those areas in the Denver region where more communitarian values competed with or coexisted with capitalist principles, far-reaching transformations of the physical environments occurred. Whatever economic and legal philosophies undergirded choices by local actors, they held the unexamined conviction that nature should be harnessed to serve humans and their material needs.[14] Eager to achieve autonomy and become competitive within the larger economy, residents used resources more rapidly and more destructively than they might have under a simple market system geared toward long-term profits. In their eagerness to compete nationally and internationally, entrepreneurs and other new settlers failed to recognize the environmental depredations they launched. They assumed that they held sway over their physical world. In time, they found their control illusory. The imposition of new human geographies brought unanticipated environmental changes and exponential devastation. In the end, it limited future activities designed to expand the region's economic bases.

Similarly, local actors' control over many aspects of their economy proved, if not delusive, short-lived. As the twentieth century began, they watched their corporate ventures fall prey to the eastern oligopolies that now dominated many of the nation's industries.[15] The struggles for urban control over hinterland development, local entrepreneurial control over outside investments, and a regulated society's control over laissez-faire capitalism created the tensions that spurred regional growth, defined cities' functions, and redistributed natural resources and the wealth they spawned. This regional transformation was contentious. By 1903, many tensions were resolved, but to the dismay of regional actors, often in favor of the modern capitalist order and outside corporate interests.

In many ways, the city of Denver dominates this narrative just as it dominated regional urban growth and environmental change. In what might be called a system of urban primogeniture. Denverites emerged early and never let go. The city became the center for directing people, resources, information, and capital into and out of the region. The first three chapters of this book focus on Denver's usurpation and maintenance of key control exchange functions and the mining frontier; its removal of supposedly "disruptive" Indian populations; and its creation, in both propaganda and reality, of an agricultural hinterland on the plains. Denver reigned, and thus, plays a preponderant role in this book.

Nonetheless, a full understanding of the environmental, legal, and social consequences of imposing a new regional urban order in the last four decades of the nineteenth century requires consideration of Denver's urban partners. Chapters 4 and 5 address Colorado Springs and Pueblo and the environmental manipulations involved in their development of new tourist and manufacturing hinterlands, respectively. Founded more than a decade later, Colorado Springs ceded Denver's leadership. Instead, its entrepreneurs carved out a unique niche as a tourist center and a home for rich tubercular patients. Having acquired wealth and prestige through this specialized function, however, the city easily expanded its influence over nearby Cripple Creek following gold discoveries there in the 1890s. Pueblo, on the other hand, developed contemporaneously with Denver and initially competed for regional leadership. Failing in its quest, Pueblo remained a backwater town until entrepreneurs developed it as one of the West's leading centers of smelting, coal, and steel. The next chapter explores the interrelated environmental changes that stretched from the mountains to the plains and examines why the Denverites' authority over their physical world proved incomplete. The epilogue examines the challenges that regional entrepreneurs faced from within by agriculturalists and laborers and from without by the power of concentrated capital.

In the end, efforts to maintain local entrepreneurial control over the region's economy, social order, and natural resources met with mixed success while devastating the surrounding ecosystems and their marginalized peoples. This book unravels the complex connections between city and country, between core and periphery, between law

8

and society, and between humans and the worlds they inhabit—that shaped the contested transition to a modern urban industrial order. It focuses on three front-range cities, but ultimately helps explain the broader processes that shaped the West and the United States as a new century began.

ONE

HOLDING THE PURSE STRINGS

Denver Emerges

*There is no doubt that Denver will always be the great city under
the Rocky Mountains. There will be many other good and healthy
towns but Denver will always be the headquarters.*

William Pierson, 1860

In November 1858, a new town emerged at the confluence of the South
Platte River and Cherry Creek. With only a few buildings, Denver
appeared larger on paper than in reality. William Pierson, however,
proved prophetic. In less than a decade, Denver ascended the region's
urban hierarchy. It monopolized the area's transportation, communications, and financial systems, created diverse tributary spheres, and
linked them to distant markets. Denver gave the region its identity.[1] Its
residents hoped to forge an autonomous economy that competed with
more established areas of the nation, but in their ambitious plans, they
faced a difficult challenge. Extractive industries defined the nascent
economy, and the capital-poor region relied on outside investments to
develop the necessary resources. Yet Denverites controlled much of
their own destiny despite this financial dependence. Building on
strong, experienced entrepreneurial leadership, the city dominated the
flow of capital, information, goods, and people into and out of the
region. Mining camps boomed and busted. Agricultural towns shepherded crops to the larger market. Denver found its *raison d'être* as the
entrepôt and emerged as a great western metropolis.

Denver's leadership, however, was not preordained. With the discovery of gold, Americans anticipated the rapid emergence of a market center along the front range. "Instant cities" arose in the presence of a natural resource worth exploiting and the abrupt introduction of a large population. This entrepôt would guide the commerce from the region's mines, a significant task. Western gold transformed the United States, moving the nation to the center of the world's economy. The question remained which new town would prevail. Denver's physical location offered no particular advantages over its competitors. Nearby placers quickly played out. Golden and Boulder lay closer to the Clear Creek mining camps and valuable coal fields. Colorado City, Cañon City, and Pueblo provided more immediate access to minerals in the Arkansas River Valley.[2] Offshoots of the Oregon and Santa Fe trails extended toward Boulder and Pueblo, respectively, while Denver lacked similar connections. Americans historically built metropolises on major waterways, and as the president of the Denver Chamber of Commerce later observed("of the three cities of the Far West which may be considered as rivals—Kansas City, Omaha, and Denver—the first two have the advantage of navigation by means of the Missouri River." In springtime, the unnavigable South Platte and Cherry Creek became torrents, even flooding Denver in 1864, yet their frequently dry riverbeds provided inadequate water for a large city.[3]

he major river

Denver enjoyed one advantage. In a form of urban primogeniture similar to San Francisco's experience, the city benefited from the fact that it appeared first and rested on the spot of the earliest finds. Newcomers associated Denver with the fortunes that awaited them. Rumors about gold had circulated for decades, even centuries. Spurred by California's success, prospectors spread out across the Rockies in the 1850s. As the summer of 1858 drew to a close, tales of success at the base of the mountains reached across the plains. An army teamster returned east with a small amount of dust from Cherry Creek prospectors. A trader reported that William Russell, who previously prospected in his native Georgia and in California, had uncovered gold near the confluence. These stories found receptive audiences in Missouri River towns badly hurt by the 1857 panic, but anticipating a difficult winter, most emigrants delayed their journeys until spring. Others left immediately, seeking not gold, but to build towns and "mine the miners."[4] Imaginary cities appeared as rivals platted townsites on paper. One of Russell's men observed that "before spring there were perhaps twenty cities . . . as large as New York, minus the wealth, population and buildings." Two towns, which soon merged as Denver, actually took shape. Russell's party abandoned its diggings and joined settlers from Lawrence, Kansas, in the Auraria Town Company on the west side of Cherry Creek on 1 November 1858. Ten days later, William Larimer's Leavenworth group organized the Denver City Town Company on the east side. An experienced urban booster from Kansas, Larimer named his town for its governor, unaware of his recent resignation.[5]

Western land speculators invested in townsites first because they offered greater profits. Shareholders in these two companies received dividends via sales, but many also settled along Cherry Creek as merchants, eager to sell supplies to prospectors. Historian Carol O'Connor argues that market values guided their urban vision almost exclusively. Personal gain remained at the fore, but shareholders acted as more than capitalist ideologues. Residents hoped to build a permanent community, and worked for the *salus populi,* or the people's welfare. The companies donated tracts to social organizations, including churches, schools, and the Masons, and recruited businesses that enhanced their towns' reputations for commerce and sociability. Both Auraria and Denver City invited Omaha newspaper publisher William Byers. Larimer and Byers soon organized Denver's vigilance committee to protect both property and persons from the crime associated with the transient mining population.[6]

As the primary outfitter for the adventurers, Auraria-Denver City offered entry to the mountains. Some twenty thousand people migrated in 1859 alone. Despite initial animosity, residents of both towns recognized their common concerns.[7] The mining frontier had shifted west to Clear Creek and southwest to the headwaters of the Arkansas and South Platte rivers. The Cherry Creek settlements needed to work together to maintain their competitive advantage over towns closer to the mines, and in April 1860, merged as Denver. The new polity regulated water, provided police and fire protection, and enacted civil and criminal ordinances, all for the community's welfare.[8] Consolidation enhanced the city's market position, as local merchants coordinated their efforts. To make Denver a metropolis, they began to build on the foundation of urban primogeniture by controlling exchanges of capital, information, and goods between the region and the East and capturing the region's transportation, communications, and financial systems.

Residents accumulated power in transportation even before the merger. In May 1859, one month before Golden and Colorado City emerged, Denver City secured the region's first overland line by donating fifty-three city lots to the Leavenworth & Pike's Peak Express. It soon offered daily service for passengers, mail, freight, and gold. The Express reached Denver directly on the new Republican River trail, trimming westward travel from twelve to six days. Denver's Ben Holladay bought the company within two years, while Porter relocated his Atchison operations to Denver. The city offered overland shippers one geographic advantage that historians have not considered. Stretching west to Denver, the plains slanted upward an almost imperceptible 18.5 feet per mile. Golden lay twenty miles closer to the camps, but the land between Denver and Golden undulated over a volcanic table and sandstone hills.[9] The topography lacked the steepness of the mountains, but was rougher than the plains. Locating the western terminus in Denver eliminated this difficult terrain at the end of a long journey. Holladay also established the first intraregional lines to the mountains. As the mining frontier expanded, other entrepreneurs surveyed and invested in wagon roads linking Denver with new camps and fuel sources. As the region's primary transshipment point, Denver's merchants built warehouses and determined prices. Teamsters worked regularly, and failed prospectors found employment transferring goods from wagon to wagon.[10]

The city also dominated early communications. On 23 April 1859, Byers published the region's first weekly newspaper, the *Rocky Mountain News*, beating Denver's *Cherry Creek Pioneer* by a half hour. Byers tied his future to Denver, and used his newspaper to recruit potential investors among his old neighbors. By advertising Omaha businesses almost exclusively in early editions, he guaranteed circulation there of his periodical and of information about the emerging entrepôt. Two newspapers gave frontier Denver a valuable edge over its competitors, and Byers's choice of name revealed his city's ambitions. The *Rocky Mountain News* proclaimed Denver spokesman for the region. Western Union confirmed this status in 1863, choosing the city for its regional terminus. Four years later, Byers, Porter, and other Denverites formed United States & Mexico Telegraph to construct the first line along the front range. They could not overcome Western Union's transcontinental monopoly, but planned north-south linkages to future hinterlands in New Mexico, Texas, and Mexico.[11]

Building on their transportation and communications advantages, Denver entrepreneurs participated in regional mining on many levels. Some merchants grubstaked prospectors. Others invested directly in mines or the businesses that served them. Byers platted Central City as a local trading center for the Clear Creek mines. Other Denverites guided outside investors. Merchant George Kassler boasted that eastern capitalists "are turning their attention to and investing some of their surplus Greenbacks in our gold mines. Speculative excitement naturally runs high." Many early prospectors sought deposits in streambeds or along the banks. In theory, placer mining simply involved separating free gold from dirt or gravel. In practice, prospectors employed large scale, rapid production methods. Running water agitated debris through sluice boxes. If water was unavailable, prospectors dug ditches, sometimes bringing it as far as twelve miles over mountainous terrain. Some used boom dams and other expensive hydraulic methods. These complicated operations required cooperative efforts, and increasingly, capital from outside the mining districts.[12]

The mining district, like the polity of Denver, constituted a rudimentary government. Ten years after the California gold rush, the nation still lacked a comprehensive law for lands with precious metals, forcing prospectors to create extralegal systems. Miners took ores for free, and assumed the federal government would extinguish Indian titles and grant them preemptive rights. Among other rules, district codes limited the claim size. By custom, mining claims had smaller borders than agricultural lands because the depth of the lode, not the amount of surface, determined the potential wealth. Smaller

Beautiful
illustrations

Figure 1. Early Placer Mining. Placer miners operating sluices
near Black Hawk, Colorado, illustrate the use of water and
wood resources in what became increasingly more complex
hydraulic operations. *Courtesy of Denver Public Library, Western
History Collection.*

borders also provided greater opportunities for the first wave of prospectors. Early governance remained local, cooperative, and participatory. In front-range towns or mining districts, it imposed self-regulation that both obligated and liberated. With no authorities present, Denver's municipal government initially depended on the cooperation of its citizens, not federal imprimatur. After Congress established Colorado Territory in 1861, most officials stayed in Denver, and mining districts continued to rely on their residents' acceptance of decisions. Market values pervaded the corporate law that facilitated investment in regional mining, but in the camps, the district enforced codes for the welfare of the community. Prospectors generally conformed to expectations. In this way, the mining districts represented the voluntary, democratic associations that Alexis de Tocqueville once celebrated as an American strength.[13]

Mining districts provided more than a stopgap where settlement preceded authorized governments. Prospectors resurrected the form with each new discovery. Mountain District No. 1 in Boulder County and Gregory Diggings in Clear Creek County appeared in 1859; hundreds followed over the next forty years. The first federal mining law in 1866 continued free access to minerals, which some historians contend represented a commitment to economic liberalism, but localism and community values persisted because district codes still defined surveys, patents, and claims. Consequently, the law and the districts it now sanctioned represented both promotion and regulation.[14] While gratuitous resource exploitation supported economic growth and individual gain, a district acted as a regulatory commission, ensuring systematic land use, creating early opportunities, and protecting its members from claim jumpers and, temporarily, from the intrusion of outside capital.

Placers played out early in most districts, and as the industry turned to lode mining in the early 1860s, dependence on foreign investments rose commensurately. With technology and enough capital, hard-rock mining promised greater profits. Lodes carried more ore and higher quality ore, but, locked within rock formations deep in the earth, it proved more difficult to retrieve.[15] A Clear Creek prospector described the rigors involved:

[Veins] are enclosed between two perpendicular walls,
rocks running parallel with the vein and composed of
hard granite structures. A lead may indicate a crevice
of say 3 feet and may retain that width to the depth of
20 or 30 feet . . . Workmen go down until the cap rock
closed over the whole. This cap rock is usually about
20 feet thick, stratified granite but I have known a few
cases were forty and even sixty feet thick. This must
be penetrated before the lead is again found.[16]

Once ore reached the surface, the gold needed to be separated from
the quartz rock. Initially, giant stones pulverized the rocks, but
mechanical stamp mills soon offered a slightly better profit margin.
Denver's Jerome Chaffee, the largest investor in Central City's Bobtail
Mine, one of the world's richest, established the first mill in 1859 with
his partner Eben Smith. Within five years, more than three hundred
mills appeared across the mountains. Mill owner Samuel Mallory
doubled his capacity in one year, observing in 1860 that "there is any
quantity of quartz near us, and we have already had application to
crush it."[17] While an improvement, mills still lost valuable ore.

Lode mining and the search for better refining processes drove
the recruitment of additional investors. Denver became the focus for
the capital that flowed into the region. Given its urban primogeniture,
the city attracted more and more capable bankers. In March 1859,
Clark, Gruber and Company of Leavenworth opened in Denver the
only regional bank that minted private coins for circulation, received
deposits, and honored checks. One newspaper reported:

[T]he fact that a reliable and substantial firm has
transported the extensive and costly machinery
requisite for this undertaking, and useless for all other
purposes, from one seacoast to the base of the Rocky
Mountains, and put it in operation here, will be a
sufficient guarantee for the extent and permanency of
our mineral resources.[18]

Expressing concerns about disruptions in gold shipments due to the Civil War and potential Indian attacks, Clark, Gruber soon petitioned the federal government to buy its minting operation. Local entrepreneurs sent a supportive memorial, arguing that, since the amount of gold coined in the territory increased 350 percent in 1860, it was

> evident that the whole range of the Rocky Mountains is more or less impregnated with the precious metal and [Denver] enjoys a central position from North to South along said range . . . [I]n view of the risk, delay, and inconvenience of shipping gold such a great distance for coinage it offers the best location.

In May 1863, Congress bought Clark, Gruber's operation and established the U.S. Branch Mint at Denver, the first such federal facility outside Philadelphia.[19]

Seeking another competitive advantage, Denverites flooded the federal comptroller with applications for a national bank that could issue currency. The region experienced constant cash shortages. Despite inquiries from other towns, the comptroller awarded Clark and Company (formerly Clark, Gruber) the First National Bank of Denver in 1864. Indicative of the city's growing influence, this institution's holdings exceeded those of the only other national banks west of the Missouri River in Leavenworth and Omaha.[20] The bank brought Denver greater financial security and increased its entrepreneurs' ability to reach distant investors. Bank shares were sold in the principal cities of the United States and Europe and lax federal examiners gave local managers great discretion on investments and loans. Within a decade, ten more national banks appeared in Colorado, including four in Denver, while the First National remained the largest federal financial institution in the West. Joseph Thatcher abandoned his Central City bank for the Denver National Bank. Omaha's Kountze brothers initially established facilities in Central City and Denver in the early 1860s, but soon concentrated on their front-range operation which, in 1866, became the Colorado National Bank. Since the Kountzes managed the First National Bank of Omaha and a New York financial house, their Denver facility easily recruited capital from Missouri River towns and eastern cities.[21]

*Figure 2. The Denver Mint. The first U.S. mint west of
Philadelphia stood at the end of Market Street in Denver with its
tower, battlements, and flag. It symbolized Denver's growing
financial power within the region. Photograph by Joseph Collier.
Courtesy of Denver Public Library, Western History Collection.*

The First National Bank of Denver confirmed the growing preeminence of local men in regional financial matters. Two founders hailed from Kansas, but the other officers and directors resided nearby. Jerome Chaffee (president), Henry Rogers, George Clark, and Charles Cook came from Denver and Eben Smith and Bela Buell from Central City. "This smacks of business," the *Rocky Mountain News* remarked, "and speaks like a whole volume devoted to Colorado interests. It tells well for the enterprise and loyalty of our businessmen, and supplies a necessity that has long existed." Within a few months, the Kansas men sold their stock. The directors added Denver's David Moffat, in whom Chaffee and Smith found a capable partner.[22] Moffat and Chaffee brought banking experience from New York City and Midwestern frontier towns. Chaffee had worked for railroads and town companies. Using the First National to access information on viable properties and secure capital for their ventures, the trio dominated Colorado mining for decades and made investments across the West.

With the mint and the national bank, Denver's future seemed secure, but by 1867, the entrepreneurs who envisioned a great metropolis faced their gravest challenge—the loss of the transcontinental railroad. Colorado's first territorial governor, William Gilpin, later explained that "to the very existence of civilized communities the railroad has become almost as much a necessity as is the circulation of the blood to the individual." Denverites could realize their dreams only if rails replaced wagon trails. Railroads traditionally ran to established towns, and as Denver was the largest front-range community, residents hoped that the Union Pacific Railroad would repeat this pattern. Their aspirations confronted the reality that surveyors long believed that the steep cliffs west of Denver represented too great an obstacle to construction. Grenville Dodge, chief engineer and later Union Pacific president, previously encountered a blizzard there, and advised the railroad to build "in Wyoming where the hills were tamer." Nonetheless, since Cheyenne remained a cow town with a third of Denver's population, news that the railroad selected their northern neighbor as the terminus shocked Denverites. Cheyenne's leaders boasted of Denver's imminent demise.[23]

Other urban competitors used the railroad crisis to challenge Denver's hegemony. Resentful neighbors long objected to the entrepôt's citizens assuming that they spoke for the region. Golden's William Loveland organized the Colorado Central Railroad in 1867 to connect his city with the Union Pacific at Cheyenne and to separate Denver from the East.[24] The rivalry between Denver and Golden derived from both economic and political competition, with the territory's Republican Party divided between cliques from each. Golden captured the territorial capital and its accompanying business in 1864, but Denver's leaders convinced the federal government to permanently return it three years later. Concerned that Denver would elect the first U.S. senators, Golden's clique blocked the larger city's statehood petitions between 1864 and 1870. In the midst of this competition, Loveland requested funds that Arapahoe County previously raised by floating railroad construction bonds. Denver voters vetoed his claim. Failing to raise sufficient capital elsewhere, Loveland ceded the Colorado Central in 1868 in the misguided hope that the Union Pacific would begin construction and assist Golden. The Union Pacific delayed nine more years.[25]

In 1867, of course, Denver's leaders did not know that Loveland would fail. To save their city, they tried to secure another rail line, the Union Pacific Eastern Division. Moving west from Kansas City, however, the Eastern Division faced bankruptcy. Its managers threatened to bypass Denver unless the city paid the railroad one million dollars. Denverites rejected the blackmail. Having lost these two railroads, Denver's decline seemed inevitable until William Byers and John Evans, the former territorial governor and an experienced Illinois railroad builder, called a public meeting on 13 November 1867 that reinvigorated the city:

> The people of Denver saw that the trade that had given their city importance, and concentrated capital at that point, must soon be diverted to Cheyenne on the north, and some point on the Eastern Division road to the southeast, thus building up rival cities . . . It was under these circumstances that the Board of Trade of the city of Denver resolved to depend upon others no longer.

21

With the Board's support, Evans, Byers, Moffat, Porter, and others associated with the First National Bank incorporated the Denver Pacific
Railway to build the city's own Cheyenne connection. Within one day,
in sums from 50 dollars to 10,000 dollars, Denverites launched the
company with 280,000 dollars and secured their city's future.[26]

Denver's strong entrepreneurs had outmaneuvered their rivals
once again. Their railroad broke ground in May 1868. Parallel to the
South Platte for half its distance, the Denver Pacific traveled through
potentially valuable farmland. By lobbying old allies in Congress,
Evans garnered a forty-mile land grant along this route. Like the
managers of the Union Pacific, Denver businessmen formed an associated land company. Sales raised additional construction capital and
expanded the city's agricultural hinterland. The Union Pacific agreed
to lay part of the Denver Pacific track, but, when it failed to do so,
Evans personally assumed the remainder of the financing. The Denver
Pacific opened for business in June 1870. Evans discharged debts
incurred in its construction through the Kansas Pacific Railway.
Instead of paying blackmail, Denver entrepreneurs had assumed
control of the Eastern Division and reorganized it as the Kansas Pacific
in 1868. Evans liaised with Congress to obtain a six-million-acre grant
and, in turn, guaranteed that the Kansas Pacific reached Denver
instead of the city's southern competitors. In seeking investors, the
Kansas Pacific emphasized Denver's diverse hinterlands: "The mountains and pastures of Colorado alone will afford a handsome east-
bound business in coal . . . lumber from the spurs of the Rocky
Mountains and the pinery south of Cedar Point; wool, live stock,
silver and other ores."[27] The Kansas Pacific arrived in Denver in
September 1870. With Denver's railroads secured and his own
Colorado Central facing delays, even Loveland acknowledged his
rival's ascendancy, opting to lay track that connected Denver, through
Golden, with the Clear County mining camps later that same year. As
one visitor observed, "the Territory is awaking wonderful prospects,
and Denver has added a quarter to her population since I was here last
year. The three railroads which now center here will work wonders."[28]

The response to the railroad crisis constituted a transcendent
moment. A few merchants initially fled to Cheyenne, but the majority

joined Denver's financiers and mining entrepreneurs in this urban survival strategy. Nothing guaranteed the success of Denver's new railroads; across the nation, local lines frequently failed. Although associated with the First National Bank, successful investors such as Chaffee and Moffat could have withdrawn their money and managed their properties from Cheyenne. They chose to bind their fortunes to Denver.[29] The decision involved complex motives. The Board of Trade and the railroads represented a commitment to community consistent with the *salus populi,* and suggested that the obligations of a regulated society need not be conservative. Their society emphasized progress over stagnation. This sense of public purpose coexisted with market values that shaped economic interactions. Yet these initiatives highlighted their ability to control capital. Along the front range, only Denver could make local railroads a reality. Its entrepreneurs accumulated sufficient resources and maintained the essential connections with eastern capitalists and Washington politicians. And, while they risked much, the potential for profit remained great.

The new railroads also changed the city's orientation to the national economy. In 1867, with few exceptions, the country's business followed an east-west alignment. People traveled along the transcontinental railroad, and communications via Western Union. Trains carried the West's natural resources to eastern manufactories and returned with finished products. When Union Pacific officers left Denver off this most important axis, its citizens recognized that regardless of their immediate reliance on outside capital, autonomy must be their goal. They envisioned enhancing their nascent empire's competitiveness in the global marketplace through the integration of increasingly more distant hinterlands. The Kansas Pacific provided a vital eastward link and Denverites regularly recruited eastern investors, but the Denver Pacific suggested the possible benefits of conducting business on a north-south axis.[30] Over the next four decades, new regional railroads and other industries physically forged this reorientation. By the 1870s, for example, Denver and Pueblo smelters drew ores from the entire Rocky Mountain range which, along with the Rio Grande, defined the new economic arc.

Just as Denver stood at its crossroads in 1867, mining entrepreneurs contemplated an important transition. The predominant shift to lode mining brought a greater reliance on corporate financing, heavy equipment, and the expertise of engineers and metallurgists. These required substantial money, but after the Civil War, investments ebbed because mechanical stamp mills failed to separate enough metal to cover the greater expenses. A newcomer finally solved the problem. Nathaniel Hill, a Brown University chemistry professor, traveled west in 1864 to survey Gilpin's mineral lands and investigate mining opportunities for eastern capitalists. After personally investing in mines, Hill traveled to Swansea, Wales, where he learned how to reduce crushed rock by concentrating gold ores on copper mattes under extreme heat. Backed by Boston investors, he began the Boston & Colorado Smelting Company in 1867 in Black Hawk, Colorado. With Hill's smelters, the Rockies yielded more valuable commodities. One prospector observed, "The expense of getting mills out here and the uncertainty of having poor quartz together with continual experimenting has ruined many. Now all feel confident and the great secret of saving gold has at last been discovered."[31]

Denver dominated the new boom launched by the smelters. With the city's strong financial institutions, its businessmen recruited and guided investments, increasingly employing the more flexible corporate structure. With few restrictions on entry, duration, and management, the corporation became the dominant form of commercial organization, allowing entrepreneurs to release their creative energies. Its economies of scale and mobility of capital proved particularly vital to the Denver region given the scarcity of cash. The corporate form also protected Denverites from personal liability when some mines failed. By controlling information on mining opportunities, often gained through the First National Bank, men such as Chaffee, Smith, and Moffat influenced where, how, and when outside capital was applied. At the same time, Denver-based mining corporations established branch offices in New York, Chicago, St. Louis, Philadelphia, and Baltimore. Denver also dominated linkages within the region, with its residents offering an array of services that supported mining.[32]

Hill's smelter cemented mining's centrality in the region's economy. In addition to many foreign investments, mining accounted for 40 percent of Colorado's domestic corporations by 1873. Unfortunately for

Figure 3. *The Region's First Smelter. Nathaniel Hill's Boston &*
Colorado smelter with the large black smokestack occupies the near
foreground. Other processing mills cover the creek and denuded hills,
but the refining process introduced by Hill in 1867 gave regional ores
new viability as commodities. Photograph by W. G. Chamberlain.
Courtesy of Denver Public Library, Western History Collection.

regional mining interests, a financial panic swept the nation that same year due, in part, to eastern bankers' use of short-term credits for railroad expansion. Within two years authorized stock in Colorado mining dropped 71 percent.[33] Cash shortages undermined investments across the country, but the precipitous decline in mining stock suggested an even greater hesitancy to participate in highly speculative ventures during difficult financial times. This boded poorly for mining camps that performed one urban function. While Denver's leaders took steps to diversify the region's economy, the city's ties to mining left it similarly vulnerable. Its fortunes ebbed and flowed with the industry.

The national depression lingered for six years, but carbonate silver discoveries in 1877 provided a true bonanza that attracted new investors to regional mines. Strikes in old camps like Oro City, rechristened as Leadville, and new ones such as Aspen, Silverton, and Creede, fixed the region as the nation's leading producer of both gold and silver. The number and size of corporate holdings grew commensurately, aided by the fact that the territorial legislature had eased already lax regulations on entry one year earlier.[34] Denver entrepreneurs promoted their own mining properties, and participated in trade associations that boosted the whole region. Financial success, they believed, flowed from an expansive metropolitan economy. As the president of the Chamber of Commerce later espoused, "The growth of a city really depends upon its relation to its tributary country and upon the character of that country and its population." Thus, Byers organized the Territorial Board of Immigration, Charles Kountze participated in the Colorado Industrial Exposition Association, and others served with the Denver Manufacturing and Mercantile Bureau.[35]

In this new era of carbonate silver, Denverites possessed the requisite experience, expertise, and access to information to remain at the forefront. Henry Wolcott, the Boston and Colorado's manager and a mining investor, summarized the situation: "Formed a connection two or three years ago with some New York and Boston men that has been growing more intimate ever since. They are men of great wealth and are too willing to invest any amount of money upon my recommendation." Denver's mining entrepreneurs acted as more than conduits for outside capital. The Bald Mountain Mining Company, for example, maintained offices in New York, drawing many shareholders from there, New Jersey, and Massachusetts. Officers of the First National Bank of Denver, however, issued its stock and managed the mines. Other entrepreneurs pooled their own capital, developing projects primarily with local financing. Regardless of the origin of the capital, Denver's share of the corporate wealth rose. Between 1883 and 1886, for example, two-fifths of all domestic and foreign corporations registered in Colorado, holding 65 percent of the state's capitalization and with operations across the West, headquartered in Denver.[36]

Chaffee, Moffat, and Smith embodied Denver's dominance. In some combination or another, this trio organized more than one hundred mining ventures, initiating their partnership with the Caribou silver mine in Boulder County. In a typical pattern, mining engineer Smith assessed the Caribou's potential while Chaffee and Moffat recruited a group of Dutch shareholders. The First National Bank underwrote the shareholders' almost three-million-dollar investment. After securing this capital, Chaffee started rumors that the lode offered a small yield. Unwilling to throw good money after bad, the Dutch investors closed the mine. The Denver trio formed a new corporation and purchased the Caribou at a sheriff's sale for seventy thousand dollars. Under Smith's management, they realized substantial dividends for three years and then sold their stock for almost one million dollars to New York investors, retaining a small interest. At the same time, the First National Bank, now under Moffat's presidency, acquired promissory notes on adjacent claims. Within a year, new gossip circulated about the Caribou's declining yield. Most New York investors sold their shares, and the Denver partners suddenly held the largest block of stock. After the bank called the notes on the adjacent properties, the trio merged them with the Caribou, and Moffat reported the viability of the combined claims. Stock prices rose and the trio sold their shares for a large profit, leaving behind overvalued, played-out properties. Businessmen across the nation commonly used such predatory, yet legal practices.[37]

This trio soon played a major role in the carbonate silver boom. In 1878, Chaffee bought the claim adjacent to Leadville's richest property, the Little Pittsburgh Mine of Horace Tabor and August Riche. Tabor's rags-to-riches-to-rags story was legendary. Once a Vermont stonecutter and Kansas farmer, he tramped about Colorado camps for twenty years with his wife Augusta, shifting between mining and mercantile activities. In 1877, he grubstaked the Little Pittsburgh prospectors, and with Riche, bought them out before the mine eventually produced more than ten million dollars. The Tabors joined the region's elites in Denver. He served as lieutenant governor and U.S. senator, became a vice-president of the First National Bank, and invested heavily in mining and Denver real estate. One of the nation's wealthiest men in the 1880s, Tabor lost everything when silver bottomed out in 1893. He prospected until friends secured his appointment as Denver's postmaster shortly before his 1899 death.[38]

Chaffee and Moffat partnered with Tabor to buy Riche's share of the Little Pittsburgh in 1878, and backed by the First National Bank, merged it with adjacent claims to control the four most productive mines in Leadville. The partners opened a New York office, and investors leapt at their initial offering of fifty thousand shares at twenty dollars, although the partners retained the controlling interest. As production declined, they delayed an engineering report and sold their shares at thirty dollars. With the report's subsequent release, and to the dismay of other shareholders, stock prices dropped to $7.50. New York prosecutors found the Denverites' dealings more counterfeit than shrewd and tried Chaffee and Moffat for fraud. Despite their trial and subsequent acquittal, they continued to attract investors. The Denver partners generated profits for many depending on the timing of their stock purchases and sales. Moffat's bank presidency and Chaffee's service as a U.S. senator supported their good reputations. R. G. Dun & Company called Chaffee a "straightforward, upright businessman, worthy of unlimited credit" and Moffat a "man of excellent character and capacity."[39]

To expand their Leadville interests, the Denver trio sought London subscribers in 1882 for the Henriett and Maid of Erin Mines on the basis of Moffat's reputation. A British solicitor commented that "in securing his services the new company obtains the best guarantee of success, independent of the large supply of ore in reserve." In 1887,

Moffat and his Denver partners reorganized these properties under a new corporation. Even with an influx of fresh British money, Moffat, Smith, Tabor, and Kassler remained the corporate officers. Chaffee had died the year before, but as executor of his estate, Moffat conveyed Chaffee's interests to a joint trust through which he managed the Denverites' majority holdings. When deeper veins called for greater expenditures, the partners sold their stock to English investors for a large profit.[40] Moffat, Smith, and Chaffee, before his death, turned the security of the First National Bank to other camps. Aspen boomed in 1884 with the discovery of a rich vein and the rapid influx of Denver money. In addition to managing mines, the Denver partners began to vertically integrate operations, practices they would employ in other districts. Greater profits could be realized if they controlled the source of the ore, reduction works, transportation systems, and ancillary services. In Aspen, they formed the Deep Mining and Drainage Company. Moffat and Smith invested in thirty-five mines and the Woring-Lexington smelter at Rico, and in the 1890s, financed a Leadville smelter.[41] *good stuff*

Aspen also provided the arena to test the 1872 federal mining law. Under the law, prospectors still claimed federal land without paying for minerals, but Congress tried to replace the diverse regulatory codes of individual districts with uniform standards, including the apex doctrine. Under this doctrine, the claimant who located his claim at the top of an exposed vein, its apex, possessed the right to follow the continuous vein, even under others' surface claims. Most districts simply ignored the law. Leadville juries hostile to its monopolistic potential rejected the apex principle. Districts clung to the sideline principle that allowed miners to take ore from veins underneath their surface claims. With more than five hundred claims filed, Aspen residents similarly resisted. David Hyman, a Cincinnati lawyer who settled in Aspen, owned the Durant, which covered the apex vein in Aspen mountain. In 1885, he sued Jerome Wheeler, the owner of the claim that sidelined the Durant, for ore that Wheeler removed from the vein. Denver mining investor Albert Reynolds financed Hyman's litigation, extracting a quarter-interest in Hyman's properties. Since only two Aspen claims covered the vein, most residents supported

fascinating

Figure 4. Aspen. *This camp became the arena for the
litigation of the apex doctrine. This photograph reveals
the frame mill buildings, iron smokestacks, log retaining*

walls, and tailings common to all mining communities.
Photograph by William Henry Jackson. Courtesy of Denver Public
Library, Western History Collection.

Wheeler.[42] In theory, the sideline seemed to represent a more equitable, regulated society in which no individual unfairly disadvantaged others. It provided more opportunities for more people. The apex doctrine, on the other hand, allowed the wealthiest a monopoly and signaled an end to community prosperity.

Jack Atkinson, who had labored in Colorado mines since 1860, complained that "the trouble is Reynolds and Hyman, capitalists and men of that ilk, nonresidents of Pitkin county say 'you miners have developed a good thing over there; we have got more money than you miners and we will try and take your claims away from you.'" Atkinson's comments contained some irony. Hyman lived in Aspen and actively participated in its civic affairs. His opponent, Wheeler, lived in Colorado Springs and New York. Wheeler married Randall Macy's daughter in 1870, but lacking any authority in the family business, sought other ventures. Two years after Hyman had arrived, Wheeler created a vertically integrated operation in Aspen mines, smelters, and banks and the Colorado Midland Railroad. He owned 25 percent of the New York-incorporated Aspen Mining and Smelting Company; New York investors controlled the rest.[43] Wheeler had little in common with Aspen residents who lionized him.

Given the earlier verdicts in Leadville, the Pitkin County court stunned Aspen residents when it ruled for Hyman and upheld the apex. Of course, by the time Wheeler unsuccessfully appealed in federal court in Denver, the actual litigants reached a compromise that protected the wealthiest investors on both sides. Nonetheless, the verdict held implications that few historians have considered. The apex doctrine promoted those who possessed the greatest potential for dynamic production, and effectively placed the interests of individual property ahead of community welfare. To some historians, the law that promulgated the apex doctrine continued economic liberalism by privatizing resources and redistributing wealth.[44] Its erratic enforcement was more revealing. Although enacted in 1872, no court enforced the apex doctrine until 1886, and well into the next decade, prospectors created districts that adhered to local customs. Many regional residents, like Atkinson, invoked the equity of a regulated society in their criticism of the doctrine. In their litigation, however,

Hyman acted not as a capitalist ideologue nor Wheeler as a proponent of localism and traditional values. More complicated, more pragmatic motives guided them. Other entrepreneurs realized that, more than anything else, the imposition of the apex principle meant expensive, time-consuming litigation. Denver's Dunbar Wright, for example, owned the Park-Regent Mine over an apex vein. When owners of an adjacent claim threatened a lawsuit, he simply bought them out. Avoiding the cost of litigation mattered more than establishing the primacy of market principles embodied in the federal law.[45]

Local entrepreneurs and distant investors contested similar transitions in the region's transportation systems. New railroads extended Denver's reach to every western mining frontier and to increasingly diverse hinterlands. The city blossomed and its population soared to more than 106,000 by 1890. William Jackson Palmer had launched the Denver & Rio Grande Railroad, the most successful regional line in the early 1870s. Like the Denver men, Palmer envisioned "a natural economic unit in a long longitudinal productive area." With new avenues for interregional and international trade, he argued, the thousand-mile haul from St. Louis offered a

> natural tariff protection for the native production of the Colorado-New Mexico area. Thus, a self-sufficient western empire would develop around Colorado whose natural commercial orientation would be toward Mexico City by way of settled communities at the base of the Rockies and down the Rio Grande Valley.[46]

John Evans founded other railroads that competed with Palmer's, but also attempted to reorient the region's economy and diminish its dependence on the East. With the Denver, South Park & Pacific, he hoped to reach Leadville, and then run along the Arkansas River toward the San Luis Valley, the San Juan mines, and the Pacific Ocean. Evans proved particularly adept in securing local investments: "I tell the merchants and capitalists of Denver that I am under no more obligation to build the South Park road than they and if they want it they must help . . . I tell my associates that there is no use of going away from Denver for the money and that we will have to get it right here." When the Atchison, Topeka & Santa Fe Railroad reached Pueblo in 1876, Evans played on fears that Denver's trade might be diverted southward. He wrote his wife, "we have got the thing before the people in such shape that it is regarded as a matter of life and death with Denver." With a substantial domestic investment, he successfully sold his railroad's bonds in London.[47]

Evans vied with the Denver & Rio Grande for Leadville traffic, while Jerome Wheeler's Colorado Midland challenged Palmer for Aspen. Regional railroads regularly competed for access to new camps, but miners rarely waited for them. Prospectors continuously scoured the mountains for the next big lode, and settlements appeared with each new discovery. Since counties lacked construction funds, enterprising individuals converted narrow paths into wagon roads and reaped quick profits. These private roads fulfilled an important market function, but community values persisted in various forms. When exorbitant charges or poor maintenance occurred, counties assumed control of, or otherwise regulated, toll roads for the welfare of the community. This authority to remedy malfeasance, even on private highways, undergirded traditional American law.[48] Hard-rock districts reached peak production after railroads arrived, but toll roads sustained camps for years. The Denver & Rio Grande reached Leadville more than three years after the first silver finds, and along with the Colorado Midland, took almost eight years to connect Aspen. Rails finalized the integration of existing hinterlands into distant economies.[49]

Mining towns performed an important function in the regional urban system, but their trade remained tied to one volatile extractive activity. Physical settings limited options. The surrounding terrain precluded commercial agriculture, and tightly contained towns attracted few manufacturers. Black Hawk prospered as the site of the first smelter, but became just another mining camp after Hill moved his plant to Denver in 1878. While many factors influenced his departure, the inability to expand facilities played a role. The narrow gulch afforded only one street, and back doors literally opened into walls of solid rock. Mining towns also housed the region's more transient elements. Despite systems of self-government and participatory

34

democracy, failed prospectors regularly departed for new digs. Successful miners and entrepreneurs, such as Tabor, headed to Denver with its friendlier climate, cultural amenities, and access to capital.[50]

When a series of national and international events rocked the region's mining towns and Denver in the 1890s, the carbonate silver boom ended abruptly. The crisis began, in part, with a 1873 federal decision to stop coining the silver dollar because the price of silver had risen to $1.15 an ounce, and people hoarded coins. The United States followed most European nations in adopting a gold standard since the price of gold rarely fluctuated. In 1878, following the carbonate discoveries, western congressmen pressed the Bland-Allison Act, requiring the government to purchase two million ounces of silver each month at market prices. During the 1880s, as Colorado, Nevada, and Montana mines overproduced silver, the government purchased only this minimum amount. By 1889, the market price fell to ninety-four cents. Given the region's dependence on mining, its entire economy suffered. Total investments in Colorado peaked at just under one billion dollars in 1881, but declined to less than seventy-seven million dollars nine years later. In response to these conditions, Colorado's Senator Teller helped enact the Sherman Silver Purchase Act to increase the government's monthly purchases. Mining rebounded briefly, but by 1892, silver dropped to eighty-seven cents.[51] When the national depression hit the next year, more than five hundred banks closed nationally and unemployment soared. Many interrelated factors sparked the depression, including overexpansion of railroads, an agriculture slump, and the collapse of British investments in the United States, but westerners blamed the demonetization of silver. To their chagrin, President Cleveland successfully sought the repeal of the Sherman Silver Purchase Act, hoping to secure the gold standard and prevent the collapse of the treasury's reserves. Silver reached new lows, and twelve Denver banks closed. Moffat kept the First National Bank open by securing its debts with his own resources. Within one year, 337 local businesses failed, 435 mines closed, and 45,000 regional residents lost their jobs. Tabor's fall from power epitomized the region's tumble.[52]

Gold discoveries at Cripple Creek salvaged the regional economy in the 1890s. Given its proximity to the new district, Colorado Springs emerged as a financial and wholesaling entrepôt for the mines, but Denver and Moffat and Smith remained at the fore of corporate investments. They used systems of vertical integration, developed in earlier camps, to control the profit-making machinery of mining and its attendant industries. The partners first purchased the Anaconda and Victor Mines with loans from the First National Bank. By overcapitalizing, or establishing for their company a greater value than needed, they recruited funds for additional projects. With absentee investors and misconceptions about the costs of mining technology, this was a common practice. Moffat and Smith owned two Cripple Creek banks, sold town lots, stripped the surrounding forests, and participated in some twenty companies engaged in mining, reduction, or drainage. They realized their greatest success with the Florence and Cripple Creek Railroad and Reduction Works Company. The pair refused to ship, or allow any partners to ship, ore on the Colorado Midland, hauling it instead two additional miles to their terminus. Smith, of course, owned the dray line.[53] At Cripple Creek, Moffat and Smith again demonstrated the ability of local entrepreneurs to control capital by controlling information. They "appropriated," from a British company awaiting a U.S. patent, a cyanide process that recovered almost 98 percent of the gold. When their Metallic Extraction Company expanded its stock in 1897 and British investors balked at purchasing more at par value, the duo simply printed excess shares at lower prices to ensure more smaller purchases and their majority control. After working the Victor Mine for early dividends, Moffat and Smith sold it to Boston investors. The First National Bank held liens against the mine that it immediately exercised against the new owners to force a sheriff's sale, where Moffat and Smith repurchased the mine debt-free at a bargain price.[54]

Moffat and his partners typified Denver entrepreneurs who invested their own money, recruited outside capital, and utilized personal ties to financial institutions to dominate almost every Rocky Mountain mining district. Walter Cheesman, a director of the First National Bank and Moffat's frequent investor, controlled the Smuggler, one of Leadville's most profitable mines. He also invested in Aspen, Central City, and Creede, diversified in mills, smelters, and Leadville real estate, and served as president of the First National Bank of Aspen. Reynolds, the financier who supported Hyman, owned or invested in more than three hundred properties in most Colorado mining communities and others across the Rockies. With Joseph Thatcher of the Denver National Bank, he seized the Pueblo Smelting and Refining Company from Boston investors. Reynolds, who began as a merchant and rancher, succeeded because of his ability to mobilize outside capital.[55] James Dexter first tried prospecting near Central City, but moved to Denver in 1872 to form the Union Bank of Denver. In frequent partnerships with Thatcher, Dexter secured investments from distant capitalists who relied on his mining expertise and technological knowledge.[56] When properties opened in the southwestern San Juan Mountains in the 1880s, Tabor underwrote the Bank of Gunnison and the Bank of Crested Butte. A decade later, Dennis Sullivan used insider information from the First National Bank of Denver to purchase abandoned Cripple Creek mines and others in receivership.[57]

As Denver expanded its population and financial strength, city entrepreneurs reached beyond Colorado and mining. Denver banks supported their ventures in urban subregions across the West. Travel guides linked Santa Fe trade to Colorado's front-range cities. Denver realtor A. G. Bowes invested in Salt Lake City and Ogden real estate. Kountze used his position with the Colorado National Bank and his brothers' Omaha and New York institutions to buy mines and other land in Nebraska, Texas, Montana, Nevada, Alaska, and California. Smith's Mine and Smelter Supply Company operated plants in Denver, Salt Lake City, El Paso, and Mexico City. Through purchasing Mexican land grants, Porter owned ranches and general stores in New Mexico and Arizona. He bought Mexican silver bonds and sold them to a London concern. He developed orchards and residential lots in Los Angeles in 1893, utilizing that city's original charter regarding water rights to double his land.[58]

While their international influence never matched that of San Francisco's elites, Kountze and other entrepreneurs organized coal, timber, mining, and irrigation projects in Mexico and Nicaragua.[59] Geographically centered within the United States, Denver's railroads gave the landlocked city access to foreign markets. In the 1880s,

Evans organized the Denver & New Orleans, later known as the Denver, Texas & Gulf, which shifted traffic away from East Coast power centers toward the ports at Galveston and New Orleans.[60] Before his financial collapse, Tabor's investment company opened offices in London, Amsterdam, Paris, and New York and organized mining investments in Central and South America. Yet, like other entrepreneurs grounded in nineteenth-century community values, Tabor maintained a strong commitment to the Denver region. In addition to serving as president of the Chamber, he invested money locally when greater profits were available elsewhere, and left a permanent legacy with the Tabor Opera House in Leadville and the Tabor Block in Denver.[61]

Tabor acted much like Moffat, Chaffee, Byers, Evans, and the other entrepreneurs who initially secured Denver's position atop the urban hierarchy and continuously developed new tributary spheres for the emerging metropolis. By controlling regional finances, communications, and transportation, the city surpassed urban rivals and dominated mining across the Rockies. Market values underlay the entrepreneurs' decisions. They believed in redistributing wealth to men like themselves who put natural resources to their most dynamic, productive uses. They sought an autonomous economy, but also hoped to bequeath a thriving, stable society as a testament. Many committed their fortunes to the welfare of the community in the early days when there was no guarantee of financial success. These entrepreneurs, along with prospectors in the mountains, co-opted elements of traditional societies that preserved local independence and self-governance, initially created greater opportunities for fellow citizens, and benefited society as a whole. On other occasions, such as the apex fight, they encountered regional actors who possessed different notions of an equitable society. As a consequence, the region witnessed a gradual, frequently contested transition to a modern capitalist order.

TWO

VANQUISHING THE INDIANS

Denver Clears the Plains

(handwritten note: " Writes in financial section of paper " places like)

The benefit to Colorado of that massacre, as they call it, was very great for it ridded the plains of the Indians.

John Evans, 1884

Gold provided the immediate impetus for the large migration to Denver and its mining camps. Yet, from the city's earliest days, its boosters recognized that minerals alone would not ensure their prosperity nor their posterity. A diversified, and thus more competitive and autonomous, economy required a viable agricultural sector. Moreover, urbanites believed that farmers and their families provided a social stability badly needed in their raucous frontier town. They hoped to recruit farmers to the region, and to this end, began to rethink the nature of the adjacent plains and to reconsider their relationship with the Native Americans who lived there. Once city residents believed Denver strong enough to expand its hinterlands, they targeted the Indians. When the federal government hesitated to act, they organized a territorial militia to control their own destiny. They violently enforced their new regional vision that had no room for Indians, as Evans revealed in subsequent comments about Sand Creek. Denverites permanently altered the human landscape of the plains, facilitating the entrance of agriculturalists whose crops and livestock changed native ecosystems and linked the plains to distant markets. While other historians have addressed the social and cultural

(handwritten margin notes: "actually Oct for"; "need to know")

tensions within the weakening tribes, this chapter addresses the relation between urban expansion and Indian removal and examines the
market values and communitarian aspirations that underlay Denver's
strategy.[1]

Eastern Americans lacked a cultural context to understand the
varied life forms sustained by the plains or the socioeconomic systems
that Indians developed there. Zebulon Pike compared the grasslands
to "the sandy deserts of Africa." Major Stephen Long described them
as "almost wholly unfit for cultivation, and of course uninhabitable by
a people depending upon agriculture for their subsistence." His maps
bore the misnomer "the Great American Desert," and textbooks
repeated it for generations. Emigrants to California and Oregon scur-
ried across the seemingly hostile terrain. Early travelers to Denver
echoed such assessments. Peter Scott found the plains "all alkali
having an appearance as if salt were sowed," while Frank Hall judged
farming an unlikely activity. As he approached Denver, Nathaniel Hill
noted, "For the last 300 miles, the principal production of the soil is
the prickly pear." Outside Pueblo, he wrote, "The soil is as dry as our
carpets." Even William Byers, an early promoter of regional agriculture, confessed, "the dry dusty plains were uninviting to all and
discouraging to the husbandman."[2]

Denverites, however, quickly began to reinterpret the plains.
American traditions suggested that farmers vitalized a competitive
urban economy. Agriculture, Byers contended, offered "the only means
by which our mines can be developed, for unless we can become self-
sustaining, we may not hope that the necessities of life can be furnished
here at rates that will warrant extensive mining operations." In the
decades that followed, new arrivals imposed their agrarian schemes,
filled with the rhetoric of manifest destiny, by introducing new animals,
plants, and irrigation systems to the plains. The Denverites who had
pushed for this diversification made the city their permanent home.
Farming would improve their economy, but of equal importance, they
accepted the common notion that farmers supplied what Byers called
the "conservative element of all national and political and social
growth." Such sentiments stretched across the country and its history.
Thomas Jefferson, for example, opined that working the soil nurtured

the virtue, competency, and independence essential to a free govern-ment.[3] Denverites assumed that tillers brought about a better civiliza-tion through the productive taming of wilderness, the regenerative force of land, and the construction of schools, libraries, and other institu-tions of social maturation.[4] Whether the myth matched reality, many nineteenth-century Americans believed that a viable, egalitarian soci-ety depended on widespread landownership by farmers.

Another aspect of the agricultural economy convinced Denver residents that it would secure their community welfare. Frontier farms involved families, and depended on women's productive and repro-ductive efforts. During the early gold rush, the region possessed a predominantly male and transient white population. In June 1859, one emigrant found only five white women in Denver. A 1860 census identified sixteen hundred women in the territory, but men outnum-bered them twenty to one.[5] Bachelor societies, such as Denver and its mining camps, engendered some violence. Disgruntled prospectors filled the front-range city where the ready availability of firearms and alcohol precipitated confrontations, although dime novels later exag-gerated their frequency and mortality. In 1859, Byers personally rented a building for the city jail, and with Denver's founder, William Larimer, established vigilance committees to address crime. With these commit-tees standing in lieu of an official police force, Denver adopted the antebellum era's narrower, more organic conception of "police" as governance for the public welfare.[6] As entrepreneurs, these men valued the protection of property, but their quasi-legal associations also instilled habits of restraint and self-control, represented the nascent origins of municipal governance, and attempted to reorder the community by imposing a public morality. Denverites' continuous promotion of agriculture confirms the importance of these nonmarket objectives. Farm families seemed to offer a benign, civilizing influence as a counterpoint to the rowdy masculine frontier. Women and chil-dren changed the moral climate as well as the demographics. Thus, both market values and tenets of a regulated society defined Denver's drive for an agrarian hinterland.[7]

Frontier entrepôts became dynamic centers of social change. If no hinterland existed for a city like Denver to dominate, it created one.

Regional farming and ranching had begun almost immediately, but on a small scale along the South Platte, the Arkansas, and their tributaries. Some newcomers came west specifically to feed the miners. In other cases, prospectors abandoned unproductive claims for farming. In 1859, David Wall grew vegetables outside Golden, drawing Clear Creek water through an irrigation ditch. Thomas Skerritt settled two 160-acre tracts three miles south of Denver that same year and bought more farmland beside Cherry Creek. In 1861, Irving Howbert gave up mining to farm near Colorado City. The Hodgson family claimed squatters' rights along the South Platte forty miles northeast of Denver, later legalizing their homestead. George Hodgson remembered that "within ten miles, the white population consisted of about ten pioneer families." Farmers prepared fields about one-half mile deep along streams that flowed from the mountains and provided dependable water. Small ranches fed cattle off the rich native grasses that surrounded creeks with more erratic flows. Overall, however, production lagged. The region depended more and more on Nebraska and Kansas agriculturalists.[8]

Urban boosters hoped to guarantee immediate sustenance, but made grander plans for their hinterland. Believing commercial agriculture vital to long-distance trade, Denverites looked to the "empty" plains east of their city, rethought the nature of this land, and took the promotional lead, forming the first Colorado Agricultural Society as early as 1859. Byers's editorials extolled the newly discovered agrarian possibilities of the plains. The *Denver Tribune's* Robert Strahorn published the *Colorado Agricultural and Stock Journal* celebrating (and exaggerating) the limited successes of early farms and ranches. Books and pamphlets designed to attract prospectors and mining investors devoted chapters to the potential profits of piedmont and plains agriculture. The Denver Board of Trade joined the chorus shortly after its founding, issuing a call to stock growers:

> innumerable herds of Buffalo, elk, antelope and deer which have from time immemorial subsisted by pasturage alone on these plains, suggest that they will not only be capable of furnishing stock and wool needed for a dense population within the territory, but also for a large portion of the continent.[9]

farming obstacles

These boosters rarely outlined the obstacles that the prospective farmer or rancher faced. Despite the high prices their food brought, local agriculturalists struggled to turn a profit because of the small size of their crops and herds and the difficulties of transport to mining camps prior to the railroads. Climatic events also undermined their efforts. The flood that hit Denver in 1864 washed away Skerritt's Cherry Creek farm. Observing the high waters of the South Platte, Hall wrote:

> [T]he river is in ordinary times a very harmless insignificant muddy stream . . . but [the flood left] only a small tract of land [from] which our farmers obtain their vegetables, hay, corn and other little articles of subsistence . . . Our agricultural resources are very limited and owing to our tremendous floods can only be cultivated with extreme care and much risk.

Engorged streams deluged narrow, steeply sloped piedmont lands almost every spring, highlighting their finite capacities and the need to expand agriculture onto the plains.[10]

At the same time, in the East and the Midwest, the Civil War "siphoned off" young laborers and increased the demand for farm products, raising both wages and prices. Denverites advertised the benefits of the plains, but easterners saw little incentive in abandoning profitable conditions for the uncertainty of farming in the "Great American Desert." More significantly, and regardless of the boosters' protestations to the contrary, people already occupied the plains. The Cheyenne and Arapaho Indians lived and worked on the land that Denverites coveted. Consequently, to realize their metropolitan dreams, local entrepreneurs faced two tasks. They needed to change prevailing American perceptions of the plains and lure a large contingent of farmers. Before they could embed the commercial agricultural sector that might follow, they needed to rid the plains of the human element that threatened their vision.[11] To this end, the city orchestrated a virulent rhetorical campaign against the Indians that culminated in violence and their removal.

In 1858, three primary Indian groups lived in the area that became Colorado. They possessed strikingly different human geographies than the newcomers who soon wanted to supplant them. The Utes had lived in the region the longest. Having long abandoned farming for hunting, they frequently participated in the bison market and regularly traded in Santa Fe. The western slope that the Utes called home initially held little appeal to most Americans and Mexicans. Although the Grand River (now the "Colorado") drained the Colorado Plateau and the Rio Grande flowed through Southern Ute territory, grasslands intermingled with sagebrush, and areas distant from riparian zones appeared desert-like. The Utes survived by hunting the mule deer and elk that frequented the interspersed montane parks. The surrounding mountains offered forests of aspens and ponderosa and lodgepole pines, and allowed the Indians to supplement their diet with fruits, nuts, and other plants. When the Utes ventured to the plains east of the Rockies in search of more bison, they experienced a very disparate physical environment, rarely seeing trees and shrubs. Grama and buffalo grasses (shallow-rooted plants indigenous to areas with little moisture) dominated the vegetation, feeding bison and antelope and providing forage for horses.[12]

The Utes encountered two Indian societies there. The Southern Cheyennes and Arapahos lived as one on the plains, between the North Platte and the Arkansas in what later became southeastern Wyoming and eastern Colorado. One Arapaho man observed that his people joined with the Cheyennes against common enemies and because "our religions, our stories, our way of doing things in camp and on the hunt and the warpath were very much alike." These Plains Indians hunted in extended family units, relying on bison for food, shelter, clothing, and tools. After 1820, the fur trade more than doubled the human population of the plains, as revolutionary market forces shaped new migrations. The Cheyennes and Arapahos fought intermittently with the Utes or the Kiowas and Comanches for territory, but rarely with American, Mexican, or European trappers and traders.[13]

With the appearance of American traders such as William Bent and Charles St. Vrain, the Arapahos, Cheyennes, and Utes became willing market participants and less dependent on the products of the local ecosystems. In exchange for beaver pelts and bison robes,

Indians received flour, textiles, liquor, lead, powder, axes, rifles, and knives. When the beaver market collapsed in 1838, traders built forts to treat and store bulkier bison robes. Indians performed all the labor-intensive chores in this culturally stimulating economy, but the profits flowed to the traders. Within the Plains Indians' societies, many of these new tasks became women's responsibilities. Just as Denverites in the 1860s thought the women of farm families would contribute to their cultural development, Native American women played vital roles in the economics and diplomacy of the fur trade. French, English, and American trappers frequently married into Indian communities, creating what historian Elliott West calls "bridges of kinship" that stabilized trade linkages.[14]

The bison economy, however, proved short-lived and undermined the herds. By the early 1850s, the market declined and traders deserted the forts. The Arapahos and Cheyennes faced greater challenges, spending half the year in near-starvation while anticipating the supernatural return of large numbers of bison. The gap between the Indians' faith and their reality was jarring. The animal no longer provided a reliable food source. Incursions by overland emigrants exacerbated the Indians' desperation, and they periodically threatened traffic on the Oregon and Santa Fe trails. The Indians viewed their thefts and less frequent acts of violence as recompense for the destruction of bison and grass. Historians suggest a more complicated story for the bison's decline. Drought, market hunting, cow selectivity, human migrations, bovine diseases, and increased grazing competition combined to diminish the herds.[15]

Isolated confrontations with emigrants prompted the U.S. government, which gained control of the region following the war with Mexico, to create the Upper Platte and Arkansas Indian Agency. Agent Thomas Fitzpatrick, a veteran trapper and trader, helped organize the Fort Laramie Council in 1851 for more than ten thousand Indians. Under the resulting treaty, the Southern Cheyennes and Arapahos received the area from the Continental Divide to western Kansas and Nebraska, and from the North Platte to the Arkansas. Emigrants could still cross the Indians' land, but in return, the treaty required the agent to distribute to the Indians fifty thousand dollars in goods annually for fifteen years. Congress subsequently reduced this to fifteen thousand dollars and rarely provided even that small amount. The Arapaho and Cheyennes continued to hunt bison, relying on the resource even as this dependency undercut their society.[16]

The Utes signed a treaty in 1848 recognizing U.S. sovereignty in exchange for unimpeded access to their traditional homeland. Hispano and white settlers nonetheless moved north from New Mexico to the San Luis Valley, frustrating the Utes with their usurpation of resources.[17] Cattle stealing became a necessary occupation as the fur trade ebbed. Tensions escalated, and on Christmas Eve 1854, an episode known as the "Fort Pueblo Massacre" resulted in the death of eleven settlers. When U.S. soldiers killed forty warriors in retaliation, the Utes agreed to a new treaty that reduced their holdings to the land west of the Continental Divide into Utah, north to the Yampa River, and south to the New Mexico border. The Utes retreated farther into the Rockies, relying on summer hunts for deer and antelope in the high country to compensate for dwindling food supplies. Even with Indians' growing desperation, the region remained relatively peaceful as the 1850s drew to a close.[18]

The gold rush and the cities it spawned challenged this peace. As the fifty-niners charged across Indian lands and as the plains began to play a prominent role in Denver's agrarian promotions, the Cheyennes and Arapahos felt the impact of the new activities more keenly than the Utes. The latter's western-slope home initially held less strategic significance to the newcomers, but disruptions began on the plains immediately. Prospectors worked along the South Platte in the summer of 1858, where the Cheyennes and Arapahos frequently wintered. These bands had dealt with Europeans and Americans for decades, but gold brought greater numbers. The Indians worried about sharing the limited resources of their winter sanctuary with miners and the men laying out city streets. By the end of 1859, with emigrants to and from Denver and the camps exceeding sixty thousand, the Plains Indians found themselves "compressed into a small circle of territory, destitute of food," according to William Bent.[19]

Yet, under the strong leadership of their chiefs, the Cheyennes and Arapahos offered restrained responses to the increasing pressure.

Some engaged in an unbalanced roadside trade with emigrants. The Indians sought things for survival; emigrants wanted souvenirs like moccasins. At other times, some Cheyennes and Arapahos tried to extract tolls from migrants who disrupted the movements of animals and consumed large quantities of water and grass essential to the Indians' survival. Emigrants and Indian agents viewed the tolls as extortion, but most fifty-niners cared more about finding mineral wealth than combating Indians. As long as the Indians did not interrupt the flow of commerce, Denverites left them undisturbed and occasionally welcomed their trade. In May 1860, Byers observed:

> [A] great number of Indians have been in and around town for some days past. They are mostly Arapahos and Cheyennes disposing of Buffalo robes and peltries. They are very orderly and peaceably disposed, but we learn are still able to obtain whiskey some place in town. The man or men who furnish it to them, should be taken in hand by the citizens and put through, as he deserves.[20]

In the city's earliest days, the *Rocky Mountain News* more quickly criticized those who distributed liquor than the drunken Indians, although it rarely mentioned Denver's more frequently besotted white residents. The new arrivals showed little respect for their Indian neighbors. Interactions reflected the racial beliefs of most nineteenth-century Americans. Before the Civil War, growing agitation over the place of African Americans in the nation spilled into the ethnological study of Indians. Some Americans believed in innate human variations, while others argued that environments dictated actions, including missionaries who hoped to "civilize" the Indians. By midcentury, however, many accepted pseudoscientific explanations of racial differences. For example, Charles Caldwell, a professor of natural history, and Samuel George Morton, a physician, contended that Indians' biological deficiencies marked them for extinction.[21] While few Americans actually read these authors, such works filled ideological needs by constructing the illusion that human difference was preordained. Racial divisions permeated American society and justified the self-serving aggression of manifest destiny. According to racist theories, nature doomed nonwhites to subordination or extermination. Racism privileged whites in the social order, as if God chose them to conquer the continent.[22]

Colorado's William Gilpin celebrated Aryan races "that have acquired new territory and have planted new colonies, that have made grand discoveries in the scientific world and have invented machines, that have written books which the world will not willingly let die, and have collected the wisdom of the ages in vast libraries." The people who joined Gilpin in the pursuit of gold assumed the truth of such racist myths and scorned the interracial marriages that previously stabilized the fur trade. These unions once defined power on the plains, but also intimately linked the Indians to the more powerful, less sympathetic white society that arrived after 1858. City builders sought Indian assistance during their first difficult winter, but once Denver and other towns took root, the protective purpose of white-Indian marriages disappeared. The bison trade, which barely sustained the Plains Indians in the preceding decade, sat on the distant periphery of the region's new economic order. Families supported the social stability of both Native American and white communities, but Denverites, anxious to show easterners that their new town was civilized, derogatorily labeled white husbands "squaw men." The newcomers considered how to remove this blight and illustrate their mastery of their physical world and its indigenous people.[23] In the Denver area, as throughout the nation, racist suppositions vindicated the expropriation of Indian lands essential to domination.

Despite the racist assumptions of the white society, timing remained important. As they built their towns and created trading networks, the emigrants initially lacked the strength and desire to suppress the region's Indians, and saw no immediate reason to act. The Utes mostly stayed on the western slope, and the impoverished Cheyennes and Arapahos posed no threat to the city. Indians, as a topic, appeared infrequently in the early editions of the *Rocky Mountain News,* although the few references revealed common racist ideas and nationalist ideologies. The Indians would "melt away" before the "advancing tide" of a "white empire" that replaced its "inferiors, physically, morally, mentally." Samuel Mallory, the stamp-mill operator, concluded that the Indians "all seemed friendly," but he showed little empathy for their dire condition. "They stand in fear of the whites, and seldom trouble them except by their constant begging."[24]

Byers initially argued for restraint and promoted "peaceful relations" with the Indians, suggesting that "a civilized and enlightened people should avoid an aggressive and tyrannous course." Shortly after their arrival, Denverites hoped to encourage investments and migration by diminishing eastern concerns about an Indian menace. Byers squelched rumors about a supposed raid by Cheyennes and Arapahos in August 1860: "We have no doubt that a large party of Indians are in the neighborhood, but have no idea that they mediate any harm, other than their natural dispositions to beg and steal." Byers blamed irresponsible individuals in the white community when confrontations occurred: "[should] a few soulless miscreants, who wish to make favorable bargains with half-drunken savages be permitted to sow firebrands . . . over this now peaceful country?" As late as 1862, Fort Lyon's Colonel Albert G. Boone reported that the new settlers caused most of the Indian-white tensions. "If the government would put a guard around the white people and keep them from shooting Indians, there would be no more Indian troubles."[25]

While hoping to allay fears that might undermine early economic development, Byers and others laid the groundwork for the removal of the Indians at a time when Denverites gained the capacity to control the eastern plains. The Civil War presented them with this opportunity. In an effort to keep the region's gold firmly behind the Union, President Lincoln appointed Gilpin the first governor of the newly formed Colorado Territory in 1861. Gilpin, who explored the region with Frémont in the 1840s and lectured on its viability in the 1850s, was an avowed unionist. Gossip about a possible coalition between the Plains Indians and the Confederacy began almost immediately, but Gilpin worried more about a contingent of Texas Rangers supposedly marching north to join local secessionists. These rumors proved unfounded. More than 70 percent of the region's non-Indian population migrated from northern states and territories, and pro-Union Republicans easily won the 1861 territorial elections. Neither

Confederate guerrillas nor secessionists constituted a true threat. Yet, despite the dearth of evidence concerning a Confederate-Indian alliance, Denverites persistently suggested the possibility, failing to appreciate the irony of comments such as these in the *Rocky Mountain News:*

> We should not forget that there are a few tribes whose restlessness and mischievous disposition may prompt them to accept the propositions of unprincipled men who claim to act on the authority of the Confederacy . . . . A subtle and malignant agent of the Secessionists might succeed in convincing the tribes around us that we are infringing upon their rights.[26]

Roused by such concerns, Gilpin raised a militia in autumn 1861. The First Regiment of Colorado Volunteers arrested a few suspected Southern sympathizers, but saw action in only one battle and it involved no Indians, guerrillas, or secessionists from the region. The Confederates sent regular troops through New Mexico in an ill-fated attempt to seize Colorado's gold. Joining federal troops at Glorieta Pass in March 1862, Major John Chivington and his Colorado Volunteers ensured the Union victory when they cut off Confederate supply lines. A former Methodist minister, Chivington had chosen command over a chaplaincy. Gilpin, however, failed to obtain advance approval for the militia, and when the federal treasury refused to honor bonds he issued for its expenses, Lincoln replaced him with John Evans.[27]

Rumors persisted that Indians in league with the rebels hoarded ammunition, even after the Plains Indians rejected the only known Confederate overture. George Bent, William's half-Cheyenne son, later wrote that

> [S]ome officers try to get Cheyennes, Arapahos, Kiowas, Comanches and Osages to join Texas troops in 1863 to go up the Arkansas and take Forts Lyon and Larned. Some Chiefs . . . had been to Washington and had just got back in spring of 1863, and were told to keep out of war and not to pay any attention to anyone that would try to get them into it, so that stoped [sic] the whole thing.[28]

Although no realistic threat to Denver existed, the rhetoric directed toward Indians changed. The *Rocky Mountain News*, the region's most popular newspaper, shifted from conciliation to antagonism. As the Civil War progressed, Denverites grew more confident of their community's permanence, and focused on removing the Indians. The *News* reprinted stories about Indian violence in distant places, especially the Sioux conflicts in Minnesota in 1862. The Cheyennes and Arapahos initiated no hostilities in the Denver region, but they became "treacherous vagabonds engaged in predatory operations."[29]

Denver's leaders supported Governor Evans's initial plan to extinguish Indian land titles through treaties rather than violence, but by 1863, grew increasingly frustrated with the Arapahos and Cheyennes, whom they perceived as an obstacle to agrarian development. More virulent rhetoric emphasized the Indians' naturally sordid character rather than their corruption by immoral whites. The *News* regularly discussed extermination. Confrontations in nearby New Mexico received substantial attention. According to Denver papers, Americans there fought the Pueblo Indians, "a dissolute, vagabondish, brutal and ungrateful race [that] ought to be wiped from the face of the earth." Byers added that while Colorado's Indians remained "on friendly terms, those best acquainted with Indian character do not guarantee [their] amity and goodwill."[30] When the Utes refused to negotiate a new treaty, he used the occasion to criticize the Plains Indians. A few had robbed some travelers, and although no one was injured, Byers conflated the two events, arguing "the tribes have sworn to exterminate all whites who dare to attempt to settle their country. There is reason to apprehend serious difficulty with the redskin vagabonds, and we cannot be too vigilant and guarded in all our intercourse with them."[31]

The Cheyennes and Arapahos, in turn, worried about the expanding front-range settlements. The new emigrants showed no interest in forging socioeconomic bonds with the Indians. Passenger and freight traffic repeatedly disrupted hunting, and the government rarely provided necessary supplies despite its treaty obligations. The territory's permanent non-Indian population remained around 35,000, but more than another 100,000 crossed the plains to and from Colorado during the Civil War. White hunters, for food or sport, depleted

51

already dwindling game preserves. In response to food shortages, the Cheyennes and Arapahos engaged in isolated episodes of theft from wagon trains and ranches throughout 1863.[32]

Although the Plains Indians and the Denverites disagreed about its provisions, Governor Evans tried to enforce the 1861 Fort Wise Treaty. Evans contended that the pact extinguished the Indians' title to all land except for a small triangular-shaped reservation between the Arkansas River and Sand Creek. He favored moving the Plains Indians to this reservation and teaching them to farm. The Indians believed that the negotiations included their traditional hunting grounds along the headwaters of the Republican and Smoky Hill rivers, and assumed that the government cheated them when Congress finalized the treaty. Most rejected the small reservation. It held insufficient game and they lacked the tools, seeds, skills, and inclination to be farmers.[33] When negotiations failed to secure a binding agreement, Evans besieged Washington with reports of Indian hostility and unanswered requests for military support. The *News* accelerated its rhetorical battle by early 1864. Unfavorable stories about livestock thefts in Colorado and new rumors of a Plains Indian–Confederate alliance filled its pages. Local newspapers regularly called for extermination. Ovando Hollister, the publisher of the *Black Hawk Daily Mining Journal*, joined the campaign, describing the Indians as "wasted creatures . . . baking human excrement on shingles for food." He suggested "utter and speedy extinction as the only cure."[34]

An early campaign for statehood by Republicans in Denver also accelerated tensions. Evans called a constitutional convention as soon as Congress created enabling legislation allowing Colorado, Nebraska, and Nevada to petition for statehood. The Denver clique nominated Chivington for the House and Evans and Golden's Henry Teller for the Senate, hoping the latter's inclusion would mollify criticism of Denver's leadership across the region. In addition to seeking agricultural lands, Evans, Chivington, and Byers promoted the "Indian" problem in an effort to secure a greater federal presence and increase the public's confidence in statehood. Hollister, and his co-editor Frank Hall, led the opposition, arguing that statehood would increase taxes. They agreed that "if there be one idea that should become an axiom in

American politics, it is **That the Red Man Should be Destroyed**," but accused the Denver trio of inciting fears to further its political ambitions.[35] The motives of the Denver clique, however, were more complex than a simple grab for political power. Since arriving in Colorado, Evans had pursued interests that dominated his career in Chicago. In his first official speech, the governor foresaw the development of a railroad and along its tracks, agricultural communities that would supply food for the region's populace and commercial products shipped through Denver to distant markets.[36] Despite a mild slump during the war, Denverites believed their mines vast enough to secure the city's future. Confident of their power to attract more participants and capital, they no longer felt compelled to assuage emigrants' fears or investors' concerns by stressing the peaceful nature of their Indian neighbors. By 1864, Denverites needed land for the large influx of farmers they anticipated. The Indians posed an obstacle, and new policies of violent suppression, relocation, and extermination found a receptive audience in the racist society at the base of the mountains.

At the same time, the circumstances of the Cheyennes and Arapahos worsened. Diphtheria and whooping cough epidemics followed droughts in 1861 and 1863. Cut off from their normal front-range sanctuaries, more militant Cheyenne Dog Soldiers fought with the Utes in the mountains or the Pawnees and Otos to the east to control dwindling resources. Desperate Indians took things from white settlers with greater frequency. Indian Agent Samuel Colley wrote that the only solution was to "place [the Indians] above actual want. Remove from them the necessity of theft—we cannot successfully preach peace and patience to a starving savage." When the government failed to provide the requisite supplies, violence ensued. The Colorado Volunteers who fought at Glorieta Pass had replaced regular army troops at Fort Lyon (formerly Fort Wise). In spring 1864, they clashed with Dog Soldiers accused of stealing four mules. Two Volunteers died. Other minor skirmishes followed, generally when Indian resources ran scarce.[37]

An incident on 11 June 1864 finally provided Denver's leaders with the basis to move decisively against the Cheyennes and Arapahos. Although no one knows how the confrontation began,

Arapahos traveling to a village on the North Platte killed Nathan Hungate, his wife, and two daughters at their ranch thirty miles outside Denver. Hoping to engender public approval and expedite federal support for the creation of a militia, the city's residents displayed the bodies. Byers vividly described the gruesome exhibit:

> It was a solemn sight indeed, to see the mutilated corses [sic], stretched in the stiffness of death upon that wagon bed, first the father, Nathan Hungate, about 30 years of age, with his head scalped and his either cheeks and eyes chopped in as with an axe or tomahawk. Next lay his wife, Ellen, with her head also scalped through from ear to ear. Along side of her lay two small children, one at her right arm and one at her left, with their throats severed completely, so that their handsome heads and pale innocent countenances had to be stuck on, as it were, to preserve the humanity of form. Those that perpetuate such unnatural, brutal butchery as this ought to be hunted to the farthest bounds of these broad plains and burned to the stake alive, was the general remark of the hundreds of spectators this forenoon . . . [38]

These images reinforced for Byers's audience (which extended beyond Denver) the immutability of Indian savagery. Such portrayals of white victims ignored the atrocities committed against the Plains Indians and justified the conquest that followed.[39] The presence of a white mother and children among the victims gave the episode greater poignancy. The possibility of random violence scared Denverites and disrupted economic activity, but the slaughter of white women and children threatened the moral center of the new social order they hoped to create.

Some contemporary observers, however, recognized the purposeful manipulation of white fears in response to the incident. Recent arrival Nathaniel Hill wrote his sister:

> [B]ut the "big scare" (I use the language of the Denverites) I am yet to describe. There is some tragedy

54

mingled with it, but much that is comic. The day after
we arrived here, the bodies of a family of [a] murdered
ranchman were brought in and exposed to view in front
of the Post Office. It was done by authority to excite the
people, so most of them were incredulous in regard to
Indian troubles . . . Well, the Indians occasionally make
a raid on these ranchmen to steal their cattle. They do
not murder them unless they have some revenge to
gratify. The indian [sic] mode of revenge is peculiar. If
any of their men are killed by a white man, they will
kill the first white man they meet. A short time ago
they were attacked by some soldiers. Two or three indians [sic] were killed and 150 ponies taken from them.
It is supposed that they murdered the family from the
double motive of revenge and booty. All day long a
crowd of men, women and children gathered around to
see the dead bodies of the father, mother and two children. They were shot with arrows and scalped. The
desired effect was produced. Everybody was swearing
extermination to the red skin.[40]

Stoking the rhetorical fires, the *News* repeatedly reported an imminent
attack on Denver. No organized Indian band contained enough
members to mount such an assault, but raids on the plains periodically
interrupted the movement of freight and food.[41] Evans used the
Hungate affair to remind Washington that the region needed a greater
military presence, but he did not wait for federal authority to act. The
governor issued a message "To the Friendly Indians of the Plains" to
move to places of safety because "the war on the hostile Indians will
be continued until they are all effectively subdued." At the same time,
Evans sent an "Appeal" to each settlement to organize for its own
protection and announced that "any man who kills a hostile Indian is
a patriot." Evans lacked the authority to declare war or to deputize
urban guards, and he effectively sanctioned murder since he offered no
means to distinguish between friendly and hostile Indians. It also
remained unclear whether the governor's message, printed in various
newspapers, ever reached the Indians. Byers supported the governor's

extralegal edicts: "Self-preservation demands decisive action, and the only way to secure it is to fight them in their own way. A few months of active extermination against the red devils will bring quiet and nothing else will." Finally, on 13 August 1864, Evans received federal approval to organize a voluntary cavalry regiment for one hundred days.[42]

Chivington organized the new Third Regiment as the territory prepared for a 12 September vote on statehood. Despite agreement with Evans's long-range objectives toward the Indians, the *Black Hawk Journal* and other newspapers undermined his credibility by opining that he and Chivington politicized the issue. To counter this, Byers printed the governor's correspondence to show how long Evans worked for a peaceful solution. Instead, the delays evident in the letters raised questions about Evans's influence and whether statehood effectively guaranteed protection. Evans's ticket lost three to one. Events subsequent to the election, however, confirm that the statehood campaign alone fails to explain the antipathy toward the Indians. Denverites continued to call for military action, even as Major Edward Wynkoop, Fort Lyon's commanding officer, escorted seven Arapaho and Cheyenne chiefs to Denver for a peace conference on 28 September 1864. Cut off from the bison, the helpless Indians faced starvation. Their chiefs sought peace. At the conference, Evans blamed the Indians for all hostilities and offered little assistance. Wynkoop, however, asserted his military authority and sent them to a winter camp on the Sand Creek land reserved by the Fort Wise Treaty, presumably under his protection. Denverites criticized Wynkoop's leniency, but with more militant chiefs and their followers at a Smoky Hill camp in Kansas, no substantial nor imminent Indian threat to any Colorado settlement remained by October 1864.[43]

Nonetheless, the region's white population remained committed to a violent resolution. Even citizens who opposed statehood wondered why Chivington's Volunteers, disparaged as the "Bloodless Hundred Dazers," saw no action. Racism comprised the kindling, but Denver's search for an agricultural hinterland provided the essential spark. By 1864, the city possessed the power to absorb the plains, but could not extend its reach to the western slope that the Utes called

Figure 5. Camp Weld Council. In September 1864, just outside Denver, Major Wynkoop (kneeling, front left) met with Arapaho and Cheyenne leaders, including Black Kettle (sitting, center). Wynkoop promised them protection at Sand Creek. Courtesy of Denver Public Library, Western History Collection.

home. Byers distinguished them as friendly Indians.[44] The continued presence of the Plains Indians presented the immediate obstacle to economic growth and community stability; the Utes did not.

Prompted by the quest for more agricultural land, the disparaging comments, and Chivington's desire to recapture lost glory, the Third Regiment pushed into action. Chivington chose to march against Sand Creek instead of the more militant Smoky Hill camp. The Third might have lacked authority to act in Kansas, although Denverites had exceeded their jurisdiction before. Sand Creek presented an easier military target. Over the objections of Fort Lyon's officers, the Third launched a dawn attack against the peaceful camp on 29 November 1864. Chivington claimed 500 Indian casualties, but George Bent, who managed to escape, estimated 163 deaths, including 110 women and children. Outgunned, the few warriors in camp tried to flee. According to Bent, "Black Kettle had a [American] flag up on a long pole, to show the troops that the camp was friendly; then the soldiers opened fire. . . . Men, women and children were lying together and many had already been scalped and mutilated by the Colorado One-hundred-days men. . . . The killing went from dawn to dusk. No prisoners were taken." The Third Regiment raced home where Denverites accepted Chivington's contention that Sand Creek teemed with armed warriors prepared to initiate hostilities. Byers called the attack "the most effective expedition against the Indians ever planned and carried out." Merchant George Kassler remarked that "there were four or five hundred of the copper colored race killed. I do not believe any regiment of hundred day men have done much better." The territorial assembly praised Chivington, and Denverites enthusiastically displayed the Indian scalps.[45]

The members of the First Colorado Cavalry from Fort Lyons who witnessed the event offered a different perspective on the carnage. Lieutenant Colonel Samuel Tappan noted that the Indians "were to all intents and purposes, in law, in equity—prisoners of war, on parole. An attack upon them was in defiance of all law, justice and decency . . . a wanton breach of military discipline and courtesy." With respect to Denver's celebration, he testified, "Nearly, if not all, the women in Denver, approve the massacre of Sand Creek, and applauded the horrible cruelties practiced. If their words and threats could be compounded into deeds, they would excel the most savage of the Indians in brutality and torture."[46] Reports from the First Cavalry, such as James Clancy's accounting of a Third Regiment lieutenant who scalped three women and five children already in custody, prompted an investigation by the Congressional Commission on the Conduct of the War. Wynkoop averred that Chivington incited his troops to "diabolical outrages" and physically threatened officers who tried to intervene. Chivington's aide, Captain Silas Soule, testified against him.[47] Condemned by the commission for having "deliberately planned and executed a foul and dastardly massacre which would have disgraced the veriest savage," Chivington escaped a court-martial by resigning his office before the investigation ended. Although Governor Evans was away from Denver in November 1864, the investigators criticized him for provoking hostilities. President Johnson requested his resignation.[48]

Most Denverites read Byers's summary of the commission's report, which only included statements supporting Chivington. They believed that Sand Creek served a larger purpose. Denying indiscriminate killing, the Third's Irving Howbert argued for the appropriateness of "a few cases of summary punishment such as we gave them at Sand Creek." He correctly saw Sand Creek as part of an organized program to remove the Indians from the plains at any cost, even extinction. Morris Coffin confirmed that he and the other Hundred Day Volunteers understood this objective:

> At the time the 3rd Colorado regiment was raised, the idea was very general that a war of extermination should be waged; that neither sex nor age should be spared . . . and one often heard the expression that "nits make lice, make a clean thing of it." . . . Officers and soldiers but carried out the general sentiment.[49]

Some historians have suggested that Denverites erred in attacking Sand Creek because Cheyenne Dog Soldiers retaliated two months later. They attacked the northeastern Colorado settlement of Julesburg, killing forty whites, and temporarily blockading Denver.

Assessing the success of Sand Creek by this immediate aftermath, however, assumes that Denverites sought peace. As Howbert and Coffin recognized, they maintained other ambitions. Grounded in the racism that precluded the Cheyennes and Arapahos from their expansionist plans, urbanites wanted the plains emptied. Denverites viewed Sand Creek as necessary to gaining this land and effectively realized their objective by 1865. The Plains Indians lacked the resources and population for a sustained battle. For a few years, Dog Soldiers used "hit and run" tactics, rarely slowing Denver's expansion.[50] The city's leaders understood something else. Although federal officials condemned actions at Sand Creek, they would not tolerate Indian acts of vengeance, particularly those that threatened gold shipments. The army returned in full force to contain the few remaining Dog Soldiers. By October 1867, almost all Cheyennes and Arapahos lived on a reservation in Indian Territory.[51]

Sand Creek and its consequences reveal the complicated nature of white-Indian relations in Colorado. Pervasive racism contributed to violence only when the people of Denver prepared to regenerate their socioeconomic order. By the mid-1860s, they had the capabilities to pursue the plains, but lacked the capital and population to draw the western slope within their network. The Utes avoided significant criticism at that time, but Denverites laid the groundwork for future usurpations. The Utes' reservation covered almost one-third of Colorado Territory, and they soon felt new pressures. In 1863, Evans obtained the Utes' cession of the San Luis Valley where small farming communities long vexed the Indians. U.S. geological surveys in the late 1860s identified agricultural and mineral lands on the western slope. Colorado's formal policy banned white settlers from the reservation, but as information about resources circulated, even before publication of the surveys, prospectors launched speculative forays. Denver capitalists wanted to invest in new lodes. Recognizing the inevitability of white settlement, the most visible Ute leader, Ouray, sought peace. The Utes repeatedly ceded smaller portions of their reservation, trying to preserve some presence in their traditional home. A 1868 treaty guaranteed the Indians the San Juan Mountains, which supposedly would "belong to the Utes forever."[52]

Five years later, mineral discoveries in these mountains prompted new migrations. With increased pressure on food sources from squatters who illegally poured across their lands, the Utes struggled to feed their people and relinquished part of the mountains that belonged to them "forever" in exchange for annual subsidies. By the 1870s, Denver's entrepreneurs prepared to incorporate the entire western slope into the regional economy, and in the absence of provocative acts by the Utes, looked for other means to seize the Indians' land. Byers and other city residents promoted resources within the reservation, while simultaneously launching a rhetorical campaign, calling the Utes "queer specimens of humanity [who] live dirtily."[53] *The Denver Tribune* reported on the Indians' lack of productivity and the sin of wasting valuable commodities. "The Utes must go" became the rallying cry in Denver. After statehood in 1876, San Luis Valley settlers and state officials in Denver repeatedly petitioned the federal government to purchase the reservation and ensure the development of the western slope.[54] When the government failed to act, local residents initiated conflict. Farmers illegally settled in the Grand Valley in December 1877. Leadville prospectors founded Aspen by illicitly entering the Roaring Fork River Valley. By 1880, the census revealed, "miners have spread over the whole mountain region, till every range and every ridge swarms with them." At the same time, white farmers and prospectors accused other bands of Utes, who had not signed the treaties, of unlawfully killing game and setting fires outside the reservation.[55]

Cultural tensions escalated when Nathan Meeker, the inexperienced agent at the White River Agency, promised to starve reservation Indians who resisted farming. Meeker questioned whether the Utes appreciated their dismal future:

> I doubt that they understand what is to be their fate, that is, to be overrun by prospectors and others. It is impossible for them to hold so large a territory, especially when they are off it so much of the time. A railroad will come through here soon and other inroads will be made all of which really is of more interest to Colorado than to the Government.

Violence erupted in 1879 when Meeker sought military assistance to overcome lingering renitency. As Major Thornburgh's column approached the agency, some Utes ambushed it, killing thirteen men. The Indians returned to the agency, killed Meeker and eleven white men, and took five women and children captive. Ouray quickly arranged the release of the hostages and the culpable Indians' surrender, but it was too late. Non-Indian residents had lobbied Congress for three years, and the Meeker incident ignited a more insidious rhetorical campaign. Denverites revisited the recurrent theme that white women and children played a redemptive role in their society. Menacing them laid the foundation for the white retribution that followed. Within weeks of the tragedy, the *Denver Tribune* published *The Ute War: A History of the White River Massacre and the Privations and Hardships of the Captive White Women among the Hostiles on Grand River.*[56] By early 1880, the United States forced a treaty which reduced Ute land in Colorado to a small strip in the southwest corner of the state, and relocated most bands to reservations in Utah over the next two years. The treaty prohibited homesteading prior to 1882, but whites continued to ignore Indian rights. Well in advance of opening day, town promoters, fruit growers, and irrigators flooded the valleys of the Grand, Uncompahgre, and Gunnison rivers as Denver expanded its agrarian hinterland once again.[57]

To vitalize their new urban-based economy, Denverites attempted to diversify through commercial agriculture. Farms also promised the moral gravity of families and white women. From the perspective of the gold-rush emigrants, the Cheyennes, Arapahos, and Utes represented, at best, relics of the past and, at worst, impediments to future growth. When their capabilities allowed them to do so, Denverites used incidents of violence against white women and children to launch nonconcordant acts of retribution and seize larger swathes of Indian lands. Racist theories justified episodes like Sand Creek, by focusing on the "innate" deficiencies of their Indian neighbors. Albeit with less mayhem and expediency, Denverites succeeded in marginalizing the Utes and all but eliminating "the last traces of Indian blood" from the region.[58] The front-range entrepôt gained land for agricultural development, and set about to attract the farmers whose production could help Denver emerge as a metropolis and whose families could make the city a community.

THREE

TAMING THE DESERT
Denver Turns to Agriculture

*Northeastern Colorado has changed from an arid plain to one
of the garden spots of the world.*

George A. Hodgson, 1932

With the Civil War over and only a few scattered Plains Indians
remaining, Denverites prepared to convert the Great American Desert
into "one of the garden spots of the world." Complex motives
compelled this ecological transformation. Regional farmers and the
urban entrepreneurs who recruited them believed in the market, but
their commitment to laissez-faire capitalism was neither constant nor
all-consuming. Boosters also wanted yeoman farmers to provide
William Byers's "conservative element of all national political and
social growth." Governor Alva Adams later observed: "Gold was the
germ of this mountain empire but agriculture is to be its abiding nour-
ishment. . . . The miner was John the Baptist of a new dispensation,
the farmer the herald of the home. The one represents the radical, the
other the conservative; one pioneers, the other perpetuates."[1] Regional
farmers engaged in commercial production, but also settled in cooperative societies in the 1870s and formed mutual stock companies in
the 1880s to guard against corporate interlopers. Extralegal livestock
associations established standards that enhanced the marketability of
regional beef while protecting members from others' injurious acts.
Laws transformed natural resources into commodities, but their

64

enforcement by state courts frequently reflected a commitment to local interests over outsiders' more dynamic uses of resources. A contested, protracted transition to agrarian capitalism accompanied the environmental conversion of the plains.[2]

As they had with the mining frontier, Denver's entrepreneurs shepherded the region's agricultural community toward maturity through their own investments, the direction of local trade associations, and the recruitment of farmers and outside capital. As early as 1859, the *Rocky Mountain News* promoted winter grazing and Denver formed a short-lived agricultural association. When the Colorado Agricultural Society reorganized in 1863, only three local farmers joined its directors and officers. The others included a newspaper editor (William Byers), a mining lawyer, a manufacturer, and three merchants, all from Denver. From its inception, the Board of Trade posted committees to research and promote new crops.[3]

Despite earnest desires to attract the more "conservative element," the first large-scale agricultural activities involved ranching. In 1859, John Dawson drove the first cattle herd from Texas to Denver. Trailing cattle to Colorado remained profitable throughout the Civil War. Blockades closed off Confederate markets, while Texas beef sold at inflated prices in Denver due to its growing population and constant food shortages. After the war, the national cattle market boomed, and ranchers looked to western ranges to feed their herds. With the land cleared of Indians, they saw economic potential in Colorado's plains. Its low-growing grama and buffalo grasses provided nutritious winter fodder and survived trampling, close grazing, and drought. In 1861, John Wesley Iliff, who sold his Denver grocery store to start a small ranch outside town, bought eight hundred head from Texan Charles Goodnight and moved his operations onto the plains. Although they still hoped to attract farmers, Denverites aggressively advanced the open-range livestock industry that Iliff typified. The Board of Trade boasted that "these plains [are] capable of furnishing stock and wool needed . . . for a large portion of the population of the nation." Evans's Kansas Pacific echoed the Board's assessment of Denver's hinterland.[4]

These promotions reflected a commitment to market principles. One emigrant noted:

I could easily make myself independent in five years
out here by hard work and economy in raising stock.
It is the best paying business in Colorado and requires
the least labor . . . I can commence here with $1000
and in five years clear $15,000 and that is more than a
man can do in the states with that amount of capital.
Stock requires no feed in the winter or summer and
the cost per head to keep them here $1.50 a year.

While these comments underestimated the requisite amounts of capital and labor, Denver's cattle industry offered relatively inexpensive
entry. With an abundance of Texas cattle, ranchers obtained herds with
small investments. A cow and calf needed forty pounds of grass and
twelve gallons of water a day, free for the taking on the public domain
not yet preempted.[5] Although its use of a cash-generating policy suggested the influence of free enterprise, in dispersing federal lands, the
government hoped to increase opportunities for Jeffersonian farmers
in the arid West. Whatever their intended purposes, the laws initially
expanded options for ranchers. Luke Cahill remarked, "Land did not
interest me, for all the earth was mine."[6]

A man could legally claim 160 acres, an inadequate amount for
maintaining a commercial herd. Consequently, stockmen imple-
mented extralegal systems to control larger sections of the plains.
Dummy entrymen, usually ranch hands, filed claims, swearing the
land was for their own use. In reality, employers provided the
purchase money and ultimately received the property. Once farsighted
ranchers seized sections bordering streams, adjacent rangeland
possessed little value. "On my own ranch (320) acres I have two miles
of running water," observed a local stockman. "The next ranch down
from me in one direction is 23 miles; now, no man can have a ranch
between these two places. I have control of the grass the same as
though I owned it." And contrary to popular myths, cattlemen used
barbed wire first to illegally fence usurped public lands.[7] This extralegal system reflected regional ranchers' desire to control their destinies.
For them, the federal system was untenable. To legitimately purchase
land required more capital than local actors possessed and would have
involved outside investors. Although an expansive industry became

dependent on eastern and British capital in the 1880s, this system initially rewarded local ambitions. Despite Denver's many promotions, eastern farmers were slow to change their perceptions of the Great American Desert and arrived in great numbers only in the 1870s. In the interim, ranchers learned how to produce wealth from the plains.

The open range involved a diffusion of market values, but also followed regulatory traditions begun in the absence of a territorial government. Early small farmers, imitating squatters on frontiers to the east, formed claims clubs to secure public acceptance and quasi-legal endorsement of their titles. The Colorado Agricultural Society attempted to regulate land on a larger scale, but proved inadequate for ranchers. Roaming herds mixed together, complicating individuals' sales. Rampant theft and disease undermined the industry. In November 1867, ranchers organized the Colorado Stock Growers Association to self-regulate their activities. The association headquartered in Denver, "the trading center of the high plains regions." The largest ranchers managed operations from Denver because it remained the biggest city along the front range. Urban entrepreneurs secured the association just as they organized the Denver Pacific, and used their market connections to distribute the region's beef. Association minutes reveal both the power of the marketplace and the persistence of regulation. Big operators dominated, imposing rules that facilitated private economic gain. The association also fostered cooperation between participants and protected their interests vis-à-vis outsiders for the community's welfare with brand books, communal roundups, and quarantines.[8]

Colorado's largest operators realized great profits. From Denver, Iliff managed fifteen thousand acres of the public domain, running thirty-five thousand head along the South Platte River from the Rockies to Kansas. John Wesley Prowers learned the grazing value of the plains when he drove the Santa Fe Trail for the Bents. Starting with one hundred Herefords, he eventually owned 80,000 acres on the Arkansas, allowing him to control another 320,000. Jared Brush abandoned prospecting for ranching in 1862, earning success that later brought him the lieutenant-governorship. These cattle kings and smaller stockmen played a new variation of an old theme, introducing domestic grazers just as the Plains Indians did with their horses. And like the Indians, their dependence on a precariously balanced ecosystem foreshadowed environmental disaster. In the interim, however, Denver-based ranches experienced tremendous growth. Some 147,000 cattle roamed Colorado's plains by 1867. Mining towns and front-range cities provided local markets, while occasional drives to Kansas railheads made the region a competitive force, although it still trailed Texas's production. The arrival of Denver's railroads in 1870 sparked more growth. Within two years, 355,000 cattle fed on nearby grasses. Denver annually shipped forty-six thousand cattle alone, valued at one million dollars.[9]

At the same time, Denver entrepreneurs exploited old Mexican land grants to push their stock industry beyond territorial borders. To protect Santa Fe commerce in the 1830s and 1840s, the Mexican government granted loyal citizens and influential foreigners lands from Mexico's northern border to the Arkansas, with many grants exceeding the ninety-six thousand acres allowed by its law. The Maxwell grant (originally Beaubien and Miranda) covered some 1,700,000 acres, while the Sangre de Cristo encompassed another 1,000,000. These larger grants overlapped communal grants in which most New Mexican farmers held diminutive individual plots. When the United States took possession of New Mexico in 1848, Congress agreed to protect established property rights there, and removed these millions of acres from the public domain without recognizing the potential for conflicting claims, setting the stage for large capital takeovers. William Gilpin and Englishman William Blackmore organized local, British, and European investors to purchase the Sangre de Cristo in 1865. To facilitate land sales, Gilpin directed the Trinchera Estate Company that controlled the northern half of the grant. A Dutch group held the Costilla Estate Company, although Denver-based managers supervised its southern half. These companies traded livestock, sold irrigation rights, and extended Denver's reach. Backed by American courts, Gilpin and his fellow investors treated established Hispano community settlers as squatters, forcing them to buy property that some had worked for decades. The arrival of Denver-based railroads and irrigation companies in the 1870s brought a large influx of white farmers.[10]

Mining entrepreneur Jerome Chaffee aimed for the Maxwell Grant with its existent grist mill, mines, and toll road and its rich timber, coal, and grazing resources. In 1870, he formed the Maxwell Land Grant and Railroad Company with Stephen B. Elkins, a lawyer and member of the infamous Santa Fe Ring, to buy the property. The pair dominated the new First National Bank of Santa Fe, which handled their company's securities along with Chaffee's First National Bank of Denver. They used the latter institution to secure a mortgage from Dutch investors. When the Secretary of the Interior ruled that the Maxwell grant covered only the 96,000 acres allowed under Mexican law, rather than the 1,700,000 Chaffee and Elkins claimed, the company declared bankruptcy in 1875. A cooperative judge, however, permitted a "friend" to purchase the company in a government sale to cover tax debts, and then sell it back to Elkins, allowing him and Chaffee to avoid foreign creditors and retain control. While representing New Mexico and Colorado in Washington, respectively, Elkins and Chaffee resubmitted their case to the land commissioner in 1879. Congress confirmed a new survey reinstating the 1,700,000 acres.[11]

Numerous "squatters" sued the Maxwell Land Grant Company over the years, but the challengers lacked unifying objectives. Oscar P. McMains, a minister who organized white farmers, ranchers, and miners in the Anti-Grant Mutual-Protective Association, hoped that their claims would be recognized under preemption laws. Hispanos living under communal grants asked the courts to uphold their rights under Mexican law and the Treaty of Guadalupe Hidalgo. Margaret McBride, a white rancher's daughter, recalled:

> Settlers from the states had come in and homesteaded lands in good faith, but heirs and derivative claimants of the Maxwell-Beaubien estate appeared and claimed the lands under the old Spanish title. . . . The two factions finally came to open war. The homesteaders, called "squatters" by some, organized the White Caps . . . The Maxwell Land Grant faction had its night riders also, and there was shooting on both sides.[12]

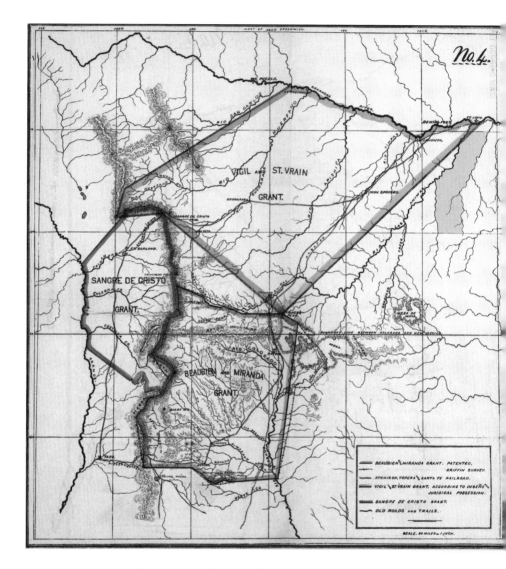

Map 2. Mexican Land Grants. This map highlights three large land claims over which Denverites asserted financial control. They faced court challenges from Hispano communal grant holders and white squatters over the size of the Sangre de Cristo, Beaubien and Miranda (Maxwell), and Vigil and St. Vrain Grants, but these properties allowed them to expand the city's influence and gain personal wealth. U.S. v. Maxwell Land Grant Co., Appeal from the Circuit Court of the United States for the District of Colorado, T. A. Schomberg Collection. Courtesy of Colorado Historical Society, Denver, Colorado.

The challengers ultimately lost when the U.S. Supreme Court upheld the larger patent in 1887, ruling that since the original grant deviated from Mexican law, Congress made a grant *de novo* by confirming the 1879 survey. The company intensified agricultural, mineral, and timber land sales, and forced the squatters to pay or leave.[13]

Similar to other conflicts in the Denver region, the land grant struggle failed to present clearly defined lines between ruthless corporate capitalism and the common man. Small ranchers and farmers who purchased property from the Maxwell Land Grant Company in good faith championed its claims and the Supreme Court's decision. While men like Chaffee and Elkins exercised influence, other grantholders did not equal their success. The federal government offered more than lockstep support of those who seemingly presented the best potential for productive wealth. Colorado's Vigil & St. Vrain Grant passed through a series of wealthy owners who ordered surveys to support a four-million-acre claim, but in 1861, Congress limited the grant to ninety-six thousand, and over time, Pueblo's surveyor general, President Grant, and the U.S. Supreme Court upheld the smaller acreage. In the 1870s, when Trinidad's citizens decided to incorporate their town, they discovered that the remaining Vigil & St. Vrain grant covered the townsite, but Pueblo's land office rejected the owner's claim.[14]

Henry Porter typified Denver's participants in Mexican land grants. An investor in the original Maxwell Company in 1870, he owned and operated the Cimarron, New Mexico, store and bank that served as its local headquarters. Following the company's reorganization, Porter loaned substantial sums and managed its cattle operations, which he later absorbed into his other ranching interests. Porter also managed the Red River Cattle Company, which purchased the 400,000-acre Nolan Grant, although later surveys reduced it 75 percent. The triumphs of Porter and others attracted more ranchers and investors, despite litigation over the Mexican grants.[15] At the same time, cattlemen encountered new competition for the open range they had seized through extralegal means.

Local boosters gradually attracted farmers to the plains as Denver's first decade drew to a close. Removal of the Indians seemed to guarantee safety. Rail transport for perishable products eliminated an imposing obstacle to commercial farming. Well-circulated advertisements argued that the success of cattle dispelled the myth of the Great American Desert. The final task involved overcoming the cost of irrigation, which was beyond the means of individual farmers. Making an analogy to railroad lands, regional entrepreneurs lobbied Congress as early as 1864 to authorize grants from the public domain to irrigation companies. These efforts embodied notions of economic liberalism. Denverites asked the federal government to create property rights for businesses that only conveyed water to those who used it. Local leaders hoped to attract farm families and their morally superior white women, but prepared to privilege irrigation corporations that seemingly offered more productive wealth.

These Denver men acted as pragmatists. When Congress rejected their grant scheme, they returned to the communitarian traditions of more regulated societies to draw farmers. They highlighted Mormon experiences in Utah and Midwestern settlement projects to boost agricultural colonies as the most viable option for the plains. Under cooperative ventures, individuals could combine their money and talents in expensive, time-consuming irrigation construction and maintenance. Denverites who owned land most suitable for irrigation, such as the National Land Company, which Byers and others formed to sell Denver Pacific and Kansas Pacific properties, negotiated higher prices with colonists who pooled their capital or attracted outside investors. Land companies more easily sold sections distant from waterways because colonies possessed adequate money and technology to irrigate it. In the 1870s, the National Land Company located more than twenty colonies in eastern Colorado and western Kansas.[16] Colonies were not new to Colorado; New Mexicans founded Guadalupe Colony in the San Luis Valley in 1854 and dug irrigation ditches still used today. The first of the new cooperative communities, the German Colonization Society, settled in March 1870 thirty miles southwest of Pueblo. Its failure within a year revealed what survival required. These colonists hoped for a congressional land grant, and failed to pool their resources when it did not materialize. Individual land purchases captured inadequate water supplies. They lacked a binding moral imperative and the social cohesion that might have allowed them to overcome these land-tenure problems.[17] The more famous Union Colony soon launched a larger, more permanent agricultural migration by avoiding these errors.

Nathan Meeker, whose death in 1879 sparked the Utes' removal, was Horace Greeley's agricultural editor when he traveled to Colorado ten years earlier. His famous employer advocated the Homestead Act as "a reform calculated to diminish sensibly the number of paupers and idlers and increase the proportion of working, independent, self-subscribing farmers in the land evermore." Agreeing with most Denverites, Greeley accepted as truth Jefferson's proclamation that "those who labor in the earth are the chosen people of God." For them, the open spaces of the West defined the nation's destiny and offered redemption after the Civil War. Utopian colonies also appeared in California and around Puget Sound.[18]

Meeker asked Greeley to support an agricultural colony that blended market values with a cooperative community spirit. Greeley, who visited Denver in 1859, quickly backed Meeker's plan. Byers convinced them that the confluence of the Cache la Poudre and the South Platte rivers offered the best opportunities for growth given its proximity to the soon-to-be-completed Denver Pacific. Despite Greeley's faith in the Homestead Act, Union Colony members obtained only a small portion of their property through preemption. The National Land Company sold the colony twelve thousand riverfront acres for its town and storage facilities. To maintain cohesion, individual members bought from Byers sixty thousand acres surrounding the town. A substantial investor in the railroad, Byers became the local manager of the National Land Company in 1869. Since his arrival ten years earlier, he consistently promoted the region's agricultural potential, founding booster organizations and publishing articles that exaggerated the production of local farms. Denverites, who voted 500,000 dollars in railroad bonds and invested in the Denver Pacific, urged Byers to sell more and more land grant property. The *News* and other local papers quickly celebrated Union Colony, his first important buyer.[19]

Almost three hundred Union colonists arrived by June 1870, including many experienced farmers from New York and other eastern and midwestern states. They paid a 155-dollar admission fee and accepted farmland of five to eighty acres depending upon their initial contributions. Guided by past participation in commercial agriculture and with the help of outside investors, they established the town of Greeley as the colony's market center. They shared beliefs in temperance, Protestantism, and the Republican Party. The colony's constitution emphasized cooperation and prohibited artificial membership tests, although it excluded African Americans and Irish Catholics, who supposedly went "in harmony" with whiskey. And work on outlying lands did not excuse members from supporting schools and town improvements.[20] With its families and potential for profitable farming, Union Colony seemed to strike a balance between market values and the associative spirit of a regulated society that Denverites hoped to engender in their agrarian hinterland.

Morality partially shaped Union Colony and other cooperatives, but community settlement also provided in this arid climate the practical means for irrigation, the expensive basis of plains agriculture. Union Colony's first ditch followed the bottom lands of the Cache la Poudre for ten miles. Reflecting rapid technological advances, the colony's second canal, finished in 1871, lifted water from the flood plain onto higher bench lands removed from streams, stretched twenty-seven miles, and watered twenty-five thousand acres through elaborate lateral canals. Union farmers harvested crops for local and remote markets in these first years. A regional agricultural revolution had begun, and Denver remained at its forefront. The National Land Company sent circulars across the country. Byers responded to distant inquiries about climate, soil, and stockraising. To illustrate the "unlimited" opportunities, he pointed to Union Colony's success, the availability of land, and the region's continuing need for more flour, corn and oats.[21]

The Chicago-Colorado Company soon imitated Union Colony's efforts. This association's promotions suggested that Denver's new human geography had taken hold. Favorable perceptions of the plains proliferated. The *Chicago Tribune* observed that with irrigation in the Great American Desert, the new colony had "the richest farm land in the world." Colonists built Longmont on part of fifty thousand acres

Figure 6. *Plains Irrigation Ditch. Viewed from downstream, water flows through the wood-slatted sluice in this irrigation ditch typical of Colorado's eastern plains. Fenced farmland occupies the flat, nearly treeless horizon. Photograph by Louis Charles McClure. Courtesy of Denver Public Library, Western History Collection.*

from the public domain and the National Land Company in the Big Thompson River system. Byers managed the colony's affairs until Denver's William Holly, secretary of the Colorado Stock Growers Association and owner of Arkansas Valley ranches, assumed those duties.[22] Longmont's farmers struggled their first year, failing to complete an irrigation ditch. A few inadequately watered acres yielded a poor harvest. Colony men worked in mines or cut timber to support the community while wives and children ran the farms. By the next season, they completed a ditch, conducting water eight miles from the South St. Vrain River. Longmont developed more slowly than Greeley, but gradually prospered.[23]

The National Land Company sold property to Denver rancher and future governor Benjamin Eaton to establish the St. Louis-Western Colony at Evans, but it always remained in the shadow of Greeley, its prosperous neighbor four miles away. Union Colony member David Boyd attributed the St. Louis-Western Colony's limited growth to its allowance of alcohol. He blamed "suitcase farmers" who lived in town and "neglected" their farms. The new colony lacked the social cohesion that marked Union Colony's early years, but proximity to Greeley retarded its development. Farming communities supported one supply center, and the Denver Pacific designated Greeley the local stop. Short of capital, its members claimed only thirty-two hundred acres, fewer acres with access to water, and consequently, less success.[24]

These different colonies reflected the complex mix of values and the struggles for control that shaped the Denver region. They simultaneously incorporated social-regulatory elements and economic-promotional dimensions. Public jurisdiction over the American infrastructure, prevalent for a century, emerged on the plains. Citizens constructed ditches that promoted the economic needs of private landowners. Yet irrigation benefited the entire community and associations of colony members, acting with the authority of the law, regulated its use. This self-government involved what historian William Novak calls "a broader, more substantive understanding of the freedoms and obligations accorded citizens as contributing members of self-regulating communities." It required at times the submission of individual interests for the welfare of the community, and existed in various forms in New England towns, Wisconsin lumber camps, and Denver's mining hinterland. Self-government encompassed more than the water system. In Union Colony, it touched upon the community's character through temperance policies and religious and racial restrictions. This self-regulation of morals was omnipotent and omnipresent in nineteenth-century America.[25]

New farm towns appeared across the plains at Sterling, Fort Collins, and Lamar in the 1870s. Denver entrepreneurs seeking quick profits often used the rhetorical label "colony" to lure more farmers. The Platte River Land Company, in which Byers was a major investor, boosted its Platteville "colony," but did not establish membership requirements that enhanced social cohesion. "Fountain Colony" became the tool to sell town lots in Colorado Springs, a fledgling resort. "Southwestern Colony," a speculative venture twenty-seven miles downstream from Greeley failed after its boosters attempted to sell five thousand lots in Green City, but never developed farmland. Pamphlets included a picture of a steamboat, suggesting Green City's commercial possibilities and ignoring its location on the South Platte, an unnavigable river.[26] At the impetus of Denver businessmen, the territorial government created the Colorado Board of Immigration. Headquartered in Denver, the Board proved instrumental in drawing new farmers as its promotions diminished problems such as the limited types of cash crops available, internal social tensions, and the increased cost of irrigation on less arable land. Some contemporaries, focusing on the welfare of the community, criticized the Board for attracting and then failing to help poor, unprepared immigrants, but expansion continued. The number of farms in Colorado almost tripled in the 1870s. With farming and stockgrowing to supplement mining revenue, Denver's population grew sevenfold, reaching thirty-six thousand by 1880.[27]

A closer examination of Union Colony, however, illustrates the obstacles that even successful farmers encountered and confirms that Denverites, impatient to sell land, created an unrealistic image of regional agriculture. The colony immediately abandoned plans to grow lucrative tropical fruits that floundered on the plains even with irrigation. To sustain the colony in its early years, they cultivated less profitable potatoes. Discontent also spread over water. Based on eastern experiences, Meeker and the other officers anticipated expenses of twenty thousand dollars to irrigate twenty thousand acres. Their first canal cost fifty thousand dollars and watered only three thousand acres. Colony officers repeatedly asked members for more money and sought additional outside capital, threatening to undermine local control. When the colony completed its irrigation system for 400,000 dollars in 1883, the value of its water rights increased tenfold, but the officers oversold them, leading to litigation. Cooperative irrigation constituted the colony's economic and social foundation, and these mistakes shook the community. In the midst of these troubles, Meeker had left for the White River Indian Agency. Union Colony members hoped to finance cooperative agencies that controlled banks, feed and hardware stores, and sugar refineries; instead, revenue from town sales went to ditch construction. Eager newcomers provided these other enterprises, but not as cooperatives. Many newcomers rejected the colony's morality. The officers faced a common problem of such utopian communities—balancing the benefits of cooperation and group cohesion against the profits of individual initiative. Like most colonies, Greeley also had its share of malcontents who had been unhappy in their old homes and constantly complained in their new one. As members turned to the courts to resolve water rights, the colony's synergetic nature faded away.[28]

Eastern farmers were accustomed to riparian rights that permitted owners of land adjacent to streams to use as much water as necessary as long as they did not unreasonably injure downstream users. In the Denver region, they encountered the law of prior appropriation, which gave the first person who put water to a beneficial, continuous use a permanent right, regardless of the proximity of his land to the stream or the impact on downstream users with later priorities. Used sparingly in California, this system took hold in Colorado's mountains where miners diverted often plentiful waters. The territory extended it to the arid plains. When Colorado garnered statehood in 1876, Greeley and other established agrarian communities successfully sought Article 16 which protected appropriative rights and favored agricultural uses over manufacturing, reflecting persistent beliefs in the need for stable, prosperous farming communities. Four years earlier, the territorial court outlined similar priorities. Chief Justice Moses Hallett concluded that the arid environment created appropriative rights; statutes only confirmed them. "Rules respecting the tenure of property must yield to the physical laws of nature, whenever such laws exert a controlling influence." Based on this opinion, some historians conclude that appropriative rights flow from nature.[29] In this, they echo John Wesley Powell and Walter Prescott Webb, who believed aridity defined the West. Prior appropriation, however, developed in response to local efforts to balance tensions between community welfare and unrestricted capitalism, not as a monolithic natural entity predestined to triumph. The great diversity of western laws captured under the prior appropriation umbrella corroborates the power of localism. Laws served the needs of particular participants. Hallett employed "aridity" to justify elevating one user's rights over another's. When Colorado's supreme court upheld Article 16 in 1882, it dropped this artifice of environmental necessity and legitimated the state's regulation of resources through its police powers.[30]

With Article 16, the framers hoped to resolve existing debates over water. During the dry summer of 1874, for example, Union Colony sought an injunction against Fort Collins's farmers twenty-five miles upstream on the Cache la Poudre. Greeley's farmers drew insufficient water for their crops, while canals at Fort Collins stayed full. Union colonists possessed prior rights, but in a compromise, dropped their injunction when upstream competitors agreed to release more water. The potential for conflict remained, however, and the early years of statehood revealed that Article 16 left many questions unanswered. Courts allowed the most profitable use of water to determine priorities as frequently as the age of appropriations. In 1878, the Colorado Mortgage and Investment Company began construction of the fifty-three-mile Larimer & Weld Canal to irrigate fifty thousand acres in the Cache la Poudre watershed. Known as the "English Company" due to heavy British investments, it headquartered in Denver and its incorporators included many of the city's agricultural entrepreneurs, including Eaton. Fearful of the big canal's implications, downstream irrigators at Fort Collins and Greeley joined other farm- ers in an irrigation convention in Denver. They recommended that the Colorado legislature abandon prior appropriation and attach water rights to land because a riparian system seemed to favor local farmers over large corporations.[31]

The state legislature rejected the convention's recommendations and, instead, created irrigation districts to distribute water according to priorities established by the courts. Under this litigious system, the wealthiest, most political district members exerted great influence over its officers. For example, Eaton easily obtained more water from the "overappropriated" Cache La Poudre for his farms. The legislature failed to place limits on the amount an appropriator could take and to measure the volume of rivers and canals. Courts frequently granted more water than necessary in anticipation of expansion. Farmers accepted the maximum for fear that they would be limited in the future. Problems arose as farmers turned to more profitable crops with longer growing seasons and greater water demands. In choosing the courts to determine priorities, the legislature rejected an alternative recommendation from the convention for the appointment of a statewide water commissioner to sort out rights. Denver entrepreneurs and foreign capitalists, who made increasingly greater investments in irrigation companies, successfully lobbied against the convention's recommendations. It seems unlikely that the legislature would have overturned the existing water system or stripped courts of their distributive powers under any circumstances, but the debates exposed the different opinions in the Denver region over control. Farmers opposed the authority of concentrated capital. Denver investors who still participated in local management seemed willing to adopt the more liberal approach to water distribution.[32]

California experienced a similar debate in the 1850s. On one side, miners claimed water as a fundamental right and advocated a position of free access. Corporations that dug ditches alternatively argued that providing water constituted a legitimate profit-making enterprise. When California's supreme court tacitly recognized that water rights could be separated from mining rights, water became a commodity.[33] In Colorado, as farming colonies completed their first projects, they often found the construction and maintenance of larger canals beyond their means. Without more extensive irrigation, distant arid lands hovered outside Denver's reach. At the same time, front-range cities needed to quench the thirst of their growing populations by tapping rivers at their mountain sources. Regional water systems became the targets of wealthy outsiders. Incorporation records reveal the extent of new investments. Before 1880, only 338 water companies incorporated in Colorado. Most involved limited city works or small canal and well companies that captured local water. After 1880, twice as many corporations formed and aggregate capitalization grew sixfold. Corporate dollars made a profound impact. In addition to the Larimer & Weld Canal, which sparked the convention, the English Company built the 2,500,000-dollar High Line Canal from the South Platte Canyon to Denver and the Loveland & Greeley Canal from the Big Thompson River to new farms. Other companies searched the western slope for water to bring east through transmontane tunnels. Most companies located in Denver, but power began shifting away from its entrepreneurs.[34]

These new corporations anticipated substantial profits with state courts supporting their more dynamic use of limited water resources. They were disappointed. Despite substantial migrations, settlement proved insufficiently dense to ensure steady dividends. Moreover, the Colorado Supreme Court rejected companies' claims for priorities in the water they transferred. Instead, it elevated the rights of local farmers and other users over the absentee owners of canal companies. Article 16 provided that "the waters of every natural stream, not heretofore appropriated, within the state of Colorado, are hereby declared to be the property of the public." Since water belonged to the public, it could only be converted to private property when used beneficially. Canals only carried water, and thus, ditch companies could not become proprietors of water rights. The court concluded, "The carrier becomes the consumer's agent, and its labors clearly inure to his benefit."[35]

Canals generated wealth, but Colorado prioritized the needs of the local community. The inability to own and thus transfer water rights diminished the profit-making power of these irrigation companies. As investors shied away, companies tried to offer better rates of return by imposing higher charges on farmers for the transportation of water to their crops. When these charges failed to return adequate dividends or cover maintenance costs, corporations imposed royalties, reserving perpetual shares of the farmers' profits. Denver entrepreneurs, who worried about their diminished roles and the irrigation companies' use of imperious methods, joined local farmers in seeking legislative and judicial relief. The Denver-based Colorado Agricultural Society pushed through an antiroyalty law in 1887, prohibiting surcharges on the water supplied, although companies employed inflated assessment fees to hide extra charges. With advance knowledge, these enterprises created subsidiaries that claimed, through entrymen, properties that would benefit from the new water projects. Sales of these lands remained their most lucrative source of income.[36]

Efforts to curtail the power of outside capitalists illustrate the ambiguous coexistence of market values and tenets of a regulated society in the region—what Donald Pisani describes as the balance between enterprise and equity. The Chicago-Colorado Colony, for example, initially celebrated "parties with capital and experience" who helped in its early days, but its members later condemned the English Company. The state legislature's rejection of the irrigation convention's recommendations seemed to signal an end to a regulated approach to water usage. The supreme court recognized water as a commodity, but then secured its availability at lower prices for farmers and limited corporate ownership of appropriative rights, emphasizing the welfare of the local community. Restrictions on fees and water rights combined with high overhead to curtail profits, and corporate activity in irrigation declined by almost 50 percent in the 1890s. Other private irrigation systems reorganized as cooperative mutual stock companies, developing by-laws to determine the amount of water each stockholder earned through assessments.[37]

Despite these unresolved tensions, Denver's agricultural hinterland grew. After the Utes' removal, the city's private land companies, its Chamber of Commerce, and the Board of Immigration recruited new farmers to the San Luis Valley and the western slope. Emphasizing the benefits of irrigation, Denverites promoted these areas as agricultural havens even as ditch corporations abandoned the region.[38] The protected valley of the Grand River proved particularly attractive. It held 250,000 acres adjoining streams, seemingly sufficient irrigation water for distant acres, and a climate and soils suitable for horticulture. Always the entrepreneur, Byers "homesteaded" claims at Hot Sulphur Springs, and officials named his small town the county seat. Grand Junction, originally known as West Denver, stood at the favored confluence of the Grand and Gunnison rivers, and the arrival of the railroad in 1887 secured its position as the western slope's urban center and Denver's primary trading partner.[39] The Grand Junction Fruit Growers Association, a cooperative organization, combined the produce of its members for transport and imposed quality standards. As fruit production boomed, Denver agents guided the association's distant shipments and mediated prices. The Colorado State Horticultural and Forestry Association emerged in 1884 to promote and regulate western-slope orchards. Confirming Denver's dominance, the entire executive committee and all but five of its forty-eight life members hailed from the metropolis.[40]

Horticulture represented just one of Denver's expanded marketing functions. Its residents established flour trusts and other agricultural cartels to engender growth and secure higher prices for regional products. In 1870, for example, the value of flour manufactured in Denver was 75,000 dollars; twenty years later, it reached 1,800,000 dollars. Only production from Denver's smelters exceeded its flour mills.[41] With its members heavily invested in the agrarian hinterland, Denver's Chamber of Commerce published bulletins on milling, fruit growing, dairying, and cattle canning. The number of farmers increased 300 percent in the 1880s and the bulk of their products flowed through Denver. Fruits and potatoes traveled on regional railroads to Mexico and New Orleans, and on transcontinental lines to Chicago, New York, and San Francisco. The Chamber's standing committees researched new crops and irrigation to avoid the happenstance of Union Colony's discovery that the plains did not abide fruit trees.[42] The Chamber selected the sugar beet as its primary research experiment. As early as 1866, the *News* promoted cultivation of the plant. No region in the country dominated the national sugar market or challenged Europe's near monopoly on worldwide production.

Figure 7. *Irrigated Fruit Orchard. Mature pear trees, watered by an extensive irrigation system, bloomed near Grand Junction, the leading agricultural community of the western slope. Photograph by Louis Charles McClure. Courtesy of Denver Public Library, Western History Collection.*

Beets required significant water, but since 70 percent of the world's manufactured sugar came from beets, Denverites thought the crop offered the region a unique, profitable niche. With the completion of extensive irrigation systems, farmers planted more beets, believing they now controlled the key to production: water. The industry spread from Grand Junction to the South Platte and Arkansas River settlements. Sugar-beet cultivation proved so lucrative that numerous processing plants appeared by 1900. Along with Cripple Creek gold, the beet revitalized the regional economy, and the Chamber claimed credit for its success.[43]

The growth of farming and the increase in irrigated acres exerted a competitive impact on ranchers who shared agricultural lands. Following the 1873 depression, cattle prices dropped and sources of credit dried up, forcing ranchers to ship young cattle and depressing prices further. Many small operators failed. By 1880, however, the industry experienced an influx of corporate capital similar to the one in irrigation. As the economy improved, the relatively low overhead and the large profits once earned on the range made the industry an attractive investment to wealthy outsiders. Denver-based cattlemen eager to expand their base and limit their liability welcomed them.[44] More than one million cattle and other grazers crowded Colorado's range, with more spread out across the adjoining grasslands of Wyoming, Nebraska, Kansas, Texas, and New Mexico. Porter's career once again emblematized developments. With new corporate financing, he associated with the Cimarron Cattle Company in Colfax County, New Mexico, and the Red River Cattle and the Meso de Mayo Land and Livestock companies near Magdalena, New Mexico, among other properties. Porter used his vice-presidency at the Denver National Bank and partnered with the First National's David Moffat to seize Trinidad's Pawnee Cattle Company when it fell into receivership. Other Denver entrepreneurs followed suit.[45]

This influx of capital, however, also represented a shift toward greater foreign control of the industry. The Prairie Cattle Company bought out smaller ranchers and cattle king Jared Brush. Organized in 1881 in Scotland, it became the largest regional operation, controlling two million acres in Colorado, Texas, and New Mexico. Another

farming
ranching
conflict

Denver-managed operation sold its Arkansas River holdings in 1882 to the Arkansas Valley Land and Cattle Company, an English Company subsidiary. Scottish investors founded the Matador Land and Cattle Company that same year, merging ranches in Texas, South Dakota, Montana, and Canada, all managed from Denver and Trinidad. Denver offered the best rail connections, and remained "the central trading point for western livestock [where] many large deals have been made within recent times." But people outside the region increasingly made key financial decisions.[46]

Open-range ranchers soon faced greater dilemmas, although they tended to blame neighboring farmers for their problems. Farmers, in turn, made ranchers the targets of their lobbying. Just as Denverites once vilified the Plains Indians, farmers labeled stockmen as trespassers on the public domain. Colorado Congressman Thomas Patterson complained of ranchers' "baronial estates." The *Laramie Sentinel* made biblical analogies. Virtuous farmers would triumph when Cain, "the tiller of the soil," replaced Abel, "the stock grower."[47] Ranchers had more than rhetorical concerns. Irrigation canals cut off access to water. Union Colony constructed a large community fence in 1872 after range cattle trampled early wheat crops. The Chicago-Colorado Colony and other communities similarly enclosed their acres. In the 1880s, the federal government sought payment for lands that stockmen illegally fenced, albeit at less than market value. The Arkansas Valley Land and Cattle Company paid only 145,000 dollars for 700,000 acres. Since ranchers continued to misappropriate land, Congress finally forbid any fences on public lands in 1885, denying them much of the range they coveted.[48]

In other ways, the boundaries between ranchers and farmers blurred. Denver entrepreneurs like Eaton diversified their agricultural interests. In addition to founding farming colonies and the towns of Evans and Eaton, he managed the English Company's local properties and owned the Cross Ranch. While committed to commercial production, Eaton fought for regulation of the cattle industry as governor, promoting inspections and quarantines. With the crowding of the plains, he worried that land, feed, and water might dissipate without judicious conservation. He supported fencing laws and lobbied against federal policies that privileged speculators and ranchers at the expense of farmers. The Timber Culture Act of 1873, for example, allowed filers to claim an additional 160 acres if they also maintained 40 acres of trees. Based partially on mistaken theories that assumed rainfall followed trees, the law was inherently flawed. Drought, grasshoppers, and the inability of settlers to care for saplings led Congress to reduce the required plantings to ten acres within five years, but ranchers frequently blocked farmers by having their employees file false timber claims. Local speculators lured farmers to the San Luis Valley by promising 100,000 acres of "timber" lands, which could be developed with irrigation by Denver's Colorado Land and Trust Company. Given the aridity, this never represented a viable option.[49]

Moreover, federal policies ultimately contributed to the collapse of open-range ranching by encouraging corporate participants to overextend. Ranchers overstocked the range to take advantage of higher prices, increasing competition for grasslands already compressed by farms. A cycle of summer droughts and severe winters between 1884 and 1887 depleted the available beeves for market. In November 1886, the Matador's manager advised his Scottish investors of the calamitous conditions:

> The year opened inauspiciously with severe snow &
> storms, rumors of losses subsequently verified, low
> prices for corn-fed cattle, and absence of all the usual
> enterprise in contracting & general despondency.
> Rains came early & spring was for a time, very prom-
> ising, but the water to which this gave rise did not last
> long; the drouth [sic] which followed covered the
> whole area west of the Mississippi to the Rocky
> Mountains.[50]

When declining prices followed this inclement weather, investors dissolved corporations and fled the industry. The remaining ranchers abandoned large, open-range operations. Boosters told potential investors, "The new plan is a tendency to smaller herds and a better breed, a system of protection from the weather." Forced to adopt new methods, they claimed that "the fattening of stock for the market is one of the gratifying innovations of recent years." And as the industry gradually recovered, regional associations and railroads promoted Denver as the favored western location for meatpacking.[51] The Denver Union Stock Yard opened in 1886 at the impetus of the Chamber of Commerce, which reported that the yard "means much more to Denver than a substantial profit to the stockholders of the company, for the reason that kindred and dependent enterprises, promoted by local capital, have sprung up in the shape of packing houses and other plants." Western ranchers grew more dependent on markets that Denver created. By 1900, Denver's packing companies slaughtered fifty thousand cattle each year, with more than half coming from feed lots in Kansas and Nebraska. Other cows fed on corn at the Union Stock Yard to increase their weight and quality.[52] Denver entrepreneurs found new means to expand and dominate large parts of the West's agriculture.

Regional agriculture changed dramatically in the decades following the discovery of gold. Perceptions of desertlike conditions and the presence of Indians initially left Denver's plains underused by market standards. Denverites altered the human geography of the plains by violently removing their human occupants and endlessly promoting their agrarian possibilities. Over time, Denverites similarly cleared and developed the western slope. Regional entrepreneurs recruited farmers, sold land, founded colonies, researched more profitable crops, built canals, and managed ranching properties throughout the West. They guided the enactment of water laws that seemingly promoted the most productive use of arid lands and made water a commodity. Within the agricultural hinterland, however, localism and regulation persisted. Ranchers formed extralegal organizations to regulate the open-range industry when unrestricted market principles threatened chaos in the fledgling industry. Urban entrepreneurs helped farmers halt distant corporate interlopers' efforts to secure appropriative rights, and the Colorado Supreme Court supported their cause.

Despite the booms and busts experienced by farmers and ranchers, Denverites wove their agricultural and mining hinterlands into an increasingly far-reaching, integrated, diversified regional economy. One booster observed:

Figure 8. Denver Union Stockyards. The stockyards, nearby meatpacking plants, and railroad tracks facilitated Denver's expansion of its agricultural functions in the 1890s. The Omaha and Grant smelter smokestack, a symbol of Denver's industrial might, is visible in the background. Photograph by Louis Charles McClure. Courtesy of Denver Public Library, Western History Collection.

Colorado is the nucleus, the kernel of the great commercial empire stretching from the Missouri River to the Pacific Slope, from Canada to the Gulf, in which Denver reigns without a possible commercial rival. . . . Silver, you say and gold; with agriculture leading them both, and irrigation, with its magic touch and tremendous possibilities back of it.[53]

FOUR

CREATING A VALUABLE NICHE

Colorado Springs and the Tourist Trade

Climate and scenery are valued beyond many natural resources that have a dimension and gravity. Some day this climate will be recognized as an asset, as real and tangible as the product of field or mine.

Governor Alva Adams, 1887

nice point

The region's farmers did more than change its landscape and expand its economic bases. They fulfilled important notions of social good, occupying the middle state between the savage and the refined.[1] In 1894, historian Frederick Jackson Turner argued that across a series of primitive frontiers, pioneers became both part of nature and its conquerors, and in the process, learned to be Americans. His essay captured long-standing national lore about the frontier's regenerative importance and new fears about overcrowded, industrial cities as wilderness seemed to fade away. Citizens wanted the United States viewed as a maturing nation with a sense of gentility, but also longed for "authentic" frontier experiences and looked for ways to re-create them. In this context, tourism in the American West assumed greater cultural meaning than simple recreation. Many Americans imagined that the wilderness experience could only be found there, even if their excursions rarely matched the reality of its inhabitants. The tourist became an important participant in the West after the 1860s, when the nation, free from its sectional crisis, periodically awash in industrial prosperity, and teeming with new railroads, could afford to send consumers in search of adventures.[2] A western city that controlled the tourist trade created a viable economic niche. The people of Colorado Springs seized this opportunity.

Denverites recognized the tourist's value and quickly jumped into the trade. Their city became the transfer point for visitors seeking the natural wonders of Colorado and the Rocky Mountains. Yet, while tourism formed a small part of this metropolis's economy, it defined Colorado Springs.[3] Its founders envisioned a resort that combined the advantages of nature and civilization. Colorado Springs existed for consumers seeking the gracious amenities and genteel qualities of an elite city and the primitive, sublime wilderness of its environs. Its entrepreneurs proved particularly adept at marketing to wealthy consumptives the restorative powers of climate, altitude, and other natural resources lacking "dimension and gravity." A few denizens of Colorado Springs considered challenging Denver's hegemony, but a rivalry never developed. As a visitor observed in 1892, "Denver and Colorado Springs pretend to be jealous of each other; why, it is impossible to understand. One is a city, and the other a summer or health resort; and we might as properly compare Boston and Newport, or New York and Tuxedo."[4]

Cities existed in relation to each other, and the residents of Colorado Springs, founded twelve years after Denver, hoped to create a community that contrasted markedly with perceived notions of frontier boomtowns, avoiding the social and environmental problems associated with Denver and the region's extractive industries. Although Colorado Springs became the headquarters of the Denver & Rio Grande Railway, the company's subsidiaries in steel and coal called other towns home. Colorado Springs proffered a new way of living to its inhabitants and visitors.[5] Its organizers invested heavily in regional mining and transportation, but foresaw for Colorado Springs a unique position within the urban hierarchy, complementing the larger, more diversified metropolis. Long before Governor Adams mentioned the value of such assets, Colorado Springs entrepreneurs packaged amorphous natural elements, and sold them as commodities like the ores of the mountains or the crops of the plains. In the process, market values came to dominate the development of Colorado Springs's hinterlands more than other segments of the regional economy.

The emergence of Colorado Springs is inevitably linked to William Jackson Palmer and his vision of a regional empire. While scouting a possible southern route for the Union Pacific Eastern Division in the 1860s, Palmer traveled through southern Colorado and neighboring New Mexico. He became convinced of their economic potential, and by 1870, began to execute his plan for the "material conquest" of this wilderness. Palmer told his fiancée of his "wide awake dream": "I thought how fine it would be to have a little railroad of a few hundred miles length all under one's own control with one's friends."[6] He had big ambitions for the Denver & Rio Grande. His scheme departed from accepted railroading principles in two ways. First, the Denver & Rio Grande ran over narrow-gauge tracks. Palmer easily attracted local stockholders, but eastern investors grew skittish after small regional railroads failed in other parts of the nation and a tightening English money market limited overseas options for capital. Palmer and his British-born colleague, William Bell, proposed narrow-gauge tracks, which cut construction costs by a third and allowed them to successfully recruit British investors. Narrow gauge also proved well suited for steep mountains and narrow passes, and soon became the region's norm.[7]

The second departure from railroading principles lay in its geographic perspective. Railroads generally ran along an east-west axis to support exploitation of western resources by eastern industrial centers. Having witnessed the Denver Pacific, Palmer believed that another north-south line opened alternative avenues for intraregional trade. He shared his vision with potential British investors in *The Denver and Rio Grande Railway of Colorado and New Mexico*. His "little railroad" would skirt the Rockies, exploiting gypsum and coal deposits along its route, while branch lines penetrated mining camps and traversed cattle ranges as far away as Texas. Palmer and Bell contacted William Blackmore, Gilpin's partner in the Sangre de Cristo, to exploit investments in Mexican land grants. They established a "pool" to finance the railroad's initial construction from Denver to Colorado Springs, while Blackmore pursued additional British and

Dutch investors. Jerome Chaffee and other Denver financiers invested in the Maxwell Grant in anticipation of the railroad's north-south route and installed Palmer as their first president in 1870 to ensure that it reached their property.[8]

Palmer elaborated his intentions in the railroad's *First Annual Report*. The thousand-mile haul from St. Louis, he argued, served as a "natural tariff protection for the native production of the Colorado-New Mexico area. Thus, a self-sufficient western empire would develop around Colorado whose natural commercial orientation would be toward Mexico City by way of settled communities at the base of the Rockies and down the Rio Grande Valley." His "Mountain Base Railroad" would be "a natural economic unit in a long longitudinal productive area marked off from the east by the 400-mile strip of wasteland and from the west by a mountain wilderness. Thus, the new road will have an adequate commercial area to serve and natural features to protect it from competition." Palmer hoped to trade Colorado fuel, manufactures, and produce for the riches of semitropical Mexico, and added, "The heart of that republic with its 9 millions of people (and 110,000 in New Mexico) is as naturally our objective point, as the Pacific slope of the United States with its 700,000 population was the proper objective of the Pacific Railroad when it started across the plains from the banks of the Missouri." To complete his vision, Palmer later organized the Mexican National Railway with ambitions of shipping Mexico's tin, zinc, silver, cotton, and corn to Colorado's front range for processing there.[9]

For Palmer, the railroad offered more than a mode of making money. He planned to solve "a good many vexed social problems." Employees of every rank would share in the company's stocks and profits. Growing prosperous with the railroad, workers would live in model towns without class strife.[10] Market values, which required the most productive exploitation of resources, shaped Palmer's regional vision, but his aspirations for improved labor relations, albeit never realized, suggested a concern for equity and community stability. Like Denver's entrepreneurs, Palmer hoped to establish a lasting legacy. If his railroad stood as a testament to capitalism, Colorado Springs would mark his commitment to a better social order.

A series of cities along the railroad undergirded Palmer's plan. He anticipated that population would follow Denver & Rio Grande expansion, and understood the importance of strategic urban locations in controlling resources and accessing markets, although Palmer and his associates faced a difficulty other railroads did not experience. The government awarded substantial land grants to the transcontinental lines, the Denver Pacific, and the Kansas Pacific; Palmer's road received only a narrow right-of-way. Consequently, the Mexican land grant interests of Palmer, Bell, Gilpin, Chaffee, and other entrepreneurs frequently dictated the railroad's route. In addition to the Maxwell and Sangre de Cristo grants, Palmer and his associates held shares in the Nolan, Las Animas, Conejos, and Tierra Amarilla properties at different times. Following common nineteenth-century railroad practices, the Denver & Rio Grande purchased proposed townsites through affiliated land companies, often bypassing existing communities. Under duress, other established towns ceded property for depots and yards before the railroad agreed to lay tracks to their borders.[11]

Construction began in Denver in the spring of 1871, and by autumn, the Denver & Rio Grande reached the vicinity of Colorado City, a supply town built at the base of Pike's Peak in 1859. Its residents never offered Denver any meaningful competition, and the railroad's subsidiary, the Colorado Springs Company, dashed any hopes for a fresh start when it platted a new city next door. The first in a series of towns, Colorado Springs offered natural amenities, as Palmer explained to his fiancée. "When I found the magnificent Pike's Peak towering immediately above me . . . I could not sleep any more with all the splendid panorama of mountains gradually unrolling itself . . . Near here are the finest of soda springs—and the most enticing scenery. I am sure there will be a famous resort here." Confident in his vision, Palmer purchased, from rancher Irving Howbert and others, some ninety-three hundred acres for the townsite even before he secured construction capital.[12]

In planning a resort, Palmer recognized a trend launched in the late 1860s. The transcontinental railroad and a nascent advertising industry exploited the West's scenic wonders, while modern mass leisure made a viable tourist trade possible. In an industrializing United

States and Europe, the emerging middle classes and the "nouveau riche" often turned to long-distance travel. Local entrepreneurs tried to seize their share of this disposable income by comparing the region to Europe. A guidebook boasted, "all the sublimest glories of the Swiss and Italian Alps, all the picturesque savagery of the Tyrol, and all the softer beauty of Killarney and Como and Naples dwindle to insignificance by comparison with the stupendous scenes that meet the gaze at every turn in Colorado." At the same time, these pristine scenic wonders offered a counterpart to a European cultural past that the younger nation could not match.[13] The ecological damage caused by mining failed to dim the lure of Colorado's mountains. To the contrary, an adoration of technology dominated the region in the late nineteenth century and facilitated tourism. Entrepreneurs, who invested in mining, tourism, and the railroads that served both industries, advertised as a sightseeing attraction the unique technology employed to conquer Colorado's high peaks. Travel guides promoted the mountainous narrow gauge as a nineteenth-century thrill ride: "It doubles in, it doubles out, leaving the traveler in doubt whether the engine on the track is going on or coming back." Even the scarred mountains offered the adventurer abandoned gold mines and ghost towns. Engineering marvels, like the Rockies themselves, offered alternatives to Europe's historical landmarks.[14]

Palmer selected a fortuitous location for his resort in the shadow of Pike's Peak. Colorado Springs residents easily commodified the western monument made famous by Long, Frémont, and other American explorers who climbed (or in Pike's case, tried to climb) the mountain. The peak gave its name to the 1859 gold rush, although few successful early mines lay in its vicinity.[15] Palmer and his associates situated "Fountain Colony," as they temporarily called Colorado Springs, at the confluence of Monument and Fountain creeks under the mountain, and carefully considered each aspect of their promotional campaign. First came the issue of a name. Palmer favored calling the city "Monument Dells" and the nearby soda springs "La Font," but the company's agents, emulating eastern spas, identified the resort as Colorado Springs, a moniker vaguely associated with an area encompassing the confluence, the springs, Garden of the Gods, and

Colorado City. Colorado Springs stuck, although the mineral waters lay five miles away. In August 1871, Blackmore encountered some Utes at the springs. Assuming that they used the water ceremonially, he suggested the name Manitou in honor of the spirit in Longfellow's *Hiawatha.* Robert Cameron, the Colorado Springs Company manager, realized that the Utes used the water to ease indigestion and rheumatism, and probably knew nothing of the Algonquin deity, but the company's public-relations man recognized both Blackmore's importance and the advertising value of this name, easily identified by the more literate visitors they hoped to attract. La Font became Manitou.[16]

As marketed across the United States, the new settlement catered to the well-to-do. Palmer hoped to spawn a community whose members would invest in his other ventures, and make Colorado Springs "the most attractive place for homes in the West." The entrepreneurial classes that emerged during the Gilded Age treasured proper manners and good breeding as signs of their social status. Eager to attract such people, Palmer cultivated the image of a genteel resort on the edge of wilderness.[17] The Colorado Springs Company issued broadsides, *Our New Saratoga* and *Villa La Font,* for readers inclined to go west in style. The company checkerboarded town lots, offering alternate "villa sites" for wealthier prospects, and holding the remainder in anticipation of rising prices as the adjacent properties sold. In 1872, the town company received nearly four thousand inquiries, and that summer, fifteen hundred visitors arrived, many staying at the new Colorado Springs Hotel, which the local newspaper billed as "the most elegant hostelry between Chicago and San Francisco."[18] Palmer and his associates also recruited the better classes of Europe. Investor and former governor A. C. Hunt suggested sending agents to Switzerland, Sweden, and Germany to seek out emigrants, but their greatest success came in the British Isles. R. B. Townsend, a visiting Englishman, praised Colorado Springs as a "very high-toned sort of new town." Known as "Little London," some two thousand English immigrants elevated Colorado Springs's social tone in an Anglophilic age. Colorado Springs blossomed; Colorado City wilted away.[19]

As Colorado Springs experienced this initial boon, it provoked criticism from others in the region. The egalitarian editor of the

Greeley Tribune observed that the resort's wealthy residents lived off the interest on investments. He complained that "while the people of Greeley are engaged in creating wealth, the people of Colorado Springs are spending it." The *Colorado Springs Gazette*'s editor worried about the implications of citizens "who are really better off out of it, people who would stay at home if there were only the prospect of an ordinary settler's life before them." Their perceived selfishness created a moral crisis for traditional, republican-minded farmers and middle-class merchants. Could American values of individualism, self-sufficiency, and democracy appear, he wondered, in a place catering to those who never experienced a pioneer's challenges? Moreover, the high cost of living in Colorado Springs excluded many Americans who preferred urban living. In the early 1880s, for example, an average furnished room rented for twenty-five dollars per month, compared to ten dollars in Denver. Tourists in Colorado Springs expected to spend money, a notion most local merchants endorsed, although a few residents warned against exploitation. The *Denver Tribune* cautioned, "Be satisfied with a moderate share of the tourist's spare cash, assured that he will give you another chance to pluck him."[20]

Such admonishments proved the exception as local businessmen began to develop the tourist trade. The Denver & Rio Grande stood at the forefront, just as other western railroads drew visitors to national parks. It offered attractive excursion rates to Colorado Springs and enticed travelers with brochures containing photographs of nearby scenic wonders, idealized etchings of Colorado Springs, and testimonials to its luxuries, often by visitors "converted" into residents. Frequent analogies to established eastern resorts such as Saratoga produced a veneer of respectability in the early days.[21] Colorado's Frank Fossett attributed the city's popularity to "a greater number of wonders and attractions easily accessible and within a short distance than any other single locality"—scenic resources sold as commodities to the touring public. Rainbow Falls and Ute Pass offered "abundance of romantic scenery." Just a few miles north sat the famous Garden of the Gods, "a set of massive, irregular sandstone formations." Within an hour's drive, picnickers found the "sparkling brooklets, streams and beautiful waterfalls" of Cheyenne Canyon. A day's ride brought visitors to the Royal Gorge of the Arkansas River, where they gazed at "the appalling view from the main walls . . . overcome by awe at the magnitude of nature's handiwork." The venerable beacon of Pike's Peak towered over everything.[22]

The ideology of capitalism pervaded this tourist trade. Capital property involved both appropriating and allocating resources. In some ways, it was impossible to own scenery or climate or altitude, but Colorado Springs entrepreneurs appropriated such resources by establishing a high standard of living for residents and visitors that limited access to the natural vistas the area offered. For a price, they allocated these resources to the wealthy. Like their counterparts in regional agriculture and mining and their competitors in California's travel industry, local resort owners relied on the national marketplace for capital and consumers. They aimed promotional materials at investors and tourists alike.[23] And like the agricultural and mining areas, the tourism hinterland involved altering perceptions of the region. A self-conscious creation, tourism required a reimagined landscape. In the search for the "authentic" western experience, middle- and upper-class travelers helped change the human geography once again. Pike and Long had described the land around Pike's Peak as a home to indigenous peoples. White trappers and traders saw a world rich with beaver fur. The early days of the gold rush presented failed placers and lodes. Under the promotional efforts of Palmer and his associates, this land became both a place of gentle amenities and a wilderness for those seeking the withering frontier.[24]

Hotel and railroad managers exploited a booming eastern market for western stories to reach these travelers. The frontier captured the collective cultural imagination of the nation, and local businessmen and their literary visitors found ways to serve each other. Palmer and his associates sought favorable reviews by inviting and catering to writers. Exploiting the national interest in the West, these travel authors used terminology common to popular guidebooks and spread the word about Colorado Springs. The city and its environs were "enchanting," "thrilling," "majestic," "spectacular," "awe-inspiring," and "uplifting in the presence of God; such dwarfing of the mortal sense."[25] The *Rocky Mountain Directory and Colorado Gazetteer*, in turn, praised the writers as "celebrated travelers, learned tourists, versatile newspaper correspondents, poets, authors and editors [who] have exhausted the vocabulary of laudatory phraseology in attempting to describe the grandeur, beauty and sublimity of the mountain and valley scenery."[26]

get

Helen Hunt Jackson, best known for her critique of the nation's Indian policies, *A Century of Dishonor*, and the novel *Ramona*, arrived in 1873 seeking a cure for chronic bronchitis. She became a permanent resident after marrying William Jackson, the Denver & Rio Grande treasurer and El Paso County Bank president. Hunt Jackson searched for transcendence in nature; she found it at Colorado Springs: "It was in the east that the wise men saw the star; but it was westward to a high mountain, in a lonely place, that the disciples were led for transformation!" Cheyenne Canyon became one of "nine places of divine worship" in the Colorado Springs environs. She saw the preservation of the world in the wildness of nature, much like Henry David Thoreau. In the sacred landscapes, she and other writers hoped to glimpse God, but like the elite tourist who came west as a consumer for both recreation and sublimity, they brought urban notions of "wilderness."[27] Looking for authentic western experiences, early visitors welcomed peaceful meetings with Utes who used Manitou until the dint of the tourist traffic forced them away in 1874. To find the sublime, wilderness travelers increasingly desired a return to a pristine nature. The Utes' departure helped tourists accept the illusion that they saw original nature as God created it. Of course, few landscapes remained untouched by human civilization. Pristine nature was a romantic invention of nineteenth-century writers such as Jackson, Thoreau, and Longfellow, but it suited the material needs of Colorado Springs's entrepreneurs and the metaphysical longings of their wealthy visitors.[28]

Figure 9 (opposite). South Cheyenne Canyon. Staircases facilitated visitors' encounter with wilderness near Colorado Springs in Cheyenne Canyon, which Helen Hunt Jackson described as one of "nine places of divine worship." Photograph by Louis Charles McClure. Courtesy of Denver Public Library, Western History Collection.

SEVEN FALLS, CHEYENNE CANON
PHOTO BY L.C. McCLURE, DENVER

good air

CHAPTER 4

(Other travelers joined Helen Hunt Jackson in seeking cures for their respiratory ailments.) Since 1858, emigrants had written of gentle winters along the front range, the absence of extreme temperatures, and the region's dry air. Samuel Bowles told his readers, "here would seem to be the fountain of health; and among these hills and plains is surely to be many a summer resort for the invalid." The Territorial Board of Immigration and other booster organizations echoed Colorado's role as a sanatorium. The migration to Colorado Springs and other southwestern spas represented one of the last expressions of medical geography that began in antiquity, a revival in the belief that the environment improved civilization and altered individuals' chemistry.[29] Tuberculosis, a disease with different meanings based on class and race, centered the new medical migrations. Before the Civil War, the rich perceived the deaths of their tubercular relatives and friends as transcendent moments between the harsh modernizing world and eternal peace. With new understandings of bacteria, romantic notions surrounding the disease changed. Tuberculosis became a degrading but treatable disease, instead of a spiritual burden. A commensurate shift from the construct of invalidism with home care to a notion of health-seeking followed. A change of residence provided the preferred treatment. The mountainous West became a restorative sanctuary, a healthful, idyllic retreat from overcrowding and industrialization. Eastern urbanites led this new migration to cities on the edge of the frontier, as historian Earl Pomeroy explains. Colorado Springs competed with Denver, Salt Lake City, Los Angeles, and others for consumptives, and by 1879, emerged as a favored destination.[30]

A group of enterprising physicians moved to Colorado Springs to exploit this health market, and often joined with Palmer's investors in other ventures. The doctors asserted that Colorado's dryness reduced the capacity of the air to conduct heat and electricity, and therefore cured pulmonary diseases. High altitudes supposedly reduced the oxygen content and replaced it with a purifying, antiseptic ozone, exciting respiration and increasing capillary circulation. The climatological elements of sunlight, aridity, and altitude could not be shipped east for industrial development, but could be marketed to those who could afford to travel to Colorado Springs. Although entrepreneurs could not take possession of such elements, they still claimed owner-ship. For example, in Colorado Springs, a visitor might purchase "sunshine insurance" from the hotels and receive a rebate if there was too much rain. While exploiting wealthy health seekers, few seemed concerned about the preservation of these natural resources for the common good.

Dr. Samuel Solly, who recovered his own health at Colorado Springs, was among the first to market its medicinal resources and the restorative qualities of Manitou's waters, which supposedly relieved dyspepsia, flatulence, nervous exhaustion, and general debility. Solly's *Manitou, Colorado, U.S.A.* launched a cottage industry of similar pub-lications. In what became the standard nomenclature, Solly included his chemical analyses of the mineral waters and detailed meteorologi-cal information to illustrate that the region offered the invalid the best opportunity for recovery. He shared inspiring testimonials from cured patients, and over time, added essays describing cultural advantages, scenic photographs, and hotel advertisements.[32] These medical boost-ers belonged to a nineteenth-century culture that placed unlimited faith in science for the solutions to human problems. Gilpin believed sci-ence divine, and joined the regional chorus on health, proclaiming "the miracle of these broadly expanded altitudes is their climatology." Charles Denison, a Denver physician with financial interests in Colorado Springs, made a pointedly elitist pitch, arguing the region offered "a salutary influence on the class of overworked brains, which, in the intensity of political, professional and business life, is quite numerous nowadays." He organized the American Climatological Association in 1884 to develop supportive scientific data, and recruited Solly and other doctors to contribute to its publication, aptly titled *Transactions*.[33] Dr. F. J. Bancroft graphically described how the aseptic atmosphere caused "the narrow in chest to become broad, the relaxed in muscle to grow strong, the thin in flesh to gain weight, and thor-oughly regenerates those suffering from the bilious diseases caused by prolonged residence in malarial districts." Recognizing the market value of noncorporeal elements, Dr. Samuel Fiske added, "there is a wealth of life stored up in the dry, sunny climate of this State, more precious than the hidden treasures which the mountains contain."[34]

Sanatoriums opened in Denver despite the fact that its factories left its skies polluted, and other local communities competed with Colorado Springs for the region's tourist and health dollars. Colorado Springs entrepreneurs quickly countered their promotions with unfavorable comparisons. They boasted that their city's air lacked industrial debris, while as Solly emphasized, Denver, "the chief manufacturing city of this region— . . . is colder, has more snow . . . and in summer is hotter." Pueblo, an emerging rival to the south, experienced excessively hot summers. Denver and Pueblo pumped muddy, polluted water from the Platte and Arkansas rivers, respectively, necessitating a "filtering process before it is fit to use, and then it is strongly alkaline, having no comparison with the exceptionally pure water of Colorado Springs and Manitou." By 1880, the flood of visitors to Colorado Springs reached 30,000 annually, and by 1890, some 200,000 arrived. Still an elite community, the city's permanent population only grew from 4,200 to 11,100 over that same decade.[35]

Other regional tourist sites saw their popularity rise in the late 1870s and 1880s, when they copied the successful methods employed in Colorado Springs. The Idaho Springs Chamber of Commerce, for example, introduced the Georgetown loop on the railroad trip from Denver, and offered sojourns to the summit of Mount Evans. Its natural setting produced "a medicinal water that is released steaming on the surface, for the cure of thousands who find no relief from other sources." In Glenwood Springs, the owners of the hot springs presented "for the Medical Profession, Invalids and Tourists, comprehensive data and information in regard to the Springs, the Climate, Medicinal characteristics of the water." The Colorado Hotel in Glenwood Springs promised the same luxuries as Colorado Springs's best facilities. Denver mining entrepreneur James Dexter developed the Inter-Laken Hotel at Twin Lakes near Aspen, boasting of its hot and cold baths, billiards, and other refinements.[36] These competitors, however, possessed neither the skills nor financial resources of Colorado Springs's entrepreneurs. And Colorado Springs rarely rested while its rivals developed their tourist attractions. Railroads, hotels, and information services stoked the promotional fires so well and invested so heavily in elaborate advertising campaigns that by the 1890s, one easterner observed,

"Colorado Springs is becoming so well known and famous that no trip to the West or the Pacific Coast is considered complete without a visit to the Springs." The city anchored Colorado's travel industry, as the state competed with California for western tourism dollars. The two easily outdistanced other western states.[37]

During the final quarter of the nineteenth century, American hoteliers offered elegant amenities while emphasizing the scenery of a particular location. The West introduced monumental natural landscapes to the industry. Solly and the physician-authors moved beyond the realm of science to join Palmer and his associates in developing such aspects of the Colorado Springs economy. To compete with established resorts in the East and in California, many urban boosters believed that Colorado Springs needed a grand hotel in addition to its health spas. Solly presided over a town meeting on 1 April 1881, advising the community of Palmer's scheme to build the finest western hotel. After the Colorado Springs Company contributed four acres, Palmer arranged a fifty-thousand-dollar construction loan, and offered to buy twenty-five thousand dollars of stock in the new enterprise if the town matched him. By evening's end, other residents pledged almost the full amount. The next day, the *Gazette* encouraged more citizens to join the enterprise "for the benefit of the entire community." Within a few weeks, the municipality took an interest, floating the business a loan. The Antlers Hotel opened in June 1883, "a new, attractive and elegantly appointed hotel, situated in the most noted of Colorado's health resorts, and affording unsurpassed accommodations." It even provided a modern hydraulic elevator.[38] An urban hotel situated at the end of Pike's Peak Avenue, the Antlers offered a panoramic view of the mountain that first gave meaning to the resort town. Palmer adopted a vigorous national advertising campaign to promote his luxury hotel, and garnered the cover of *Harper's Weekly* within three years. Colorado Springs's palaces imparted a sense of sublime wilderness blended with stylish amenities for the elite traveler.[39]

The essential development of Manitou complemented the progress of Colorado Springs's health spas and luxury hotels. Palmer and his associates invested heavily there. In the 1870s, mineral water springs carried a mystique of supernatural healing powers for differ-

Figure 10. The Antlers Hotel. The monumental scenery of Pike's Peak frames William Jackson Palmer's luxury hotel, the Antlers, offering tourists the amenities of a genteel civilization and the sublimity of nature in the city's environs. Photograph by William Henry Jackson. Courtesy of Colorado Historical Society.

ent maladies. A short-lived rivalry between Colorado Springs and Manitou resulted in mutual dependence. Colorado Springs enjoyed greater name recognition and rail connections, but Manitou possessed the waters. The Denver & Rio Grande's William Bell organized a consolidation of Manitou hotels under a land company "so as to concentrate their divided efforts . . . and provide against injurious competition either between hotels or the owners of the property for sale as building lots." The Colorado Springs Company owned a large portion of the association's land and managed the hotels through 1900. Although not completely successful, Bell's interests in the Manitou Mansion Hotel, the Manitou Avenue Hotel, the Manitou House, and the Manitou Park Hotel, as well as the Antlers in Colorado Springs, allowed him to quell much intracity competition. Bell and other investors also formed the Manitou Mineral Water, Bath and Parks Company to enclose most of the springs and control their flow. The company marketed Colorado's health resources across the country through its bottled water.[40]

Having established their city as a favored resort, local merchants and entrepreneurs exploited excellent rail connections to expand its functions within the urban hierarchy, while attempting to keep the actual industries at a distance. Colorado Springs supplied nearby mining districts, local coal fields, and ranchers on the adjacent plains and became the shipment point for products from these hinterlands. Many of its wealthier residents, such as Jerome Wheeler, the owner of the Aspen sideline claim, speculated in various Rocky Mountain mining frontiers. The Durango Trust, which developed railroads, land companies, smelters and mines in southwestern Colorado, headquartered in Colorado Springs. Yet the city's tributary sphere remained smaller than and often overlapped Denver's realm of influence.[41] A railroad battle in the 1880s demonstrated Colorado Springs's inability to offer more than limited challenges to the metropolis's hegemony. Like Wheeler, who initially left New York City for health reasons, James Hagerman came to Colorado Springs in October 1884 on the advice of his physician, who believed his tuberculosis would kill him if he remained in Milwaukee. He soon invested in regional silver mines, and became president of the

Colorado Midland Railway, incorporated by Colorado Springs men, including Wheeler and Howbert, to establish the first front-range link to Aspen and the only standard gauge line over the Continental Divide. Hagerman recruited eastern investors who previously joined his profitable ventures in Michigan's iron-ore fields. The Denver & Rio Grande had fallen into receivership in the early 1880s, and by this time, Moffat and other Denver interests managed it. They wanted to claim Aspen. Denver's superior financial resources and political influence within the state and the nation allowed their enterprise to pull ahead. Hagerman's railway arrived in Aspen in February 1888, three months after the Denver & Rio Grande.[42]

Colorado Springs could not overcome the behemoth, but it supplemented Denver's activities in transportation, and its entrepreneurs' investments created new sources of regional capital. By 1890, Colorado Springs was a stable, wealthy community. Driven by its multidimensional resort industry and smaller economic activities, it benefited from the many "capitalists, not only of this state, but of the far East and North, and even from old England, who have come here to make their homes," according to Colorado Midland promotions. Although Denver led the region's silver boom in the 1880s, Colorado Springs still profited from it. The region's denizens spent more money on leisure activities at its resorts, while these resident capitalists successfully speculated in mining ventures and expanded the city's influence. Hagerman's stock in the First National Bank of Colorado Springs, for example, gave him access to inside investment information. In addition to his railroad and Aspen silver mines, he invested in coal mines at New Castle and Elk Creek, Colorado and irrigation projects in New Mexico and Texas.[43] Having carved a profitable economic niche, Colorado Springs and its residents occupied a privileged position. It allowed them to capitalize on the last and greatest Colorado mining bonanza when gold was found in their backyard at Cripple Creek. Denver's entrepreneurs dominated this new hinterland, but Colorado Springs emerged in the 1890s as a more versatile, more influential player.

Pike's Peak gave its name to the gold rush in 1859, but when miners combed the area with little luck, the nearby mountain parks of

Cripple Creek had been turned over to cattle grazing. Only a few men persisted in prospecting. One of them, Robert Womack, brought gold samples to Colorado Springs for assaying, and by May 1891, considerable prospecting began anew. On the Fourth of July, Winfield Stratton, a Colorado Springs carpenter, marked the Independence and Washington claims and launched a new gold rush. Concentrated in ten square miles on the southwestern side of Pike's Peak, the Cripple Creek fields required only a four-hour wagon drive from Colorado Springs. A feverish race erupted to establish key town sites in the fields and Colorado Springs merchants and bankers prepared to assert their leadership. They laid out the town of Hayden Placer adjacent to Fremont, a town built by local miners. Like Denver and Auraria in 1860 or Colorado Springs and Manitou in the 1870s, residents of both communities recognized that continued urban competition undermined their efforts and quickly merged. Incorporated in 1892, their new town of Cripple Creek had almost ten thousand inhabitants (plus many transients) and became the focus of the district, although the new community of Victor and Florence, a local ranching center, also buzzed with mining investments. Hoping to avoid the busts experienced by older mining camps, these new towns formed associations, such as the Victor Chamber of Commerce, designed to promote a more permanent populace and diversified economic activity.[44]

Miners found Cripple Creek gold locked in compound tellurides that required complex chemical reductions through cyanidation or chlorination, much like the silver alloys from Leadville and Aspen. While Colorado Springs entrepreneurs eagerly utilized their proximity to the new mining districts and their superior rail connections to seize the supply lines, they did not provide other attendant services within their city's boundaries. By 1891, Denver and Pueblo already possessed large, technologically superior smelters. Colorado Springs's residents knew that they could not compete for this urban function, and claimed little desire to do so. Palmer later observed:

> When this town was started, the thought of manufactures, mills, furnaces, etc., was not at all in the minds of the founders . . . Until the development of Cripple Creek, the question came up occasionally, but was

scarcely raised with any seriousness. Those gold mines
have of course added greatly to at least the rapidity of
our growth here. Fortunately for us, they are forty
miles away, and we have enjoyed the benefits without
the self-evident drawbacks.[45]

Colorado Springs added to its fortunes as a financial center for Cripple
Creek, avoiding its polluting processing industries. Financing was a
significant task. Cripple Creek gold production began with a value of
200,000 dollars in 1891, but within six years, reached 10,800,000
dollars, and in 1900, topped 20,000,000 dollars annually, representing one-fourth of the nation's output. In 1893, the newly established
Colorado Springs Mining Exchange traded more shares than any other
exchange in the world. Bank deposits in the front-range city increased
ninefold. Its population doubled, and millionaires in residence
jumped from three to fifty. Physical proximity alone does not explain
this expanded function; Pueblo was nearly as close to the mines.
Colorado Springs garnered its new role, in part, because the entrepreneurs who founded it twenty years earlier had successfully recruited
their elite classes. Its wealthy residents, who chose the city because of
its high standard of living or its restorative reputation, grabbed the
initiative in Cripple Creek speculations and held tight.

George Buckman owned hotels and other businesses, and served
as secretary for the Colorado Springs Chamber of Commerce. When
gold was discovered, he invested earnings from these enterprises in
Cripple Creek and became vice-president of the Exchange. Charter
members of the Exchange also included Hagerman, Howbert, and
William Jackson.[46] State incorporation records confirm Colorado
Springs's emergence as a financial center. In 1883 and 1884, for example, only twenty-six new corporations headquartered in Colorado
Springs or Manitou, with only 2.8 percent of the state's authorized
capital. Few engaged in mining. By 1896, with Cripple Creek production soaring, some 350 new corporations identified Colorado Springs,
representing 27 percent of authorized capital. Another 259 corporations called Cripple Creek home. The bulk of the capital came from
shares traded on the Colorado Springs Mining Exchange.[47]

With its new role and its residents' investments in Cripple Creek gold, Colorado Springs remained relatively untouched by the depression that rocked the nation and the region in the 1890s. While individual Denverites such as Moffat and Smith succeeded, Denver profited less proportionately from Cripple Creek than Colorado Springs because many of Denver's entrepreneurs invested more heavily in Leadville and felt the impact of declining silver prices. F. W. Crocker, president of Denver's Chamber of Commerce congratulated Colorado Springs "for her sense of seeing and faith in investing in Cripple Creek. Colorado Springs, with a very few from Denver, opened Cripple Creek. We wish them a continuance of all the prosperity they have had and more." Unwilling to concede the competition, however, he added, "Nevertheless, although they have blazed the way, it is not for Denver to say that she will not partake of the feast provided." Denver still commanded the key control exchange functions and the bulk of corporate investments in the region.[48]

In defining their city's role in the regional urban economy through elite tourism, Colorado Springs's residents acknowledged Denver's primacy, but they believed that they created a better environment than their front-range counterparts. Like Denver, Colorado Springs's growth depended on linking the natural resources of its hinterland to human elements in distant ecosystems. Prior to the Cripple Creek discoveries, however, its commerce involved moving people from more heavily populated areas to those resources rather than extracting and shipping raw materials eastward. Because beautiful scenery supported the tourist trade, the physical alterations of the land that accompanied Colorado Springs's initial development were more subtle and less destructive than those in Denver's mining and agricultural hinterlands, but they still had serious implications.

For example, in early 1871, an eleven-mile irrigation ditch from Fountain Creek quenched the new city's thirst. The absence of industrial activity left the water relatively clean and the proximity to its mountain source minimized the silt and mud. But this first ditch immediately proved inadequate. More than Colorado Springs's booming population prompted construction of a second ditch in 1873. The Colorado Springs Company, in its effort to create "an oasis of culture and refinement in the wild and undisciplined west," hired a British landscape architect to beautify the town. Following traditions from the eastern United States and England, where rainfall was more regular, he introduced deciduous trees and formal gardens that catered to British migrants. Having observed cottonwood groves along the region's rivers, the architect lined city streets with five thousand indigenous trees. These aesthetic additions overburdened finite water sources. The planners failed to appreciate, for example, that cottonwoods naturally gathered near streams because of their enormous water consumption, transpiring some fifteen hundred gallons daily. Before 1870, recurrent prairie fires and flash floods limited the spread of cottonwood saplings. Converting the plains into towns, farms, and ranches, however, eliminated these natural checks. As demands for water increased, the city moved higher and higher up neighboring peaks, and by 1900, constructed reservoirs to tap distant montane aquifers.[49]

Constant efforts to enhance the city's status as the premier western resort further depleted the region's limited water. In the 1880s, Colorado Springs pumped Cheyenne Creek, which flowed from Cheyenne Mountain to the south and ran through the Broadmoor Dairy. The city lacked appropriative rights. Willie Wilcox, a wealthy scion who came to the springs for his health, and James Purtales, a German-born landowner, purchased the dairy. Modeled on European resorts, they planned a hotel and casino, but needed to remake the environment. They began with construction of an artificial lake by channeling and damming a portion of Cheyenne Creek, but struggled to maintain water levels. The city continued to steal water until the partners proved in court that a prior right attached to their property. Another problem was natural. Indigenous prairie dogs dug holes that drained the lake. The partners found a simple solution; they eliminated the prairie dogs with poison and explosives. The company, which reorganized as the Broadmoor Land and Investment Company after bankruptcy, sold its interests in August 1893 to the London and New York Investment Company, which completed the hotel and lake three years later. Gardeners selected decorative plants for their aesthetic value and contoured playing fields, erasing the natural terrain and its native grasses. Visitors gambled, played golf or polo, and shot pigeons within the Broadmoor's artificial world.[50]

Similarly, the Manitou Mineral Water, Bath and Parks Company manufactured an environment in which an admittance fee allowed visitors to enjoy the natural wonders. Its bathhouses enclosed the springs, while the company drilled artificial wells to extend the use of the mineralized waters. It called them "springs," with no distinction made as to whether humans or nature hewed the conduit. Natural springs diverted within well casings became part of an elaborate system of underground pipes that allowed the company to control the flow of Manitou water. As the popularity of the resort declined in the twentieth century, many springs fell into disrepair. Artesian pressure throughout Manitou decreased as water leaked through damaged well casings into the alluvium or fractured rock.[51]

Some of the most extensive physical transformations resulted from efforts to improve access to the scenic wonders. The technology that facilitated participation became an attraction in all its destructive power. George Crofutt's *Grip-Sack Guide of Colorado* celebrated beautiful vistas while introducing easterners to tours that snaked through precarious mountain passes on the narrow gauge. Industrial marvels at Cripple Creek offered travelers diversions from the gentility of Colorado Springs. Scenery and technology came together in one tourist enticement—the Manitou & Pike's Peak Railway. The company's founder, Zalmon Gilbert Simmons, arrived from Kenosha, Wisconsin, for a vacation in 1884. Exhausted from hiking up the peak, he proposed a cog railway to conquer the steep gradient that covered 7,518 feet in nine miles. Simmons also recognized the lure of the railway's machinery in his promotional brochures:

> The roadbed . . . is most substantial, being cut from or built upon solid rock in many places. There is no trestle work whatever; the four short bridges on the line are of iron, resting on solid masonry. To prevent the moving or sliding of the track . . . 146 anchors are imbedded into the solid rock.

Figure 11. *The Broadmoor Casino. This European-styled casino and resort catered to Colorado Springs's wealthiest guests. It sits on a large artificial lake created by diversions from Cheyenne Creek and the removal of indigenous prairie dogs. Photograph by H. S. Poley. Courtesy of Denver Public Library, Western History Collection.*

When the cog railway opened in 1891, hikers all but abandoned Old Bear Creek Trail to the summit. The railway reached the apex in two hours, but tourists found themselves farther removed from nature. They viewed famous Lake Moraine or Mount Hiawatha from a train window. With wilderness seemingly slipping away once more, some young men sought other adventures by sliding down the cog rails. Reaching speeds of sixty miles an hour, several perished.[52]

These celebrations of engineering revealed the devastation that technology wrought on the physical environment. To create a twenty-two-foot roadbed for the cog railway, crews graded steep mountain slopes and obliterated any rock formations, native plants, or animal habitats that blocked the most fortuitous route. This was nothing new. Dynamite swept away Rainbow Falls during the construction of the Colorado Midland. Ironically, in their effort to promote a "sublime" world for the weary traveler, local entrepreneurs destroyed innumerable natural structures and replaced them with the permanent infrastructure of a new human-made terrain. To make nature viable for tourists, they removed the "wild" from the wilderness. As early as 1871, Palmer donated nature areas to the city, attempting to maintain some of the natural beauty he first encountered. Thirty years later, he donated a 753-acre mesa overlooking the community, and created parks around Colorado Springs, Manitou, and Pike's Peak by redeeming areas that had become unregulated garbage dumps.[53] Palmer attempted to restore a natural environment lost forever in the Colorado Springs he helped launch.

In Colorado Springs and its hinterlands, perhaps more than elsewhere in the region, residents clearly and consistently applied the logic of the marketplace with few inhibitions. Amorphous natural resources, like altitude, climate, and sunshine, became commodities as the town sold both civility and wilderness. Its higher standard of living attracted wealthy residents who expanded the functional roles of Colorado Springs and controlled large parts of the Cripple Creek gold rush just as they dominated the resort industry. Perhaps Palmer best captured the prevailing attitude toward the utility of nature, even for those

Figure 12. Manitou & Pike's Peak Railway at Minnehaha Falls.
*Rather than gaining firsthand experience with nature by hiking
Pike's Peak, visitors increasingly enjoyed it and the technology of
the cog railway from the comfort of a car. Minnehaha Falls and
Mount Hiawatha, scenic wonders visible from the train, continued
the misapplied Longfellow references. Photograph by William
Henry Jackson. Courtesy of Colorado Historical Society, Denver,
Colorado.*

interested in its scenic and restorative values: "Never mind if Railroads and tunnels abolish poetry in some few instances, they introduce a higher and deeper and more permanent poetry into the lives of whole communities and States."[57] Nature served tourism. If natural elements, such as prairie dogs, obstructed or destroyed visitors' experiences with the pristine wilderness of their imaginations, they became expendable.

FIVE

FORGING STEEL
Pueblo's Incomplete Challenge

Obeying the laws of gravitation and attraction, the drops of
rain gather . . . running into natural channels down the steep
inclines of our mountains . . . So are the products of our mines
brought down from the mountains to these grand channels
prepared by human ingenuity and enterprise known as rail-
roads, then unloaded by them on platforms of the great ore
market of the West, the Pueblos, to be distributed to our large
metallurgical works . . . the railroad is the principal agency
that carries to Pueblo the mineral resources of the Great
Southwest.

Pueblo Board of Trade, 1883

While its founders quickly defined Colorado Springs's role within the
regional hierarchy, other towns struggled to find their places. Urban
careers were rarely stable or continuous.[1] From its trading post begin-
nings through its emergence as "the great ore market of the West,"
Pueblo's fortunes waxed and waned in response to local events like the
gold rush and broader national developments like the movement
toward capital consolidation within the United States economy.
Pueblo's entrepreneurs attempted to control complex hinterlands of
agricultural, mineral, and fuel resources, and competed, albeit unsuccessfully, with Denver for regional leadership. In the process, Pueblo
supplemented the activities of the metropolis. Pueblo coal and steel
reached across the West and into Mexico, frequently along the north-

south arc of the Rocky Mountains and the Rio Grande Valley, which its residents increasingly viewed as a natural phenomenon.

Before 1859, various settlements existed near the confluence of Fountain Creek and the Arkansas River, where Pueblo now stands. In 1833, trader John Gantt raised Fort Cass, but unsuccessful in brutal competition with Bent's Fort, abandoned it two years later. In 1842, George Simpson and Robert Fisher constructed a building called "the Pueblo." A group of independent traders soon owned it, living there with their families, tending livestock, cultivating bottomland, and bartering with Indians. More a New Mexican ranch than a fort, its location possessed numerous geographic advantages. The nearest point in the United States to Taos, it offered easy access to the Santa Fe Trail. Routes south to Mexico and north to posts on the South Platte joined at the mouth of Fountain Creek. An abundance of water and grass seemed capable of sustaining these settlers and their crops and animals, but mismanagement and overgrazing, the declining fur trade, and emigrations to Oregon and California shifted the Pueblo from prosperity to decline. New settlers, primarily from New Mexico, arrived at an almost derelict Pueblo in 1853 following news of congressional approval of a transcontinental rail route through the Arkansas River Valley. Sectional tensions, however, distracted Washington from organizing the line. After violent confrontations with the Utes, settlement along the Arkansas came to a halt in the mid-1850s and migrants again deserted the Pueblo.[2]

 The gold rush renewed interest in the confluence of the Arkansas and Fountain Creek. Two hundred Kansans claimed the east side of the creek, near the ruins of the old Pueblo, and christened their community Fountain City in February 1859. Ten months later, a new camp across the creek adopted the name Pueblo. The fledgling settlements merged within two years under the latter's name. Pleased with the mild winter climate, some prospectors opted for farming near town, while other emigrants established mercantile stores. They supplied and fed prospectors moving up the Arkansas to California Gulch and other diggings just as their counterparts in Denver serviced Clear Creek's miners. Pueblo's initial importance came as a central marketplace, a point of trade for these farms and mining districts.[3] Its founders hoped to make

Pueblo the front range entrepôt. They first sought a piece of the polit-ical pie. When the territorial legislature initially convened in 1861, George Chilcott and Jesús Barela led southern Colorado in urging Pueblo as the permanent capital, while Jerome Chaffee and other Denver leaders pushed for their northern city. Pueblo simply could not overcome Denver's urban primogeniture. The government temporarily assembled in Colorado City as a compromise, but soon returned to Denver where it remained permanently except for one three-year period. Pueblo also lagged in the performance of the control exchange functions that secured Denver's early dominance. For example, Pueblo obtained the telegraph more than a year after Denver. Nathaniel Hill summarized this urban competition: "You ask about the cities of Colorado. Denver is a city . . . Colorado City contains about twelve houses, several of them deserted. It is a city only in name. Pueblo is a city about like Colorado City."[4]

Other intraregional and external factors undermined Pueblo's goals. An initial boon, its proximity to the Santa Fe Trail soon worked to the town's disadvantage. New northerly trails to Denver allowed that city to maintain a more consistent trade during the Civil War. Pueblo, to the contrary, established its early linkages with areas in Kansas and Missouri where connections to the Confederacy hindered economic activities and outward migrations. With Colorado Territory pledged to the Union, travelers to the new gold fields generally chose the Platte River or Republican River route to Denver. From there, they took a shorter, albeit more difficult path to California Gulch across the 11,200-foot Weston Pass and bypassed Pueblo. As the social and economic effects of the war waned, Pueblo still trailed Denver and other front-range cities because the Arkansas Valley mining camps provided an insubstantial hinterland. As many as ten thousand prospected in California Gulch during the early 1860s, but within five years, placers played out and Oro City, the primary camp, stagnated. Miners located few significant lodes of gold. Lacking technological knowledge, the first prospectors failed to appreciate the value of silver-bearing lead carbonate ores that later made Leadville the center of the mining world. By 1870, only five hundred souls resided in Lake County, home to California Gulch and Pueblo's backyard.[5]

The loss of a railroad cemented Pueblo's secondary status. When William Palmer surveyed Pueblo's countryside for the Union Pacific Eastern Division, he recommended a route along the Arkansas River similar to the one contemplated in 1853. Lacking Denver's strong entrepreneurial leadership and financial connections, Pueblo never organized a promotional campaign to support Palmer's suggested route. John Evans and other Denverites, however, responded to the railroad's financial struggles and reorganized it as the Kansas Pacific. Denver became the terminus; Pueblo's options within the urban hierarchy became more constrained.[6] The remaining residents of nearby river valleys intensified their focus on agriculture. In the Huerfano Valley, eighty Anglo and Hispano farms produced corn, barley, and oats. East and south of the town, a few Anglo and Hispano stockmen maintained herds of cattle, sheep, and horses. With no other significant towns on the southern plains, these farms and ranches stayed within Pueblo's tributary sphere, although the town now operated only as a local wholesaler, providing supplies for these agriculturalists and nearby Fort Lyon. Such rapid changes in functional rank occurred regularly.[7] In Pueblo's case, external change brought about by war and intraregional factors, such as the loss of the railroad and diminished mining production, forced the transition. Denver's ascendancy seemed unchallengeable.

Pueblo's prospects appeared to improve with the incorporation of the Denver & Rio Grande and the announcement of its projected route: south from Denver near Pueblo, westward through the canyon of the Arkansas into the San Luis Valley, and down the Rio Grande to El Paso. As the county seat and largest town, residents assumed that Pueblo would be part of the new rail system. At a March 1871 meeting, they learned the startling truth: Pueblo would be bypassed. Cañon City responded to these circumstances by approving a fifty-thousand-dollar bond in an effort to draw the railroad and usurp Pueblo. Confronted with these challenges and in a new demonstration of organized boosterism, Pueblo's citizens pledged 100,000 dollars in municipal bonds to support construction to their community. The railroad sent A. C. Hunt to Pueblo in November 1871 to negotiate. If the town assumed another fifty thousand dollars in bonds, Hunt advised, the narrow

P buy1 12R

gauge tracks would reach Pueblo. Residents agreed, and the Denver & Rio Grande approached Pueblo by June 1872.[8]

In anticipation of economic expansion, Pueblo's population jumped to thirty-five hundred, and construction began on 180 new buildings. Soon thereafter, however, the Denver & Rio Grande followed its customary practices. It moved the depot across the Arkansas River to its new town, South Pueblo, occupying a small portion of the Nolan Grant that Palmer, Bell, Hunt, and Blackmore purchased. Palmer and his associates formed the Central Colorado Improvement Company ("Improvement Company") to make "a Railway Centre of our town site at the General Railway Junction opposite old Pueblo, and for its growth to as great importance as Denver, or even greater."[9] Angry that the company reneged on the agreement, the Pueblo County Commissioners refused to honor the bonds. The railroad unsuccessfully sued to recover the 150,000 dollars, and Pueblo rebounded with the court victory. Unlike Colorado City's experience with Palmer and Colorado Springs, Pueblo's distance from the Denver & Rio Grande depot was measured in yards instead of miles. Pueblo, like Denver, had a history of urban consolidation. Its boosters correctly anticipated the eventual merger with South Pueblo in 1886. And a rail connection, even on the "wrong" side of the river, meant new business. With the railroad, Pueblo reemerged in the 1870s as a manufacturing center and a significant secondary entrepôt.[10] This artificial transportation system allowed the city to regain the "natural" advantages it enjoyed at the start of the gold rush. Pueblo expanded its tributary sphere and made new forays into southwestern Colorado and northern New Mexico.

One natural advantage—coal—helped secure Pueblo's future. Its residents previously developed some nearby sources, but the Denver & Rio Grande aggressively exploited "coal lands [which] were unquestionably well selected and secured in advance of the railroad plans being made public, at a very low cost." This fuel source proved essential to burgeoning industrial expansion on regional and national levels. The government placed a higher sales price (twenty dollars per acre) on lands containing coal and excluded these fields from the Preemption Act. Despite these limitations, intrepid regional entrepreneurs found ways to access large coal beds. For example, Evans secured for the Denver Pacific a land grant that contained sources along the front range between Denver and Cheyenne, although of a lesser quality than the coal near Pueblo. The Improvement Company, following the pattern of ranchers and speculators, used dummy entry-men to purchase fields and sell them back to the company.[11]

By the time the Denver & Rio Grande reached coal fields near Florence in October 1872, the Improvement Company owned large plats in the Arkansas Valley. Under the Arkansas Pool, Palmer, Bell, and their partners raised 1,500,000 dollars to purchase more coal lands and to encourage settlement that produced a large volume of traffic for their railroad. One year later, a new federal law permitted associations as many as 640 acres of coal land for only ten dollars per acre if it was located more than fifteen miles from an established rail-road, or for twenty dollars if it was within that distance. Persons already in possession of coal mines, such as the Arkansas Pool, received preferential rights. The officers of the Denver & Rio Grande initially arranged routes slightly farther than fifteen miles from the designated land so as to minimize the cost, and then simply built spur lines to the fields after their purchases.[12] Few objected to such tactics. The government and most regional actors agreed that coal should be harvested rapidly. Despite their reliance on outside investors in the Arkansas Pool and various Denver & Rio Grande subsidiaries, control remained local. Palmer, Bell, and Hunt identified and negotiated the properties, such as the Nolan Grant, the Florence coal fields, or eighty-four thousand valley acres for agriculture. They secured the necessary bonds and credit.[13]

Anticipating Pueblo's eventual consolidation with South Pueblo, the Denver & Rio Grande and its subsidiaries promoted a united community that would become "the central town of a vast manufac-turing district in the near future." Coal from its hinterland would anchor these new activities and provide Colorado and the surround-ing states with more reliable, badly needed fuel sources. Denver and its railroads already overtaxed Boulder's coal fields. The Canon Mine, for example, shipped forty-three tons a day, with one-third consumed by the Denver & Rio Grande. The Improvement Company developed new mines at Wet Mountains and Coal Creek, emphasizing the superior quality of its coal in promotions aimed at investors. According to a Denver & Rio Grande mining engineer, his railroad burned only a ton of the more efficient Pueblo coal every 85.29 miles, while the Kansas Pacific fired a ton of Boulder coal every 39.87 miles.[14]

By 1876, Pueblo's functional role metamorphosed once again. The Improvement Company told potential investors that both Pueblo and Denver represented "local centres of trade and capital through which the great energetic North will always transact business." As the effects of the depression waned, eastern and English capitalists considered new investments. The Denver & Rio Grande provided the opportunities. Its officers organized the Trinidad Pool to facilitate the injection of outside capital, and incorporated the Southern Colorado Coal and Town Company to complete the railroad's southern extension. They built the town of El Moro five miles from the established Hispano community of Trinidad to usurp nearby coal sources.[15] Other railroads recognized the value of Pueblo's coal, but the Atchison, Topeka & Santa Fe Railroad ("the Santa Fe") stalled at the edge of Colorado when the national economic crisis constrained construction capital. With residents anxious to secure another rail connection, bond issues in both Pueblo County and neighboring Bent County supported the Santa Fe's completion. This second railroad reached Pueblo in March 1876. Denver's leaders fretted about the expansion of Pueblo's tributary sphere. John Evans wrote, "There is some trepidation in Denver business circles for fear the extension of the Atchison & Topeka road to Pueblo will divert trade from Denver." The Santa Fe next challenged the Denver & Rio Grande by building a line to Trinidad. Pueblo benefited from their competition. Evans observed:

> Denver is quite dull and there is a general feeling that
> Pueblo is to be the city of growth this year. The
> competition of the A. T.& Santa Fe Railroad to that
> point . . . and the extension of the Rio Grande road to
> Trinidad which will soon be accomplished will direct
> attention to Pueblo very largely—we see it here
> already.[16]

From Pueblo, the two railroads competed for access to Santa Fe, New Mexico, and the rest of the state. The Santa Fe Railroad sent the first construction crews to the Raton Pass in February 1878, presumptively blocking the Denver & Rio Grande from the traditional route to New Mexico. In response, Palmer and his associates built toward the San Luis Valley, reaching its town of Alamosa, 120 miles from Santa Fe, in 1878.[17] While anxious to connect with Santa Fe, El Paso, and Mexico, Palmer also understood the agricultural potential of the valley and the mineral wealth of the San Juan Mountains he visited a decade earlier. His railroad wove a path across southern Colorado and northern New Mexico through the Mexican land grant properties controlled by him and other entrepreneurs, spurring emigration there and rapidly drawing their natural resources into Pueblo's marketplace. The railroad seemed to be making their dream of a regional empire a reality.

Pueblo's fortunes also improved with the rejuvenation of California Gulch. News of lead carbonates rich in silver spurred renewed interest there. Lake County's population soared from five hundred to twenty-four thousand within a few years, with most settling in the shadow of old Oro City at Leadville. Yet California Gulch remained a difficult destination. Denver lay physically closer, but a trip from that city required traversing the Highline wagon road over the twelve-thousand-foot Loveland Pass and trudging through swampy low ground at Fremont Pass. In a minor reversal of their Civil War roles, people looked to Pueblo's longer but less arduous route to Leadville. Emigrants arrived there on the Santa Fe or the Denver & Rio Grande, stockpiled supplies, and continued on the latter's branch line to Cañon City. From there, freighters and prospectors took the Fremont County road paralleling the Arkansas.[18]

Great profits awaited the first railroad that reached Leadville and the front-range city from which it originated. Palmer, Bell, and others heavily invested in Pueblo refused to concede the prize to Evans's Denver, South Park Railway, but also faced competition within southern Colorado from the Santa Fe. Palmer assumed that a line through the Arkansas Valley would effectively thwart his rivals.[19] The Denver & Rio Grande, however, soon clashed with the Santa Fe when both railroads sent crews to the Royal Gorge of the Arkansas, a narrow

ravine with little space for tracks. Isolated skirmishes gave way to litigation, but Palmer needed quick access to Leadville to placate
investors. He advised Bell, "Any peace that stops A.T. & S.F. at South
Pueblo and gives us Leadville and San Juan, [and] prevents coal and
coke competition westward, will put D&RG on stock dividend paying
basis." In February 1880, the railroads compromised out of court. The
Santa Fe forswore plans for Leadville and Denver, while the Denver &
Rio Grande permanently abandoned Raton Pass and delayed
construction to Santa Fe, New Mexico. In the interim, Evans's Denver-
based railway, which once seemed poised to move on Leadville, ran
out of construction funds for the mountains, and instead connected
with the Denver & Rio Grande. At the end of 1880, Palmer's railroad
arrived uncontested in Leadville.[20]

The Leadville link opened new industrial possibilities for Pueblo,
although Denver-based money developed most mines there. Pueblo's
success depended on the fuel supplies that littered its hinterlands,
resources that suggested the possibility of a viable smelting industry.
Before the Leadville bonanza, Colorado miners and Denver smelters,
with few exceptions, focused on gold ores. Leadville's carbonate silver
required new smelting processes. Initially, ores went to St. Louis or
Omaha via Denver and the Kansas Pacific, but with low grade ores
and high transportation costs, mine owners wanted local refining
plants. Fifteen smelters appeared around Leadville, but eight failed
within two years, primarily due to fuel shortages. Coke from Trinidad
cost too much to transport up the mountains, and fields near Leadville
provided an inferior alternative. Leadville smelters turned to charcoal,
an inefficient option that left swaths of forests denuded. Only three
Leadville smelters remained by 1885. Industry participants recognized that the front range offered greater economies of scale. It cost
less to bring ores down the mountains than to ship fuel up. Both
Denver and Pueblo prepared to seize the smelting industry, although
the former possessed distinct advantages. Denver railroads headed in
all directions. Smelting required substantial capital, and Denver
remained the region's financial center and home to its leading mining
entrepreneurs. Denverites enjoyed access to Boulder's coal and
Trinidad's more efficient product via the Denver & Rio Grande.

Figure 13. Carbonate Hill, Leadville. Leadville's ores paid tribute to Pueblo's smelters and expanded the city's urban role. Home to some of the richest mines in history, Leadville's Carbonate Hill bears the typical scars of nineteenth-century mining: deforestation, ramshackle wooden buildings, piles of mine tailings, and polluted skies and waters. Photograph by William Henry Jackson. Courtesy of Colorado Historical Society, Denver, Colorado.

Nathaniel Hill, who launched regional smelting in 1867, relocated on Denver's northern edge and already gathered ores from Clear Creek and Summit counties and Leadville in Colorado, and as far away as Arizona, Nevada, and northern Mexico. Since the process he appropriated from Wales required copper, Hill also organized the Colorado and Montana Smelting Company, incorporated in Colorado with facilities in Butte.[21]

James Grant, Leadville's only successful smelter operator, built the second largest facility in Denver, merging with a Nebraska firm to form Omaha and Grant Smelting and Refining Company. Grant cornered a large share of the Colorado ore market by establishing sampling agencies that controlled assaying in the camps. He drew ores from Utah, Montana, and Idaho, and helped Denver edge out Omaha in smelting. The third big Denver operation, Globe Smelting and Refining, began in 1887. The Globe's production never matched the other two, but it reached silver markets in northern Idaho, California, Utah, Nevada, New Mexico, and Mexico and drew platinum from Wyoming. Among its Denver investors, Charles Kountze held almost five thousand shares, but the Globe's most significant contribution to regional smelting, and eventually to Pueblo, was the presence of Meyer Guggenheim as a partner.[22]

Even before Guggenheim's involvement, Pueblo competed with Denver to refine ores. Pueblo offered its own advantages. It commanded rail connections to the new silver towns, along the front range of the Rockies, and across the plains to eastern markets. Pueblo's Board of Trade advertised its railroads as if they were creatures of nature, "obeying the laws of gravitation and attraction" and "running into natural channels down the steep inclines of our mountains." Most important, Pueblo lay near Trinidad's coal fields, the best source of metallurgical fuel in the region.[23] Seizing the opportunities created by Leadville, partners Alfred Geist and Joseph Mather constructed Pueblo's first silver smelter in June 1878. Mather soon sold his interests in the Pueblo Smelting and Refining Company to men with substantial mining interests: Thomas Nickerson, former president of the Santa Fe, and Mahlon Thatcher, a prominent Pueblo and Central City banker. Grant's Denver operation still controlled the lion's share of Leadville ores, but Nickerson and Thatcher secured access to Aspen, Breckenridge, Clear Creek, and the San Juans within Colorado, and mining towns in New Mexico and Arizona. The company dispatched agents to Idaho and Mexico. By 1884, the Colorado Smelting Company and the New England & Colorado Mining and Smelting Company thrived in Pueblo. With each mining discovery in the 1880s, small refining plants, as many as three hundred, appeared across different mining frontiers, but most quickly faded, unable to duplicate the front range's agglomeration advantages. Once railroads reached the camps, mine owners returned to Denver and Pueblo smelters that refined large quantities of ores more economically.[24]

Pueblo's tributary sphere in smelting overlapped with Denver's, and competition between the front-range cities intensified at the end of the 1880s. Guggenheim and James Holden, his main partner in Globe Smelting, decided to erect a significantly larger facility. They preferred Denver, but found no suitable site. In an unusually weak demonstration, Denver's Chamber of Commerce failed to facilitate their search. The people of Pueblo responded in an aggressive, organized fashion more typical of their rival. Local entrepreneurs first denigrated their competitors. Leadville's location necessitated higher freight charges and possessed inadequate fuel supplies. Denver's higher wage scale increased operating expenses. The metropolis, they argued, was too far from the best coal, lime, and coke resources. Pueblo, by contrast, offered every competitive advantage: transportation, proximity to Trinidad, plentiful labor at lower wages, and a shorter commute to Mexico, whose ores became increasingly important in processing regional silver. Pueblo's Board of Trade invited Holden and Guggenheim's son Benjamin. To clinch the deal, A. H. Danforth, a local man with ranching and manufacturing interests, offered them free land (overgrazed and useless to him), while the city and county granted property tax exemptions and paid the partners twenty-five thousand dollars in cash. Construction on the Holden Smelting Company, as the new enterprise was initially known, began almost immediately.[25] With the increased capacity of the city's smelters, its assaying firms sought a larger market share. Charles Ruter, who participated in the newly aggressive Pueblo Board of Trade, sent agents from his Pueblo Sampling Works Company to New Mexico, Arizona, and Texas, challenging established relationships with local and Denver smelters.[26]

Denver smelters still outproduced their southern competitor by 43 percent in 1891, but Pueblo's operations earned substantial profits, employed thousands, and generated investments in the local economy. The permanent population of the region's most important secondary entrepôt grew to almost twenty-five thousand by 1890. Pueblo's Board of Trade tied the town's future to the smelters. Promotional materials displayed images of their smokestacks billowing furiously, a symbol of the community's productivity.[27] And anchored by the two front-range cities, smelting expanded the influence of regional entrepreneurs up and down the Rockies to almost every mining camp in the U.S. West and Mexico.

Although Pueblo's usurpation of Denver seemed unlikely, the city gathered other heavy manufacturing that guaranteed it a preeminent role. In 1879, three Denver & Rio Grande affiliates (the Improvement Company, the Colorado Coal and Town Company, and the Colorado Coal and Steel Works Company) consolidated as the Colorado Coal & Iron Company with ten million dollars in capital. Outsiders held the majority of the stock, but local men such as Palmer and Bell filled corporate offices and directed the new company's affairs. This enterprise continued town and farm sales, coal production, and coke manufacturing, like its predecessors. More important, it launched the only plant west of the Mississippi to manufacture steel.[28] With fuel and iron ore in the vicinity, Pueblo seemed the ideal location, as its first general manager, A. H. Danforth, explained, "to erect iron and steel works to supply and control the growing markets of that portion of the country." The works rose up just beyond South Pueblo, at the company town of Bessemer, and drew on six iron mines within 140 miles, all part of holdings that Palmer and his associates garnered through Mexican land grant purchases.[29]

Denver continued to perform more diversified functions, but Pueblo emerged as a leading western industrial center when the steel works opened in 1882, although few of the Colorado Coal & Iron officers called it home. The city now attracted more conventional manufacturers whose heavy capital needs might be met by the new operation. Consumers from a wider area sought a greater variety of goods and specialized services in Pueblo. Within two years, mercantile enterprises and the value of real property grew fourfold, while purchases of household goods climbed 2,300 percent, reflecting both the increased population and the presence of more people with greater personal wealth. The ability of nineteenth-century cities to prosper also depended on their ability to secure and extend credit, as historian William Cronon demonstrated with Chicago. Credit in Pueblo County more than quadrupled between 1881 and 1883.[30]

Colorado Coal & Iron garnered profits in nine of its first twelve years, and its iron and steel department helped attract these new businesses to Pueblo. Yet this department earned profits in only five of those years and failed to return the substantial investment made in its construction and maintenance. Given the nascent stage of its industrial development, the West offered only limited markets for the firm's steel. The company sold pig iron, pipe, spikes, and steel rails throughout the West, but its only reliable customer remained the Denver & Rio Grande. Moreover, Colorado Coal & Iron frequently encountered freight charges on raw materials five times higher than rates in Pennsylvania. Consequently, its eastern competitors sometimes supplied western lines with rails at lower prices despite the greater distance. On three occasions, Colorado Coal & Iron closed its works due to inactivity.[31] The company survived on profits from fuel and real estate sales within the old Mexican land grants. Merging the holdings of its predecessor companies, Colorado Coal & Iron immediately became the region's most prolific coal producer and generated better-quality coal than any Colorado company just as the state emerged as the West's leading producer. With additional purchases near Crested Butte and Durango, it controlled almost 17,500 acres of coal and shipped two thousand tons a day by the late 1880s, while its ovens at El Moro and Crested Butte manufactured the coke for smelters in Pueblo and Denver. The company's markets included Kansas, Texas, Utah, Nebraska, California, and Nevada.[32]

Coal, steel, and smelting reinforced Pueblo's industrial base and augmented regional manufacturing as a whole. With its production

Figure 14. Coke Ovens at Crested Butte. *Essentially a company town of the Denver & Rio Grande Railway, Crested Butte and its ovens extended Pueblo's manufacturing interests to western Colorado. Boxcars carry coking coal. The smoke from the ovens almost obscures the 12,172-foot butte in the background. Photograph by George L. Beam. Courtesy of Denver Public Library, Western History Collection.*

and profit imbalances, however, Colorado Coal & Iron soon faced challengers. John Osgood's Colorado Fuel Company, backed by investors from Denver and Iowa, won contracts with regional railroads and emerged as the most significant rival, although the two companies rarely allowed the mechanisms of the marketplace to solely dictate the result of their competition. Colorado Coal & Iron reached an agreement in 1887 with the Grand River Coal and Coke Company, a Colorado Fuel affiliate, to divide disputed lands in Garfield and Pitkin counties, fix sales quotas, and establish minimum prices for coal and coke where they shared common markets. In 1889, a similar pooling agreement limited competition around Leadville.[33]

Even while these companies conspired to reduce the possibility of self-defeating price wars, Colorado Fuel's aggressive practices cut into Colorado Coal & Iron's market share. In 1891, the Denver-based Colorado Fuel snagged large contracts with the Missouri Pacific and the Union Pacific, and showed net earnings of 352,002 dollars. The Pueblo-based Colorado Coal & Iron's fuel resources netted only 149,620 dollars, while its iron and steel department lost 77,091 dollars. At the same time, some Denver entrepreneurs even considered challenging Pueblo with their own steel works.[34] In an effort to avoid further diminishing profits through unrestricted competition for new Kansas and Nebraska markets, the local directors merged their two companies in 1892 as the Colorado Fuel & Iron Company. Physical operations remained in Pueblo, contributing to the city's employment ranks and its ability to attract other manufacturers. But Denver secured the corporate offices. The Board of Directors consisted of seven men from Denver, four from New York, and only one from Pueblo. The Executive Committee included five Denverites with Osgood as president. The directors looked to Denver's financial institutions, including the First National Bank of Denver, for capital, credit, and mortgages.[35]

Colorado Fuel & Iron's regional impact extended beyond Denver, Pueblo, and Colorado's borders. With the merger, it owned sixty-nine thousand acres of coal lands. Over the next ten years, the company acquired smaller operations, and accounted for 75 percent of Colorado's output as it became the third largest coal-producing state in the nation.[36] Colorado Fuel & Iron modernized its steel works, leased Wyoming iron lands, and organized the Colorado and Wyoming Railway, a wholly owned subsidiary, to transport ore. With these improvements and more favorable rail rates, it emerged a more effective competitor in the national steel industry, and by 1900, employed fifteen thousand workers across Colorado, Wyoming, Utah, and New Mexico. Colorado Fuel & Iron sold its products on the Pacific Coast, as far east as the Missouri River, and internationally in Mexico, frequently following the north-south path envisioned by Palmer and others.[37] Colorado Fuel & Iron made these capital improvements just as the silver crisis and the 1893 depression limited regional credit options and the 1894 railroad strike undercut coal profits. John Jerome, the company's treasurer, worried that overcommitment could lead to receivership, but Colorado Fuel & Iron avoided foreclosure. Its once lagging steel fortunes ameliorated, although again laissez-faire competition did not secure the improvement. In 1895, it joined a pool of steel manufacturers that set prices and established production quotas. The eastern giants that organized the pool, such as Carnegie Steel or 2nd Federal Steel, valued the much smaller Colorado Fuel & Iron because its location gave it potential supremacy in a West slowly awakening to manufacturing. Osgood's well-recognized business acumen and his skill in modernizing the Pueblo works made him a better partner than competitor from the perspective of these eastern manufacturers, many of whom invested heavily in western railroads.[38]

Given the scope and visibility of these industrial activities, most historians focus on Pueblo's manufacturing and the emergence of smaller industrial towns throughout its southern Colorado hinterland, echoing contemporary authors who observed that "it is as a manufacturing city that Pueblo has become famous and by which she will ever maintain her supremacy. Her iron and steel works are the concerns which entitle her to the title of the 'Western Pittsburgh.'"[39] Smaller smelters and coke-production facilities appeared in Durango, Gunnison, and Crested Butte, towns built or developed by the Denver & Rio Grande, Colorado Coal & Iron, or their successors.

As before, the evolution of these small manufacturing towns came at the expense of established communities. Animas City developed in

Figure 15. Colorado Fuel & Iron Company. The company's steel works helped secure Pueblo's position as a secondary entrepôt within the region and a western manufacturing center. Fumes pour from two smokestacks, a common image utilized by Pueblo's boosters to promote their town's productivity. Photograph by Joseph Collier. Courtesy of Denver Public Library, Western History Collection.

the late 1870s as a central marketplace for local farmers who fed San Juan miners. When its residents refused to accept the railroad's extortionary terms, Palmer, Bell, and their associates organized the Durango Trust to purchase property near Animas City. The arrival of the railroad in its company town of Durango overwhelmed the older community and Silverton, a larger but one-dimensional mining camp nearby. The railroad also redirected trade and communication away from towns along the old toll roads, like Highland Mary, Stony Pass, and Lost Trail. They either disappeared or shrank to the point that they were no longer found on Colorado maps. With its rail connection and nearby coal fields, Durango became a small smelting center and shipment point for a growing Animas River Valley cattle industry.[40] Crested Butte began differently, but shared a similar destiny. A local millman, Howard Smith, and the regional smelterman, James Grant, founded the town, but the Denver & Rio Grande's 1881 arrival made it an industrial hub and retail trading center. The Durango Trust purchased town, agricultural, and coal properties there, while the railroad line allowed Colorado Coal & Iron to develop extensive coal beds. These fields offered the only anthracite coal west of the Allegheny Mountains. After 1892, its successor, Colorado Fuel & Iron, guided the town's future as the largest employer and landowner.[41]

Pueblo's agricultural hinterland emerged immediately in 1859, but since its growth was slower and less spectacular than in the city's manufacturing sector, its productivity and the variety of its organizational forms received little attention. Following the original gold rush, this tributary sphere first expanded east along the Arkansas River when the railroad reached Pueblo in 1872. Dependent upon expensive irrigation, these farmers attempted cooperative ventures, like their counterparts along the South Platte and its tributaries. The mutually owned Rocky Ford Ditch Company, for example, maintained one of the oldest water priorities in the basin by buying and improving an irrigation ditch the U.S. Army originally constructed for the Arapahos and Cheyennes under the 1861 Fort Wise Treaty. The Maxwell Land Grant Company sold some property to individual farmers, but conveyed most to land and irrigation companies. These often used the term *colony* to draw farmers, but eschewed the cooperative principles that defined Greeley's

Union Colony. The Improvement Company constructed a reservoir for South Pueblo in 1874 and formed Pueblo Colony to sell agricultural lands watered by its canal. Strictly a profit-making venture, Pueblo Colony offered no communal irrigation. Colorado Coal & Iron's Bessemer Irrigation Company later promised cooperation to farmers in the same area, but maintained the rights to build reservoirs and distribute water. Under the Bessemer Ditch, farmers competed with industrial and urban users for water.[42] Even with these restrictions on water access, the agrarian sector's growth and diversification complemented industrial expansion in the late 1870s and the 1880s. As regional population grew, increased demands to produce food for local consumption and distant markets followed. Pueblo-area agriculturalists responded, even if many contemporary boosters who focused on manufacturing underestimated their contributions. In Pueblo County alone, farming acres increased from 21,731 in 1881 to 39,908 in 1883, and their value doubled. Yet Pueblo's manufacturing reputation obscured these developments. Even the 1894 National Irrigation Congress, a body dominated by agriculturalists, observed that "the (agricultural) advantages of Pueblo County have been shown very briefly that more space might be given to the City of Pueblo, which is the center of population of the middle section of the State, and ranks next to Denver in importance."[43]

Market culture values guided white farmers in the Arkansas River Valley during the formative years, according to historian James Sherow. Desirous of growth, they hoped to conquer nature by constructing dams, reservoirs, and conveyance structures. They followed priority laws that made water a commodity, all the while undermining natural water systems and degrading farmlands through salinity and siltation. Local entrepreneurs seeking more commercial participants exploited these irrigation complexes:

> The vast area of agricultural and horticultural land in
> the Arkansas Valley tributary to Pueblo [is] watered by
> the greatest system of canals and irrigating ditches in
> this country, and is capable of supporting a population
> of a half million people. All kinds of fruit, from
> peaches to apples, grapes to raspberries, can be and are

> successfully grown here. Vegetables from the Dutch
> cabbage to the Irish or sweet potato, from the juicy
> tomato to the peanut, are grown in the rich lands of
> the Arkansas Valley in Colorado.[44]

Yet Pueblo's agricultural hinterland revealed a mixture of communities and social values as it extended westward with the Denver & Rio Grande to the San Luis Valley in 1878. William Gilpin had been among the first Anglo-Americans to appreciate the potential of the valley when he traveled there in the 1840s. Long before he and other Denver entrepreneurs purchased Mexican land grant properties there, Hispanos from New Mexico established small settlements, including the first cooperative project, Guadalupe Colony in 1856. Within two years, Hispano settlements contained sufficient population and generated enough production to support flour mills near the towns of Conejos and San Luis. The army built Fort Massachusetts, later known as Fort Garland, to protect them and a few Anglo-American emigrants. Hispano settlements covered almost 100,000 acres, under old community grants from the Mexican government. The U.S. government subsequently reduced those claims almost 75 percent. Congress or the courts frequently concluded that the Treaty of Guadalupe Hidalgo did not apply and distributed their lands to others under the Homestead Act, or they upheld the larger individual Mexican land grants that superseded communal holdings. Nonetheless, the Hispano population grew, and by 1873, some twenty-six Hispano communities, or *placitas,* called the San Luis Valley home.[45]

Anglo-American settlers initially showed less interest in the valley despite the protestations of Gilpin and his fellow speculators. In addition to the absence of coal and precious metals, white farmers perceived the plateau as desertlike. The Army Corps of Engineers described "barren wastes of rock and sand; nowhere continuous forests or carpets of herbaceous vegetation." The German Colonization Company, the first of the white farming cooperatives in 1869, failed within a year there due to internal tensions, inadequate irrigation, and poor land purchases. With the Denver & Rio Grande's expansion and the arrival of irrigation companies, however, other Anglo-Americans began to rethink the area. Seventy-two Mormon converts from the American

South arrived in Pueblo in November 1877. They intended to migrate to New Mexico, but settled in the southern San Luis Valley upon learning of the impending rail connection and available land near Conejos. The relative remoteness of the area helped assuage their fears over the antipathy that Brigham Young's followers encountered elsewhere. Within thirteen years, some four hundred Mormons built four towns and irrigated forty thousand acres. Instead of applying strict market values, they adopted communal approaches similar to those employed in Salt Lake City.[46]

Alternatively, Denver entrepreneurs with substantial holdings, eagerly took advantage of the railroad, the development of nearby San Juan mines, and new irrigation systems, particularly since land sales slowed before 1880. Through their recruitment of farmers and land sales, they helped develop more intensive agriculture, but given Pueblo's proximity, the two cities' hinterlands overlapped. Denver's Colorado Land and Immigration Company, for example, handled the sale of the large Daigre & Moore Ranch outside La Veta, sixty miles south of Pueblo, emphasizing timber, meadow lands, and early water rights under an existing irrigation ditch. At the same time, industrial development at Pueblo and other manufacturing centers from Bessemer to Durango provided ready markets for San Luis produce and meat.[47]

Expanded agriculture in the San Luis Valley and mining in the San Juan Mountains altered the physical landscape with profound implications for Native Americans and Hispanos who had long occupied the area and brought different values to the land. Ute lands had continued to shrink until their eventual removal from all but one small southwestern Colorado reservation. In addition to pressure from Denver's western-slope expansion and the metropolis's virulent rhetoric, the Utes faced the relentless extension of railroads from Pueblo and the search for coal and coke to feed the city's industries.[48] An American notion of progress underlay these changes, an assumption that the new settlers put the region's resources to more productive uses. Although the Mormon colonies and their neighboring Hispano communities cooperated with each other, the latter suffered as a consequence of Pueblo's growth. Groups led by Palmer, Chaffee, Gilpin, and other entrepreneurs from Denver, Colorado Springs, and Pueblo gained access to water through purchases of the old Mexican land grants, while most Hispano settlers lacked the capital to invest in these large properties. In other circumstances, racism contributed to their decline. One rancher later remembered that "the Greasers spent their time loafing about their camp." Before 1859, greater intermingling occurred between whites and Hispanos, but civilization required a form of ethnic separation similar to what the Plains Indians experienced.[49] When Nathaniel Hill's 1864 survey of Gilpin's properties brought him to Culebra and Costilla, he easily assumed the primitiveness of Hispanos' communal farming practices: "It is said that these people live just as their ancestors did hundreds of years ago . . . They think themselves well off with a piece of land 25 yards by 2 or 3 yards . . . They abound in superstitions . . . They take out a wooden God."[50] Other efforts to marginalize Hispanos were more subtle, but equally devastating. Culebra and Costilla, cities of one thousand and twenty-five hundred, respectively, appeared on none of the maps provided for Hill's survey. He criticized Mexican architectural traditions, and in describing the residents of these cities, failed to even appreciate their inclusion in the United States since 1848. He reported that Costilla's "population is entirely Mexican and a mixture of Mexican and indian [sic]."[51]

Urban entrepreneurs envisioned replacing subsistence-oriented agriculture with commercial farming and mining. Palmer, Gilpin, Chaffee, and their associates anticipated substantial profits would flow to them and their cities through these activities. Few expressed concerns for Hispano farmers whose underlying land-tenure system left them susceptible to degradation. This Spanish and Mexican system of community grants and small individual holdings imposed collective constraints that encumbered private property. It offered communal pasturage, woodlands, and water to increase opportunities for all and to ensure that no community member fell by the wayside during difficult times. These communities rarely cultivated marginal lands along mountain slopes or distant from streams. With the influx of capital via Denver and Pueblo, however, irrigation seemed to make arid land arable and attracted homesteaders, preemptors, and speculators. Hispano settlements and individual landholders, whose property had passed over generations through the social structures of community and family, possessed sufficient documentation to challenge the newcomers in court, but their concept of common lands held little favor under American law. Judges rarely sympathized with Hispano claims, rejecting the majority on technical grounds. Having lost their land, most Hispanos remained in the region as laborers or lessees. The few Hispanos who succeeded in U.S. courts owned some of the unusually large Mexican land grants. These *ricos* initially enjoyed some social acceptance from their new neighbors, but saw their influence decline over the century's final decade.[52]

Palmer's development companies issued reports that patronizingly suggested that "American" ownership of Pueblo's hinterlands saved the Mexicans by creating day-labor jobs that suited them better than property ownership. He contended that residents of the Cuchara Valley were "anxious to sell their land and find such employment."[53] The Denver & Rio Grande used the supposedly inefficient nature of Hispano communities to justify building its own towns and bypassing established communities such as Trinidad. The Improvement Company told potential investors that "all Mexican towns" were "poorly situated." Their functional role in the regional economy undermined and their mere presence marginalized, residents abandoned many communities. A Pueblo Board of Trade pamphlet summed up the attitude of many whites toward the Native Americans and Hispanos they replaced or marginalized: "all these [post-1859] pioneers seemed to be sanguine in their search for speedy fortune; and the Indian and the Mexican speedily receded before this tide of emigration until ranches, mining camps, cities and towns sprung up to give solidity, strength and beauty to one of the most inviting sections of America."[54]

Perhaps more than any other town, Pueblo's history reveals the undulations that cities experienced as members of a hierarchical system and the types of internal and external tensions that shaped functional roles within it. In its early days, Pueblo joined a string of front-range towns that unsuccessfully challenged Denver for regional leadership. Over the next forty years, entrepreneurs who invested in Pueblo contested Denver's leadership within specific industrial sectors. They never toppled the metropolis, but their city became an integral part of the regional empire that many envisioned. Its smelters and steel works stretched the influence of the front range across the West. Pueblo emerged as the region's and the West's heavy manufacturing center, while supporting increasingly more diverse agriculture. Despite the cities' competition and the persistence of some communal values among farmers, most residents of Denver and Pueblo shared similar concepts about societies, economies, and the nature that surrounded them. Both quickly labeled those with differing visions and different skin color as unproductive outsiders. And in usurping those outsiders' lands and developing other natural resources, in transforming them into commodities, these urbanites began to view their cities as natural phenomena. Geography seemingly destined Pueblo and its front-range sisters, Denver and Colorado Springs, to greatness, intimately joining their enterprises with the ecosystems from which these riches flowed.

SIX

MASTERING NATURE

Reality and Illusion

Long bloomed the wilderness, filling the air with fragrance breathed only by wild beasts themselves, which came and departed with no higher end or aim than to devour one another, and to roam through the forests, as yet untrod by men or gods. It was reserved for man alone, for the elevation of mind and the immortality of intelligence, thus to transmute the cinders and waste material of this world into the fine gold which ministers to human culture.

William Gilpin, 1890

Their residents perceived Denver, Colorado Springs, and Pueblo as cities of nature. The resources of their hinterlands combined with the skills of their entrepreneurs and the timing of their settlement to determine their hierarchical positions within the urban system. These communities imposed new human geographies, uniting the ecosystems of the mountains and plains in overlapping processes of economic and environmental change. Indeed, the existence and growth of these front-range communities depended on their ability to extract, process, and ship the region's natural capital to distant markets, or in the case of Colorado Springs, to lure health and wilderness consumers to its threshold. Traditional histories boasted that such conversions represented the American mastery of nature, a fulfillment of manifest destiny, or as Gilpin crowed, the transmutation of the "waste material of this world into the fine gold which ministers to human culture."

Environmental historians pose alternative narratives. Among the most influential, Donald Worster writes, "the drive for the economic development of the West was often a ruthless assault on nature, and it has left behind it much death, depletion, and ruin." Acknowledging this profound impact, William Cronon cautions that we carefully consider the complexity of historical change: "One of the longstanding impulses that environmentalism shares with its great ancestor, romanticism, has been to see human societies, especially those affected by capitalist urban-industrialism and the cultural forces of modernity, in opposition to nature." Modern humanity is assumed to be environmentally unstable, corrupting, and malign. In his study of the Columbia River, Richard White alternatively avoids a simple story wherein "nature" disappears with the arrival of whites and industrialization. He examines how changing notions of work, and the underlying values they implied, defined human relations with the waterway.[1]

Complicated motives influenced resource usage and the related struggles for control within the Denver region. Anglo-Americans supplanted Indians and Hispanos. Cities competed for hinterlands. Self-regulatory systems and tenets of traditionalism persisted even as local entrepreneurs attempted to hold the reins of an emergent market economy. Humans seemingly shaped the natural world in the service of their communities and personal economies. Whether these efforts reflected conventional chronicles of success, more recent recountings of depletion, or some new story can only be determined by understanding what historical actors hoped to achieve when they initiated environmental change. What values underlay their choices? Did the intended economic and social benefits justify the frequent environmental depredations? Did the actors anticipate all the consequences they set in motion? If not, was their control of nature illusory?

At some level, all human beings alter the physical world to serve their material needs. Historians have begun to deconstruct, for example, popular stereotypes of "ecologically noble savages" that fail to convey historically contingent, culturally constructed natural contexts. The Plains Indians affected and were affected by environmental change. Their religious culture fostered a belief in nature's unlimited bounty, while economic and defensive pressures pushed them into the bison market. They avidly participated, killing as many as necessary to enhance their competitive trading position. Their activities, however, unexpectedly contributed to the animal's decline, one factor in the decimation of their own communities.[2] Gold-rush emigrants believed that the region's resources should provide necessities and luxuries, which they defined differently than their predecessors. With denser, more intensely commercial populations, their demands on the mountains and plains surpassed those of the Indian cultures. Advanced technology and the increased mobility of capital permitted more rapid, farther-reaching environmental changes than anything the region previously experienced. One of the most profound alterations involved the very removal of Native Americans and their value systems.

The new arrivals deemed as wasted any underdeveloped resources. Within their own cultural constructs, they assumed that nature offered infinite rewards and possessed restorative powers. Confident of their progressive civilization, they believed that their activities actually improved natural processes.[3] Farmers and entrepreneurs like Henry Porter preached that "rain follows the plow" and celebrated the changes they initiated: "[T]he buffalo made the country arid in a long course of years by tramping down and hardening the soil . . . in what was formerly known as the Great American Desert. When the farmers came into the country and drove back the Indian and the buffalo and plowed up the soil of the country, they reversed the operation by making the whole country a reservoir to hold the rain and moisture and make the country fertile and one of the most pleasant climates to live in."[4] Nineteenth-century agriculturalists supposed moisture a normal condition, and aridity an aberration. Between 1865 and 1872, when the region's agrarian population remained relatively small, little rain fell. Precipitation increased over the next twelve years just as the number of farms more than tripled. Farmers concluded that they brought the basic climate into a healthier equilibrium, although subsequent studies revealed a cyclical pattern of droughts on the plains. The farmers, ranchers, and their urban backers had not stopped aridity, although as part of their new human geography, they transformed the plains through the substitution of sugar beets and cattle for indigenous flora and fauna.[5]

These were but a few of the environmental shifts compelled by a complex amalgam of motives and actions. The contested transition of this frontier region to a modern capitalist society involved the absorption of its natural capital into the nation's manufacturing system. Impatient to establish a competitive, autonomous economy, to diversify and extend it to more distant hinterlands, Denverites and other regional residents adopted an increasingly aggressive attitude toward nature. Market values preponderated, but even the enduring elements of a regulated society did little to secure equitable access to resources or to temper their destructive exploitation.[6] Irrigation and fencing introduced under Union Colony's utopian ideals still altered the feeding and watering patterns of wild animals and cattle.

The north-south reorientation illustrated the utilitarianism that drove resource development. Businessmen in Denver and her sister cities maintained old ties and nurtured new ones with eastern metropolises offering major sources of capital. At the same time, entrepreneurs in mining, railroads, agriculture, smelting, coal, and steel looked to the Rocky Mountains and the continuation of the Rio Grande Valley into Mexico as "a natural economic unit in a long longitudinal productive area."[7] As they integrated the hinterlands of this "organic" phenomenon into the marketplace, they linked them together environmentally. Changes in one sphere signaled modifications of others. The exaggerated use of one fuel source such as timber forced residents to turn to and deplete others like coal. Timber and coal powered the industries that expanded regional boundaries. The Denver Pacific pitched shares by emphasizing the coal fields within the railroad's land grant and the strands of trees adjacent to its tracks. The Maxwell Land Grant Company vigorously promoted its forests and the more efficient coal found in southern Colorado and northern New Mexico.[8]

Wood equaled precious metals in its importance to the region's economic development. Americans used it for buildings, transportation, manufacturing, fuel, and chemicals. Timber also undergirded the mining industry that produced the area's most dramatic environmental changes. Denuded hills became the norm along the front range and deeper in the mountains. In the early 1860s, Samuel Mallory used a cord, or 128 cubic feet of wood, each day in one Nevada City quartz mill. In one year alone, another relatively small operation, Georgetown's Silver Reduction Works, purchased 1,000 cords and 4,500 bushels of charcoal (created by charring wood in an airless kiln). Wooden toll roads provided access to the camps. Wood-burning stoves heated miners' cabins. Railroads replaced wooden ties every five years, and as they reached the camps, combustible refuse from their engines sparked frequent forest fires.[9] Placing a premium on mining production, few residents regretted the deforestation and other environmental damage described by rancher James Hoy:

> From the upper end of the [Central] city, we had a
> chance to view the country around about and a most
> dreary aspect it was; no green trees, no Indians, no
> bears, nor deer nor elk! No birds ever, no water fowl,
> no fish or anything in sight worthwhile. Here and
> there were ten, twenty, forty acre tracts of slashed
> pines; elsewhere stumps, ragged rocks, huge boulders,
> desolate, abandoned even by snakes and owls; fit only
> for gold mad men . . . This was a gold mining camp
> with no gold in sight to glitter and blind the eyes.[10]

Touring Colorado and Utah for potential investors, mining engineer Alfred Rockwell echoed Hoy's assessment of Central City. "The little houses and cabins are stuck up on the hillside like in Switzerland without any of the picturesque effects . . . There is not a blade of grass to be seen, but the hillsides are dug over and burrowed . . . The result is desolation and complete destruction of nature." With respect to Georgetown, he added, "There is no softness to contrast with the roughness—no cultivation and wherever man has been he has done his best to strip off what natural beauty of vegetation there was."[11] In California Gulch, one of Golden's founders, Mark Blunt, declared:

> It is astonishing to behold the change wrought by
> man's search for the "shining ore." Where a few
> months ago stood the primeval forest through which
> wild deer roamed and drank in safety at the crystal
> stream which here swept gracefully among the trees

and there bounded merrily over the rocks, all is
changed . . . On each side of the gulch instead of
"pyramids of green" now appear long rows of log
houses.[12]

Wood fueled the industries that serviced mining and supported its
physical infrastructure. Placer mining sought the recovery of particles
of gold or silver from exposed veins. Romantic notions invoke images
of prospectors panning along a sunlit mountain stream, such as those
in the painting that adorns Colorado's capitol rotunda. In reality, large-
scale, capital-intensive enterprises swallowed substantial timber
resources and transformed the landscape. Prospectors and, soon
thereafter, mining and ditch companies diverted streams from their
customary courses, laying bare riverbeds that might contain flakes of
precious metal. Miners sometimes torched trees to find buried placers.
More frequently, ditches carried water miles away to remove soil and
reveal nuggets left behind by long-extinct rivers. Forests yielded the
necessary construction materials. Countless trees fell, reshaped as
sluices, troughs, and flumes for the tens of thousands of claims litter-
ing western mountains. Other companies built boom dams that
avalanched water over downhill placers. While these rarely unlocked
significant riches, they always upset the soil and destroyed whatever
trees and other vegetation lay in their wake.[13]

The wood demands of lode mining surpassed those of placer
deposits. Underground lodes contained several veins of metal below
bedrock. Initially, a few miners might reach shallow ores with a hand-
operated windlass, but rock formations deeper in the earth required
corporate capital to finance more elaborate operations. Timbers
supported the shafts and adits from the surface and the miles of multi-
level tunnels that crisscrossed beneath. Charcoal and cordwood
powered steam-driven equipment—hoists, air compressors, and the
pumps that drained excess groundwater. Principles of localism and a
regulated society persisted in the limited size of claims and the sideline doctrine that dominated western mining long after the 1872
federal law. These created more opportunities, but broadened the
damage. More companies worked the land. Instead of one central
shaft from the apex, multitudes of miners created portals to the under-

Figure 16. Central City, Colorado. Platted by Denver's William Byers, Central City was one of the earliest Clear Creek camps and the main supply center for the district. The deforestation, scarcity of animals, and scarred hillsides described by visitors were evident in the town's first decade. Photograph by Harry Lake. Courtesy of Denver Public Library, Western History Collection.

ground. As assayist Stuart Lindley remarked, "the mines [of Leadville] are very thick seeming to cover the hills and gulches." Yet, even as they watched the depletion of resources, boosters still assumed nature's endless abundance. One Leadville pamphlet asked, "If then, lode mining has flourished in Cornwall for over 2,000 years, and still flourishes, then what hesitation should there be in regarding Leadville as a permanency, surrounded as she is by all the appliances of civilization?" The promoter never acknowledged that most of the two millennia in Cornwall preceded industrialization. The "appliances of civilization," steam-powered mining equipment manufactured in Denver, accelerated the scale and rate of environmental change. By 1896, eight Colorado counties alone identified almost 150,000 lode mines. Some claims were never patented and others were abandoned or consolidated over the years, but places such as Clear Creek and Gilpin counties, home to the Rockies' earliest diggings, painted a portrait of ecological chaos by the turn of the century.[14]

Early agriculturalists in the mountain parks and front-range valleys contributed to deforestation, although not on the same scale as mining. Farmers removed trees to plant crops near water. Domestic livestock, particularly sheep, rooted out bushes and saplings. Growing front-range cities developed unquenchable appetites for fuel and wooden buildings, sidewalks, and roads. Small Denver sawmills processed timber and shipped it across the region. The plains were particularly bereft of trees. Union Colony claimed supposedly "inexhaustible supplies from thirty to sixty miles west along the Cache-La-Poudre in the mountains," but farming communities in eastern Colorado and New Mexico and western Kansas and Nebraska looked to Denver mills to supply their basic needs. In later decades, as one local newspaper reported, Denver and Pueblo smelters "used prodigious quantities of wood in the production of charcoal necessary to their operations."[15]

Regional actors acknowledged the ecological changes they imposed, but accepted and even celebrated them. Senator Henry Teller captured the prevailing attitude:

> We have destroyed some timber in Colorado, but we
> have added to the sum of human happiness by doing

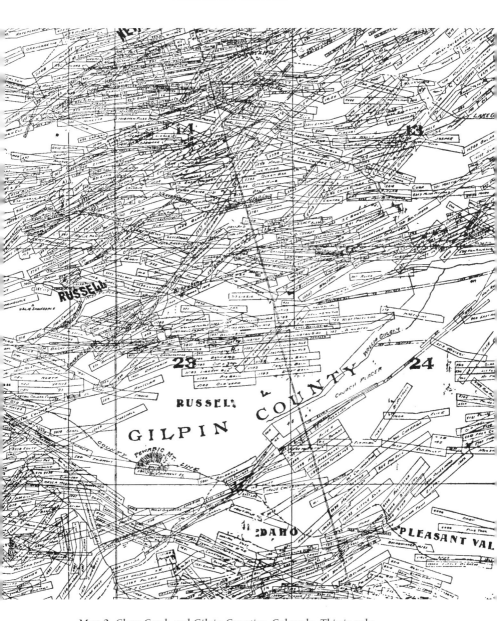

Map 3. *Clear Creek and Gilpin Counties, Colorado. This is only the northeast section of James Underhill's large map (c. 1902) of the two counties that were home to the first gold rush and various strikes over the next forty years. It reveals the chaos that defined mining camps and added to environmental degradation. Courtesy of Denver Public Library, Western History Collection.*

so. We have put into the commerce of the world a
billion dollars worth of gold and silver, and we have
made homes for thousands and thousands of men, and
we have built up a civilization that cannot be beaten in
any part of the world . . . we have something better
than timber to show for it. We have schools and
colleges and churches and hospitals and all the appliances of civilization. . . . If we have cut off the pine,
we have made a hundred orchards where we have
made a hill bare.[16]

Constituents frequently complained to Teller that the federal government denied them an even larger share of the timber market. One resident advised, "our [state] legislature is the only body that understands
this timber question. The public interest will be better served under
their management than by men who never saw Colorado." Lumber
entrepreneurs assumed that the transfer of forest lands to state control
would facilitate private access and reasonable development of
resources, as defined by the market. Others, including members of the
Colorado State Horticultural and Forestry Association, supported state
management, blaming the federal government's lax fire protection,
instead of their neighbors' exploitation, for watershed damage.[17]

Mining entrepreneurs proudly displayed their usurpation of forest
land. The vertically integrated systems that Denver's Chaffee, Moffat,
and Smith brought to Leadville, the San Juans, and Cripple Creek
depended on the capture of timber. It remained the single greatest
expense in any mining venture. Towns across the mountains published
brochures highlighting their mastery of the terrain through the imposition of these appliances of civilization. Silver Plume's boosters embodied such brashness. In their propaganda materials, they explained, "Our
object in issuing this pamphlet is not of vain glory, but of legitimate
pride of our immense treasure vaults." They offered photographs of the
district's successful operations as symbols of their domination, industrial progress, and profitability. The image of the Seven-Thirty Mines
was both typical and striking in its revelations. Workers sit among a few
scattered buildings, piles of tailings, and towering stacks of felled trees.
The timber-lined adit and drainage tunnel are visible. In the back-

Figure 17. *Seven-Thirty Mine, Silver Plume, Colorado. The Silver Plume Board of Mines and Trade celebrated such images in materials for prospective investors, residents, and tourists, showing little concern about the loss of vegetation and devastation of the ecosystem. Silver Plume Mines and Scenery [1902]. Courtesy of Denver Public Library, Western History Collection.*

ground, the hillside stands stripped of plant and animal life. Control of timber resources signified prosperity.[18]

In their pursuit of profits, mining entrepreneurs purposely modified the mountain landscapes, but in an increasingly integrated and diversified economy, the effects of this environmental devastation reached across ecosystems. In 1905, the state engineer testified that less than 20 percent of the original forest remained in Colorado. Enos Mills, the western author closely associated with the founding of Rocky Mountain National Park, offered a more dire assessment. Of thirty-five thousand square miles of forests when gold was discovered, he asserted, only five thousand remained. Historian James Sherow describes how deforestation in the upper Arkansas River Valley watershed reduced the flow to downstream irrigators. Without the protection of large trees, wind and sun reduced the winter snowpack long before warm spring weather and interrupted the steady stream of water to agricultural areas. Salinity, siltation, and decreased production plagued the plains and western slope. Although farmers rarely factored how their own irrigation practices, livestock, and crop selection affected water resources, they understood the relation between forests and rivers, and inserted themselves in the political debates on water.

> It is not the irrigation ditches of Colorado that cause the Platte to run dry in Nebraska, the Arkansas in Kansas, and the Rio Grande in New Mexico; it is rather the destruction of the forests which have deprived the sources of supply of their natural protection, and thus permanently changed the character of our mountain streams.[19]

Cognizant of the importance of both watersheds and timber as a commodity, framers of Colorado's constitution in 1876 included Article 18, directing the General Assembly "to prevent the destruction of and to keep in good preservation the forests upon the lands of the State." Despite this affirmative duty, the legislature waited until 1884 "to establish a system of forest protection" when timber shortages and other catastrophes prompted the appointment of a forest commissioner. He observed:

> Disastrous droughts, floods, snow and landslides . . .
> climatic changes, failure of crops, and other evils, can
> also be referred to this same cause. . . . In the Rocky
> Mountain region, where vegetation can be maintained
> only in the face of many difficulties, it is doubtful
> whether the native woodlands can ever be restored to
> their original state. Hence, it is clearly our duty to
> preserve the few remaining trees, and to plant trees . . .
> wherever they can be made to grow.[20]

Forest conservators at this time intended to benefit humans more than nature, and the commissioner's initial comments revealed the diversity of human activities that regional forests might serve. Agriculture had become more important financially, while its participants provided a stabilizing social element. Consequently, the commissioner recognized forest functions separate from the extraction of wood and prioritized farmers' water needs ahead of the interests of mining.

In 1893, Colorado's Populist governor, Davis Waite, formed a board "to protect and promote the horticultural interests of the state by making regulations." He related changes in his boyhood Kansas home where deforestation diminished the productive capacity of fruit orchards. In addition to the troubled economy, Waite mostly bemoaned the societal changes that followed failed farms. He found prosperity, beauty, and stability in the western slope's fruit-growing communities, and hoped to ensure that the state preserved forests that protected them and the cultural landscapes he cherished. Historian Donald Pisani explains that the moral component in Colorado's forest policies appeared across the nation by the 1880s. In addition to timber shortages and the disruptions in water flow, officials fretted about the social impact of this waste. In the romantic literature of the late nineteenth century, western mountains and their forests seemed to offer the last primeval wilderness, places of restoration and sublimity. The destruction of trees and consequent "violation of nature's law," Pisani argues, threatened "the material and spiritual foundation of American civilization."[21]

The appointment of a state forest commissioner, however, did little to stop the degradation of regional forests. Denver entrepreneurs already drew on extensive timber resources in Wyoming and New Mexico. Moreover, the system limited the commissioner's authority by leaving his office underfunded and understaffed. State laws required that a few officers prevent depredations and forest fires, but forbid them from interfering with domestic, mining, or agricultural uses that fostered the decimation. The federal government permitted similar practices on its public domain, and even granted railroads easements to cut wood on vacant lands. In the early 1900s, as private forests grew scarcer, Congress shifted policies and placed a fifth of Colorado's remaining timber under the Forest Service and its stricter rules. Teller and others complained that regulations still undermined the region's society and economy by precluding homesteaders and prospectors, although others could cut trees in national forests under certain circumstances.[22]

As they depleted their Rocky Mountain storehouses and faced more restrictive regulations, Denverites looked for new sources. Regional railroads, which played a large role in sapping nearby fuel sources, helped secure supplies from more distant hinterlands while expanding the metropolis's sphere of influence. John Evans assured shareholders that the Denver & New Orleans Railroad "will bring the products of the extensive forests of valuable timbers of Texas, so greatly needed in Colorado." The Cripple Creek fields opened in the 1890s in an area with limited timber stores due to low precipitation and earlier lumbering. With these shortages, mining entrepreneurs turned to the New Mexican forests lining the tracks of the Denver & Rio Grande or the Santa Fe Railroad.[23]

Mining's impact on mountainous environments involved more than deforestation. The geology and geomorphic history of each area dictated the form of mining. Although employed more often in the Sierras that paid tribute to San Francisco, hydraulic mining shaped some of Denver's regional landscapes. Perhaps the most damaging mining method, hydraulicking required huge amounts of water. Boom dams held large reservoirs, allowing cannons, or monitors, to release water under great pressure. It pierced stone and dislodged soil, literally washing hills and mountains into ravines and rivers. Companies intermittently used this system throughout the Rockies and the Rio

Grande valley, in Idaho, Montana, Utah, New Mexico, and most mining counties in Colorado, although a lack of water limited hydraulicking in parts of the Southwest. Faster than traditional methods, it reduced labor costs by as much as 90 percent. In the 1890s, another new technique, dredging, moved entire streams from their original courses to reveal the bed. Flat valleys metamorphosed into parallel ridges as the dredge, a steam-powered earthmover, redeposited gravel in large symmetrical piles. Redirected waterways filled multiple channels, cutting man-made ridges between the discarded heaps of stone.[24]

Proximity to mining operations also forced prospectors and speculators to locate their camps on terrain ill suited for significant human habitation under nineteenth-century notions of town platting. Cripple Creek typified the problem. Its streets dipped and rose as they crossed the broken slopes of the rugged mountainside. The main thoroughfare sloped so steeply that it separated into two terraced lanes, one fifteen feet above the other and supported by a retaining wall. Town builders partially filled the creek, which became a gutter for garbage and sewage from an ore concentration mill. With this essential artery clogged, prospectors working downstream dynamited rock formations to create new water routes to their claims.[25]

Piles of mine tailings became a common landscape element in mining hinterlands. Fifty years after the Cripple Creek discoveries, the Colorado Springs's Gazette-Telegrapher observed, "Small, round, somewhat evenly spaced, and semi-symmetrical piles of rock and gravel dot the area, the refuse of rock discarded in the search for valuable ore." Reduction works heaped smoldering slag (silicate formed during smelting) around the camps. Surrounding hills, denuded and scarred with cut marks, trapped railroad smoke with the sulphurous fumes and coal dust from mills and mines, destroying what little vegetation survived deforestation. Cyanide and other chemicals used by smelters seeped into the groundwater or were dumped in nearby waterways. Toxic topsoil could not sustain new growth. Drainage tunnels pumped out groundwater that gathered in subterranean passages. Eroded embankments filled streams with sediment, joining the other mining debris. As early as 1861, Blunt described the waters

Figure 18. Hydraulic Mining in the San Juans. The most destructive form of placer mining, hydraulicking releases high-powered jets of water aimed at the sides of hills and mountains. These methods eroded embankments and clogged mountain streams with silt. Courtesy of Denver Public Library, Western History Collection.

of California Gulch to his relatives: "The sparkling brook is now a muddy ditch, bound and fettered; being compelled by man to assist in the extraction of the precious ore and to leave its old familiar ways and to flow sluggishly through ditches, flumes and sluices." Thirty years later, little had improved. A Wisconsin visitor to Clear Creek noted that "if this is a specimen of your clear creeks, I'd like to see one of the muddy ones." In other communities, miners dangerously expanded natural underground chasms or opened unstable artificial ones, bequeathing subsidences to their descendants.[26]

Similarly exhaustive methods appeared in coal mining. Colorado, Wyoming, and northern New Mexico contained the best coking coal west of the Alleghenies, and the only anthracite coal, locked in the earth near Crested Butte. Coal had an immediate value in an industrializing United States. Production in Colorado alone increased from 70,000 tons in 1873 to 3,900,000 tons twenty years later, fueling the industries that reoriented the local economy and extended the influence of its entrepreneurs. Coal from the region powered the machines in distant hinterlands as Denverites opened mines, sampling agencies, and small smelters in Butte, Salt Lake City, El Paso, or Mexico City. And in the increasingly integrated economy, expansive coal production related, in part, to the decimation of trees. In the 1870s, a lack of timber caused fuel shortages and stimulated higher prices for charcoal. People turned to coal, which the extension of the Denver & Rio Grande and other railroads seemingly brought into an almost limitless supply.[27]

Yet, by 1883, mismanagement of these resources by private owners prompted Colorado's general assembly to implement a regulatory scheme to control abuses of nature and labor. The first law allowed miners to examine scales used to weigh coal because the amount they produced partially determined their wages. When superintendents refused to accommodate weighmen and the state failed to enforce its law, miners organized a protracted statewide strike. The Knights of Labor volunteered to establish a conciliation board. Not surprisingly, the companies (Colorado Coal & Iron, the Union Pacific, and the Santa Fe) that controlled seven-eighths of regional production rejected the offer, and this effort at accommodation, or self-regulation, collapsed. With acrimonious labor-management relations and production disruptions, the state created the office of a State Inspector of Coal Mines in February 1884. His job was to regulate the mines, secure employees' health and safety, and promote the state's coal interests—at times contradictory goals. Poor drainage and ventilation endangered workers, but Inspector John McNeil emphasized economic losses attributable to inefficient mining techniques in his opening statement. The owners had harvested coal "in a rude, miserable and even reckless manner," leaving pillars of fuel unrecoverable. "Thousands of tons of coal are lost to the State, the land owner and the operator annually, the object being only the immediate extraction of the coal in view, and every applied exertion becomes a barrier to the end of placing a mine upon the plane of its fullest producing capacity."[28]

McNeil averred that in seeking quick profits, private operators employed extraction methods that removed only the immediately accessible coal, undermining the industry's long-term gains. Coal located in deeper beds required more time-consuming techniques, and earlier recklessness made it difficult and dangerous to recoup. With greater labor organization within the industry, annual reports also contained data on accidents and suggested regulatory standards, but inspectors rarely touched on far-reaching environmental effects attributable to such methods as these were not their responsibilities.[29] Some contemporary commentators, however, questioned the principles guiding local operators and the damage to nature. Troubled by changes at Crested Butte, Helen Hunt Jackson pessimistically remarked,

> There is no accounting for differences in values; no adjusting for them either, unluckily. The men who are digging, coking, selling the coal opposite the aster field, do not see the asters; the prospectors hammering away high up above the foaming, splashing, sparkling torrent of the O-Be-Joyful water do not know where it is amber and where it is white, or care for it unless they need a drink.[30]

While coal mining and coking enveloped towns like Crested Butte in gritty soot, few local residents shared Jackson's moral sensibilities. They accepted smoke over the asters. It signified progress and prosperity. Entrepreneurs intended to alter their natural world, and believed they advanced the region, as well as their own fortunes, by developing these resources. Coal mines and coke ovens irreparably tainted Coal and Baxter creeks and left Elk Mountain stripped of vegetation, but these were the reasonable costs of doing business. Crested Butte offered multiple strata of coal that needed to be developed.[31] Durango's denizens similarly viewed the appliances of the coal industry as necessary and as modern improvements of nature. They appreciated the deleterious health effects of pollution and tried to minimize them by building the smelter outside town, but they lacked the technology to clean the air and its growing population soon reached the plant's doorstep. In Newcastle, Colorado, layers of sandstones, shales, and fossil shells contained seams of coal as narrow as twenty inches or as wide as forty feet. Miners and machines worked at different levels from 400 to 1,660 feet below the mountaintop. As in lode mining, the expansion of natural underground chasms and the creation of artificial ones altered the internal environment. Groundwater utilized subterranean channels for thousands of years, and now seeped into manmade chambers as well, weakening mine structures and threatening miners and production. Surface subsidences regularly developed. In other areas, primitive strip-mining techniques left behind gouged hillsides devoid of flora and fauna.[32] And laborers in search of steady employment chose these towns because of their economic opportunities and despite their pollution.

Smokestacks in Denver, Pueblo, and these industrial communities emitted the same dirt that fouled the skies of eastern industrial metropolises, although perhaps with greater density when trapped by surrounding mountains. Pamphlets from Pueblo's Board of Trade emphasized images of smelters and steel works expelling noxious fumes. A railroad photograph boosting Leadville's smelters revealed denuded hills, even as smokestack refuse obscured the city. The region's producers and consumers understood the centrality of coal to their competitiveness with other parts of the nation. "Emancipation by machines and fusion by railroads, reinforced by a proper climatology, are here united to urge on our people in the channels of uninterrupted progress," Gilpin recalled. Entrepreneurs and laborers alike rarely shied away from the environmental consequences that suggested the region's shift from the periphery to the core of the national economy.[33]

Haphazard coal-mining methods, however, caused environmental problems that nineteenth-century technology could not contain. Fires in gobs (spaces where coal had been mined, but combustible refuse remained) created a grave predicament. A coal mine in Boulder County burned for twenty-five years, extending over many underground acres and wasting tens of thousands of tons of coal. Carbon, sulfur, and other gases permeated the surface through chimneys, spreading noxious fumes that destroyed vegetation, affected human health, and sculpted a landscape reminiscent of "burning volcanoes." This conflagration was extreme, but gob fires occurred regularly. In the 1880s, regional coal operators often responded by abandoning these mines and others that flooded due to poor drainage. They overworked more productive mines, or developed new ones throughout Colorado, New Mexico, Utah, and Wyoming, following the same practices that inhibited future profits and placed workers and local ecosystems at risk.[34] "Moving on" became a common entrepreneurial response to environmental crises. Given the extractive nature of many economic activities, potential resource exhaustion presented an impediment to further growth. Local businessmen did not possess the luxury of time or money, nor the cultural context, to contemplate the implications for nature. They needed to act, and act quickly, to expand investment opportunities and locate hinterlands that replaced depleted resources. Smoke pollution, subsidences, gob fires, and other damages constituted acceptable and expected costs in the purposeful exploitation of valuable resources.

In the alteration of the natural world that accompanied their struggle for competitiveness, regional bankers, miners, timbermen, and farmers also generated unanticipated environmental changes that limited future activities just as careless practices inhibited further development of some coal mines. While constructing a new human geography in the pursuit of their imperial vision, local actors assumed that their efforts and industrialization itself advanced nature, putting its resources to their most productive uses. In ignoring its limits, they discovered that nature could be unforgiving.[35] For example, large human migrations, deforestation, the introduction of domestic live-stock, and the diversion and pollution of mountain streams sabotaged indigenous animals and fish. In response to these unexpected changes in regional fauna, western states authorized regulatory agencies to restore the balance of nature, "recreate" lost species, and shape tourist landscapes for recreational hunting and fishing. Game and fish soon became pawns in the market economy and in humans' often vexing struggles to govern nature.

Overland accounts during the early gold-rush years abounded with descriptions of the diverse abundance of animals on the plains and in the mountains. In 1859, Harry Faulkner compared the plains to a barn yard because "buffalo manure covers the land for millions of acres." John Hartzell wrote his family, "I have seen more than two thousand buffaloes and hundreds of deer and grate [sic] many wolves." Farmer George Hodgson recalled that "in addition to the herds of cattle there were thousands of buffalo on the range in north-eastern Colorado . . . At times as many as 100 antelope could be seen in one herd. There were also many white-tailed deer along the creeks in those days."[36] Blunt spotted a black bear in the mountains, and told his sister that wild deer roamed nearby forests. "Game was wonder-fully plenty when the [California] gulch was first discovered; they used to shoot deer right from their cabin doors." On visits to different districts, Samuel Mallory saw duck, grouse, curlew, trout, bear, elk, deer, antelopes, bison, and smaller game. On one journey, he "had the pleasure of killing two wild turkeys." Edward Garbutt, a North Park farmer, found himself "in the vicinity of such large game such as buffalo, elk, deer, bear, antelope, etc. that it is hard to resist." Dunham Wright hunted elk and bighorn sheep with Joel Estes in the mountain park that would bear the latter's name.[37]

By 1870, however, wild animals became less visible on the plains, although evidence of their past participation remained. On his first western trip, Peter Scott saw only two antelope and fifty bison, at which his party immediately fired. He described the grasslands as "literally covered with bones, carcasses in every stage of decay." Traveling to Longmont, Chicago-Colorado Colony member Seth Terry observed "lots of dead buffalo—hundreds." Terry staked out Longmont's townsite with buffalo horns.[38] Worster contends that many historians, influenced by anthropocentrism, fail to consider "a veritable holocaust" and "a landscape littered with skulls and bones, drenched in blood." In considering such issues, historian Elliott West emphasizes the "connectedness" of life in the West.[39] Many factors played a role in the dissipating native animal populations on the plains, including the substitution of cash crops for indigenous flora, the introduction of domestic livestock, irrigation projects that altered riparian systems, and fences that blocked access to water. Deforestation stripped the mountains of vegetation while human populations crowded into the valleys and mountain parks that once provided refuge for foraging animals.

Yet overhunting initially received the greatest attention as the cause of the problem. During the gold-rush days, in a predominantly male, transient, and occasionally violent society, hunting provided a diversion and supplemented the sometimes meager, always expensive foodstuffs shipped to mountain camps. Noting the abundance of deer in California Gulch, Blunt added, "It was provident that it was so, for there was no chance to buy provisions there then and many must have gone hungry if it had not been for the game." Market hunters fed front-range cities. Plentiful game sold for as little as two cents a pound even as railroad construction crews created a heavier demand at the end of the first decade. Facing narrow profit margins, market hunters killed large quantities, delivering more meat than necessary in summer and too little in winter.[40] The forces of supply and demand intermingled with a reckless disregard for nonhuman communities. Killing for the sport explained only some of the decaying carcasses that Scott and Terry espied, but residents worried by 1870 that certain species faced annihilation and sought regulations to protect them, much as territorial laws protected fish since the early 1860s. A grasshopper infestation in 1866 devastated crops. Farmers concluded that the killing of orioles, flycatchers, and other insectivorous birds eliminated a natural check on these insects. Focusing on "the wasteful cruelty and unsportsmanlike attributes which seem to characterize the professional hunter and the orthodox tourist," the territorial legislature passed the first law imposing fines for killing listed animals and birds out of season.[41] Market and recreational hunting needed to be regulated to protect regional agriculture at Greeley and other locations. Life in the West, as in all regions, was connected.

The disappearance of wild animals associated with new human geographies on the plains, however, went far beyond reckless hunting. Large herds of cattle and smaller numbers of sheep, horses, and mules reveled in its grasses. In the open-range era, stock roamed freely on the plains from Montana to Texas. For southern Colorado and northern New Mexico, for example, Pueblo became "the base of supplies and monetary and residential center for an almost boundless pastoral region." In little more than a decade, some fifty thousand sheep grazed nearby, while large parts of the Arkansas Valley had been converted to wheat. Scott mentioned that his traveling party killed a buffalo, but ten days later, while exploring Trinidad, he made a more revealing observation about the growing agricultural hinterlands: "sheep and cattle are extensively herded . . . Hay is cut in a place or two. There is no fence as everyone herds their stock. Cattle and horses thrive well on the grass and hogs on the acorns. Mr. S. has 300 cattle kept by two Mexican herders."[42]

Dramatic changes in flora and fauna also accompanied communal farming to the north. In its first year alone, Union Colony at Greeley introduced wheat, corn, hay, oats, barley, potatoes, and fruit trees, although the last failed. They brought dairy cows, and maintained small cattle herds and flocks of sheep. Hogs trampled native herbage. The Chicago-Colorado Colony mimicked Greeley's production, and planted twenty thousand shade trees to beautify Longmont—elms, maples, box elders, and scotch larches that absorbed large amounts of water. At the same time, Denver Board of Trade bulletins emphasized the pasturage potential of the plains by stressing "the innumerable herds of buffalo, elk, antelope, and deer which have from time innumerable subsisted" there.[43] Consequently, indigenous animals competed with domestic livestock just as new farms replaced more and more native grasslands. Whether the agriculturalists and their boosters appreciated the possible extinction of some species, they knew that these wild animals shared the grasslands. Their vision of a healthy, sustainable relationship with nature simply privileged more economically productive animals and plants.

Deforestation, polluted streams, and the loss of vegetation associated with mining put more pressure on wild game. In the fertile valleys and mountain parks, wild beasts competed with domestic animals again. Summit County ranchers raised Herefords, sheep, horses, and mules for sale, and swine and poultry for domestic consumption. To maintain their stock in the winter, they added timothy hay, clover, alfalfa, and wild grasses. In summer, livestock grazed for free on federal lands where they had an advantage over nondomestic animals with insufficient winter forage. Hodgson recalled, "As a result of this human invasion, the wild game steadily diminished."[44]

Private organizations and state and federal agencies confirmed this anecdotal evidence of dramatic environmental change. The Stock Growers Association reported that the first cattle boom placed 147,000 head on Colorado's plains. Cattle, sheep, and horses in Colorado grew eightfold by 1880, while farmers added dairy cows, goats, and swine to the mix, bringing total domestic grazers to nearly 1,500,000. By 1895, ranchers set aside almost 3,400,000 acres for pasturage, and farmers placed another 4,000,000 under irrigation, cultivating half of those with more than forty new crops that supplanted native grasses and plants. Comparable data on the deer, antelope, and elk that preceded this new human geography do not exist, but these numbers suggest that the region supported substantial wildlife populations before rapid, expansive, and all-encompassing exercises of species shifting superseded their sustenance. Alien organisms captured the regional ecosystems.[45] In introducing new species and extracting resources for trade, residents built a market structure that redefined the value of various plants and animals. As their harvests and livestock helped created their "natural economic unit," they increasingly viewed indigenous creatures as intruders.

Some intruders gained greater acceptance with the expansion of regional tourism, and attempts to facilitate this trade and other economic interests grounded the regulation of hunting that followed. In the 1860s, the Earl of Dunraven created a private hunting preserve near Estes Park, publicizing the area for recreational hunting and camping. Although the Earl moved on, interest remained and the upscale Estes Park Hotel appeared in 1877. Like Palmer and his

Colorado Springs associates, new entrepreneurs stepped forward to lure members of the leisure class who sought the quintessential wilderness experience in the challenge of the hunt. Denver's James Dexter used trout and salmon fishing to promote his Inter-Laken Hotel at Twin Lakes.[46] Territorial officials tried to support tourist activities by restoring particular animal populations and reversing some of the environmental changes generated by the complex interactions of other economic and social activities introduced after 1858. Economic realities dictated how, when, and which species received protection. The first was fish. Unlike settlers in the Pacific Northwest who disliked native salmon, early prospectors in the Denver region enjoyed the freshwater trout and walleye pike that abundantly filled local streams. Denver provided a ready market, prompting eager prospectors to set up nets, baskets, and seines. These devices remained in place for days with many fish rotting before they were retrieved. The traps captured so many fish that supply soon outweighed demand. In 1861, the territorial legislature banned them. Local deputies rarely indicted their neighbors for violations, so enforcement of this law was spotty, but it represented the first assertion of the state's authority over natural resources.[47]

Activities, which initially seemed to offer greater wealth, impacted native fish. Placer mining required the movement of streams, and with lode mining the number and size of diversions increased. The debris from mining and ore processing filled fish habitats with toxic substances. When discovered in large amounts and reached with relative ease, ores offered more profits than fish. Nonetheless, the territorial legislature repeatedly tried to protect this fragile living resource from the impact of human activity. It required in 1870 that artificial waterways obstructions provide passageways for migrating fish. After it was learned that sawdust killed fish, statutes outlawed dumping by lumber mills.[48] Farmers' irrigating ditches in mountain parks became unintentional traps, destroying millions of trout annually. Recognizing both the economic and social value of farming, the fish commissioner concluded that "it would be a suicidal policy to in any way hinder agricultural development." He recommended a screen that might direct fish to another channel, and suggested that when the fish migrated, the water to ditches be turned off, allowing them to travel upstream. Farmers resisted any interference with their water practices.[49]

For some citizens, fish also provided food, income, or both. Barred from using traps, they turned to a "poisonous, deleterious or stupefying drug or explosive substance." Although prohibited by law, such practices proved difficult to trace and continued as late as 1886. The commissioner observed, "The most flagrant and outrageous of these is the use of explosives. Explosives are not only cruel and barbarous, but they work a very serious injury to the fish interests of the state. They secure the wholesale destruction without giving any adequate return to those using them." Frequently, "dynamite was placed under the ice of a lake, and every fish in the lake killed, when it was impossible for the heathen who did it, to secure one in ten thousand of those killed."[50] Commissioners worried especially about young fish newly planted in streams. Given the poor compliance with and enforcement of laws, declining fish resources prompted western states like Colorado to opened hatcheries. These ensured "to all her citizens a wholesome and cheap food, and one that is prized by all classes." Fisheries raised carp, trout, and pike among others and delivered them to both public lakes and private reservoirs. Some eggs came from regional streams; others, like Ohio's black bass, came from distant locales.[51]

Everyone in the region did not embrace the principles of conservation inherent in the hatcheries. In 1894, Commissioner W. R. Calicotte reported: "Public sentiment was not in sympathy with the work. There seemed to be an idea that the business was conducted in the interests of a few sporting men from Denver, and other cities in and out of the state. At Twin Lakes, this feeling was so marked that it became necessary to guard the traps for catching spawners by day and by night to prevent their threatened destruction by citizens."[52] Populist Governor Waite appointed Calicotte, who criticized his predecessor, Gordon Land, for "wining and dining" and "accepting courtesies" from wealthy sportsmen and tourists. Issues of class frequently defined nineteenth-century conservation movements in the United States. As commercial and industrial forces altered the migration of fish and animals, fewer people procured game as part of their household consumption. Those who did tended to be poor, to live in rural areas, and to resist these regulations. Colorado hatcheries expected to produce five million fish per year by 1894. Taken as a measure of success by their promoters, these figures revealed continuing problems with depletions by poachers and poisonous dumpings, and the difficulties of restoring nature. Hatcheries needed to maintain high levels of production simply to keep recreational and commercial fishing afloat.[53]

Comparable laws protecting game animals and birds disclosed mixed motives and preferences for particular businesses and favored creatures. Antelope, elk, and deer gained much of their weight during the summer, but the hunting season established in 1876 began in June and continued through November, coinciding with the most popular time for tourist travel. In related advertising campaigns, railroads and local hotels organized camping trips for their guests, further disrupting foraging patterns. At the same time, the legislature catered to the livestock industry by placing bounties on wolves and coyotes at fifty cents a scalp. Lacking a systematic, ecologically based approach, these regulations did little to prevent the decline of some native animal populations, in part because officials still assumed that uncontrolled market hunting caused near-extinctions rather than contemplating the complex factors involved in species shifting. The law protecting livestock from wolves and coyotes removed a natural predatory check on antelope, deer, and elk, whose populations grew in some areas, although not necessarily those frequented by touring hunters. Mining, cultivation, and deforestation limited food sources and forced these animals to compete with domestic livestock for grazing lands on the public domain and private lands. At the same time, recreational hunters complained about the size and health of their targets. By 1885, and over objections from local ranchers, state officials addressed these imbalances with a seasonal system that replaced bounties on predators. Despite a series of regulations, the state found it difficult to permanently control animal populations. Bighorn sheep nearly vanished by 1877. Three years later, the state declared bison extinct in North Park, once home to large herds but now covered with cattle ranches, commercial farms, and irrigation ditches.[54]

The resort and health industries of Colorado Springs had involved a pure application of market values as they commodified amorphous elements that, for the most part, could not be processed, packaged, or shipped; they needed to be experienced. Avid promotions of recreational hunting and the wilderness experience it offered, even in the face of anti-elitism and declining animal populations, reflected the same commercial sensibilities. The legislature managed these resources according to the demands of various economic interests.[55] The laws initially penalized butchery by market hunters and others who indiscriminately killed for sport, practices that contemporaries condemned for upsetting farmers. The evolving regulatory scheme shaped the environment and its animal populations by reallocating resources for stockgrowers and a permanent tourist trade. Nonetheless, the statutes also reflected localism and traditional concerns about the unreasonable destruction of limited resources in ways that injured neighbors. Within regulated societies, rules benefited the community as a whole, not only dynamic economic producers. Consequently, game laws made exceptions "for food, and only when necessary for immediate use, governed in amount and quantity by the reasonable necessities of the person or persons killing the animal."[56] The poorest members of the community could hunt or fish out of season to feed themselves and their families. And when they attempted to sell their catch to others for profit, local deputies pursued them half-heartedly at best.

Given the variety of motives undergirding game laws, it is difficult to evaluate their ultimate effectiveness. With the panic of 1893 and the high unemployment that ensued, "many of the silver miners were compelled to resort to the rod and the gun to supply themselves with food," according to Calicotte. He joined others in seeking a more equitable system that limited the numbers of animals killed by tourists, whom the commissioner labeled "nonresident, aristocratic nabobs." On the other hand, ranchers complained because the season, which was shortened from 15 August to 1 November, overlapped with autumn roundups. When the game came down to feed in the parks and valleys, the law prohibited ranchers from killing their "winter's meat." Yet few residents noticed the racism inherent in the complete ban on any hunting by Indians.[57]

One way to consider the effectiveness of fish and game laws, Worster suggests, is from the perspective of the animals. Measured by the preservation of species threatened with extinction, the regulations achieved mixed results. Bighorn sheep resurged, increasing a hundredfold by 1900 following a complete ban on killing them. Mule deer and antelope populations remained healthy, but elk neared extermination in the region and Colorado completely closed their season in 1902. It took two decades to restore vital numbers. Many native fish perished, depleted by pollution and irrigation and replaced by state-sponsored game fish. Bison represented the most significant failure. Officials did not even record their small numbers. Predators faced equally dubious futures. Gordon Land protected bears and mountain lions in 1892 by effectively arguing that they did not present a threat, but restored the bounties on wolves and coyotes. Land, Calicotte, and other regional residents treasured certain indigenous animals for their commercial and pastoral value, but relegated others to the category of wildlife interlopers. Yet these men rarely controlled nature or all the environmental changes that they set in motion. Seasons and limits required annual adjustments. Officials could not prevent illegal and destructive poaching. Restorative efforts frequently failed because some local actors rejected them, and others assumed that game laws directed at hunting could solve problems caused by the complex interaction of different activities.[58]

The new interactions between people, animals, and their physical world during the last four decades of the nineteenth century revealed that human control was both real and illusory. Those who followed the discovery of gold brought experiences and values that helped them envision a new regional empire within the national and global marketplace. They possessed or acquired the capital and technology to physically alter their natural world in the furtherance of their dreams. In some very real ways, they controlled the environment. They redirected rivers, and removed chunks of silver, gold, and coal from the earth. They created new landscapes of railroads, cities, mines, farms, factories, and tourist attractions. In other ways, their control proved illusory. Regional residents celebrated their "improvements" of natural processes, despite the scars and shortages left by deforestation, air and water pollution, and erosion. And there were unanticipated consequences. They failed to foresee how the complex mixture of domestication, cultivation, irrigation, deforestation, and market hunting contributed to the rapid disappearance of indigenous flora and fauna, undermined future tourist activities, and challenged class relations. Efforts to regulate and restore resources brought mixed results. Water leaked into the manmade mining caverns, pillars of coal burst into flames, and nonhuman species rarely followed their prescribed path.

The struggles to control the natural world revealed the underlying tensions that defined society in the Denver region. Market forces suggested that resources be put to their most productive and profitable long-term use. Yet the desire for competitive autonomy underlay a push for the most rapid exploitation of these resources. At other times, localism and traditional values tempered resource development to protect, within limits, the welfare of community participants—coal miners, ranchers, and poachers. Commercial interests influenced policymaking by the legislature and agencies, but underneath existed the increasing recognition of the scarcity of resources and a continuing belief in their conservation and a more equitable distribution than the market allowed.

EPILOGUE

Losing Control

Denver is the center, not only of Colorado, but of a vast region extending for hundreds of miles in every direction.

Charles J. Hughes, Jr., 1902

By 1902 Denver anchored an urban hierarchy whose tentacles extended over "hundreds of miles in every direction." The metropolis and her sister cities converted natural resources into commodities, joined diverse hinterlands to distant markets, and intentionally transformed their physical world, initiating processes that linked distinct ecosystems in environmental change. Front-range entrepreneurs dominated a variety of tributary spheres, but just as their mastery over nature proved both tangible and delusive, the establishment of their vital, autonomous regional empire faced challenges from outside and within. They measured their successes in the integration, specialization, and expansion of the economy, substantial population growth, and the stability of their communities. Yet not all shared equally in the burgeoning domain, and many contested the class structure inherent in it. At the same time, shifts in the country's legal and financial systems prompted greater monopolization, undermining the tenuous balance that entrepreneurs maintained between their management of and their dependence on outside capital.

Even as some elements of local power proved transitory, Denver, Colorado Springs, and Pueblo remained central, permanent fixtures in the region and in the West. These cities moved people, capital, technology, information, trains, raw materials, and finished goods. By controlling these exchanges, they demonstrated dynamic population growth while other towns increased slowly, stagnated, or faded away. In the 1870s, Denver quickly surpassed its nearest metropolitan competitors, Cheyenne, Salt Lake City, and Santa Fe, by guiding the trade of the Rockies and the Rio Grande valley. Business leaders in Butte and Boise served smaller tributary spheres and never matched the independence, clout, or vision of Denver men. The front-range metropolis rivaled Omaha's importance as a railroad and meat packing center. By 1900, some 134,000 people called Denver home and it trailed only San Francisco in population and financial influence in the West.[1]

The complexity and rapid emergence of Denver's urban system also indicated substantial local success. Pueblo and Colorado Springs complemented the metropolis, performing important manufacturing and tourism functions. Once established, these junior partners competed with Denver in certain regional activities, like Pueblo and smelting or Colorado Springs and the Cripple Creek mining exchange. With their roles successfully defined by 1900, the populations of Pueblo and Colorado Springs reached twenty-eight thousand and twenty-two thousand, respectively, easily passing Santa Fe and Boise, cities that centered their own western subregions. Other piedmont communities, which fell behind in early competition with Denver, exhibited less vigorous growth, but made steady gains over fifty years. As secondary places within the regional system, Golden, Boulder, Cañon City, and Trinidad provided retail services for nearby mining and agricultural communities, while filling specialized roles.[2] Golden's fortunes, for example, improved or abated in relation to regional events. It once challenged Denver's dominance, but after the Colorado Central Railroad stalled and the territorial government returned to Denver, Golden lost almost half its population in the 1860s. To resurrect the town, its residents developed small smelters and attracted the Colorado School of Mines and the State Industrial School over the next two decades. Adolph Coors's brewery and other small businesses compensated for some of the town's earlier losses to the metropolis, but the volcanic tables and sandstone hills that separated the two towns only temporarily staved off Denver's outward expansion. By 1900, Golden became little more than a manufacturing suburb.[3]

Boulder City, founded in 1859, initially acted as a local wholesaling center for the enterprises that took root in the resource-rich area, but it always remained in the shadow of Denver forty miles to the south. Coal fields lay nearby, and surrounding valleys, watered by mountain streams, offered good farming soil. Flour mills sprung up in Boulder, while sawmills serviced timbermen from the foothills. Gold and silver mines played out by 1900, but entrepreneurs found other minerals, like tungsten and oil. The town's proximity to spacious mountain glens prompted a small tourist trade. Despite its links to extractive industries, education soon defined Boulder, although the town accepted what many considered the consolation prize among state institutions. The University of Colorado opened in 1877, but took twenty years to acquire its permanent campus through private donations from Boulder residents. Cañon City garnered the "superior" state reward. The territorial penitentiary arrived in 1871, providing regular employment and a steady flow of cheap prisoner labor for local businesses. While some promoters recognized that a prison could be "in some respects a detriment to the town, a payroll of $40,000 per annum [was] not to be despised." Cañon City's failed grab for the Denver & Rio Grande in 1874 had spurred Pueblo's residents into action and left Cañon City stagnating until the Leadville boom. With its merchants supplying miners there, Cañon City grew fivefold by 1880.[4]

Trinidad, just north of the New Mexico border, was the largest Hispano town when Congress formed Colorado Territory. Anglo-American merchants followed the extension of Denver's telegraph wires there, and typically pushed aside longtime residents. Racial tensions gave way to Christmas Day rioting in 1867, leaving three Hispanos dead, five injured, and one white man wounded. Federal troops restored order. In a rhetorical tone reminiscent of campaigns against the region's Indians, the *Rocky Mountain News* remarked, "The greater portion of the Mexican population vamoosed on the arrival of our 'Uncle's boys.'" William Byers blamed the "Mexicans" who supposedly misunderstood the new arrivals' motives and hoped to "exterminate the Americans."[5]

Corporate decisions further marginalized Trinidad's Hispano community when the Denver & Rio Grande erected a company town, El Moro, five miles away and the affiliated Colorado Coal & Iron Company built coke ovens there. The railroad's competitor, the Santa Fe Railroad, gave Trinidad new life when it arrived in 1876 and brought southwestern markets more securely within the region's control. Given the proximity of high-quality coal, other railroads constructed facilities there. John Evans connected the tracks of the Denver & New Orleans Railroad to his Denver, Texas, & Fort Worth Railroad at Trinidad, strengthening links to Texas and the Gulf of Mexico. Michael Beshoar, a physician, editor of Pueblo's *Chieftain* newspaper, and owner of coal and iron properties around Pueblo and Trinidad, celebrated the latter's manufacturing possibilities in typical booster fashion in *All about Trinidad*. By 1890, Trinidad supported its own coking ovens, two small smelters, a rolling mill, a cement works, three brick yards, three flour mills, two marble works, a broom factory, two saddle and harness factories, and an asphalt works. Its proximity to Pueblo limited Trinidad's growth, but by 1910 it became an important western industrial center and Colorado's fourth largest city with almost eleven thousand people.[6] These businesses privileged white Americans and left the marginalized Hispanos generally seeking employment as laborers.

While no other urban members challenged the supremacy or elitism of Colorado Springs in the tourist trade, boosters across the region recognized that the exploitation of recreational interests potentially offered profits. New resorts exploited their grand mountain scenery. Idaho Springs's prospectors appreciated the medicinal values of waters, but boosters promoted them as a tourist attraction only as mining declined. Its founders established Glenwood Springs as a resort, but it survived like Idaho Springs by supplying nearby mines in the off season. Estes Park fared differently. Given its early association with the Earl of Dunraven and the absence of prospecting in its environs, Estes Park acted solely as a tourist center. Economic activity languished during the winters, and its population remained smaller than more diversified resorts.[7]

Other secondary places with steady, albeit unspectacular, growth formed around railroad connections and agrarian communities at Fort Collins, Greeley, and Longmont. Lacking the diversified economic activity of Denver or even Boulder, these towns performed services closely linked to agriculture. Located on streams flowing from the mountains and established early in the creation of Denver's agricultural hinterland, their farmers acquired extensive appropriative rights. Unlike the quick fortunes that a few achieved on the mining frontier, local cultivators tended to realize steady profits over time, adding to these towns' stability. "The glory of Longmont is the community of intelligent thrifty farmers that surround it," according to promoters. Longmont businesses in 1890 included three grist mills, two elevators, four blacksmiths, a creamery, a canning factory, a fish hatchery, and agricultural implement stores. Just as Golden, a mercantile town for mining, grew with the Colorado School of Mines, Fort Collins's residents vigorously lobbied for the Colorado Agricultural College under the Morrill Act. Later known as Colorado State University, it opened in 1879 and contributed to the town's prestige and financial strength.[8] The wholesaling centers that were established with agricultural expansion into the San Luis Valley and onto the western slope shared similar experiences. Alamosa, the Denver & Rio Grande company town, emerged as part of the railroad's strategy to reach Santa Fe, but also gave the line access to products from San Luis Valley farmers and ranchers. As the Utes left the western slope, the railroad wove its way to Grand Junction. Located amidst rich agricultural and horticultural lands, this town also became an important link in the trade with Utah once the railway reached Salt Lake City in 1883.[9]

With the successful promotion of the sugar-beet industry by the Denver Chamber of Commerce and others, some agricultural towns grew anywhere from 33 to 50 percent over the 1890s. The Chamber and the Colorado Agricultural College hosted a sugar convention in 1892 and distributed beet seeds to recruit more participants for the nascent industry. With improved irrigation and newly researched cultivation techniques, more regional farmers grew beets, but they sent their crops to refining plants in Nebraska and Utah. In 1899, local entrepreneurs sought more control by opening a processing plant in Grand Junction. By 1903, factories appeared at Las Animas, Rocky Ford, and Lamar in the Arkansas River Valley and at Longmont, Greeley, Fort Collins, and Sterling along the South Platte and its tributaries. Beet farmers in western Kansas and Nebraska paid tribute to these new facilities.[10]

Absent refining plants, early appropriative rights, entrepreneurial leadership, or rail connections, agricultural communities like Evans and Julesburg struggled. Towns closely associated with ranching shared that industry's mixed fortunes in the 1880s. Iliff and Brush served the cattle kings and the corporations that succeeded them as nothing more than company towns. Even at the height of the open range, such places attracted few merchants or citizens because large cattle operations were self-contained. With the opening of Denver's stockyards and packing plants in the 1890s, many like Trail City, where herds once crossed the Arkansas River on their way to Kansas, disappeared. Culebra and Costilla, marginalized by the development of Alamosa, faded away.[11]

Reversals of urban fortune occurred most commonly, however, in mining. Tents popped up with each new discovery. Most vanished just as quickly, while some prospered for a few years or even decades before their inevitable decline. None flourished permanently nor consistently through the booms and busts that plagued the industry. Central City, platted by Byers, anchored early mining efforts at Clear Creek. Rich lodes in the surrounding mountains allowed it to maintain a relatively stable population as a local supply center when the new century dawned. Nearby Black Hawk profited from Nathaniel Hill's decision to locate the region's first smelter there, but when the industry shifted to the front range, he shut down the operation and the town lost a third of its population. Mining activity supported one local supply center, and Central City, only a mile away, filled this position. Neighboring Georgetown began as a gold camp in the 1860s, boomed again during the silver carbonate era, and struggled in the 1890s when bimetallism failed. It avoided Black Hawk's more precipitous tumble because its merchants diversified to a limited extent, celebrating the Georgetown Loop, a famous tourist attraction.[12]

No town better exemplified the tumultuous career of a mining town than Leadville, mirroring the rise and fall of its most famous alumnus, Horace Tabor. Mining began nearby with the initial gold rush, but there was little early success. When prospectors discovered that lead carbonates held rich silver deposits, they launched a new mining era. Leadville replaced little Oro City and boomed, emerging within three years as Colorado's second largest city with almost fifteen thousand people by 1880. Uncounted transient miners also crowded Leadville, "the leading silver producer of the world." Civilization followed with churches, schools, elegant residences, newly paved streets, and the grand Leadville Opera House. Boosters claimed a different future for Leadville: "Mining camps may come and go, but Leadville goes on forever." Forever proved ephemeral. Sinking silver prices shrank the town's population by a third and left the city gasping after the 1893 panic. Despite a slight resurgence following investments by Moffat and Smith in 1895, Leadville's days near the top of the urban system ended abruptly.[13]

Cripple Creek and its neighbors snatched the glory that once belonged to Leadville. Almost immediately, thousands arrived hoping to strike it rich, while hundreds of merchants prepared to mine the miners. In the end, these towns followed the same path as previous camps. When the mines played out, they declined. By the 1940s, Cripple Creek joined Black Hawk, Central City, and others in the *Ghost Towns of Colorado*, a book from the Writer's Program of the Work Projects Administration. Before they became "crumbling and often quite deserted cities," however, they performed important functions in the regional urban system, supplying surrounding mining districts and providing essential claim and assaying services. They lacked the long-term stability of farming communities, but housed miners' courts that organized filings, meted out justice, and established local rule and democratic traditions. These communities secured a semblance of order for an otherwise rootless population.[14]

With the permanent ascendancy of the front-range cities, the social stability of the agricultural communities, and the temporary utility of mining towns, urban control of diverse hinterlands became a concrete reality. Yet the susceptibility of the mining towns to remote events, such as national economic panics, revealed that other elements of regional control were more arbitrary. In his study of Aspen, Malcolm Rohrbough argues that the power of concentrated capital from national and international markets threatened regional autonomy. The very enterprises businessmen used to reorient the regional economy and become competitive proved to be their undoing. In a familiar late nineteenth-century tale of the West in particular and the United States in general, the region's railroads, smelters, and steel plants fell prey to monopolistic takeover from concentrated capital located far from Denver. The corporate structure that became commonplace in the last three decades and allowed for an entrepreneur-driven economy gave way to a realignment of economic power.[15] Denverites and other regional residents clung at times to vestiges of localism and traditionalism, but the commodification of natural resources that they more frequently promoted had linked the region and these industries to outsiders. With the concentration of large amounts of capital, these distant participants increasingly looked at mergers and consolidation rather than competition as the most effective means of realizing profit. In the process, they frequently shut local investors out of management.

Outsiders first targeted regional railroads. In 1873, Jay Gould gained a controlling interest in the Union Pacific as the national depression pushed the transcontinental line toward bankruptcy. John Evans, William Palmer, and other local railroad men condemned Gould, and William Gilpin wrote that the railroads could have done no worse "than in the hands of those who have made their hundreds of millions by fraudulent contracts, by excessive charges, and by the employment, in every way they could conceive, of the money obtained from the people for extorting from the people yet more money." Historians also vilify Gould and his compatriots. Robert Athearn labels him "an eye-gouging, gut-stomping brawler," and refers to his "bag of tricks," "dazzling display of deception and deceit," and "usual method of wrecking established lines and buying up the remains." Keith Bryant suggests that traditional portraits of Gould and other robber barons unfairly demonize eastern capitalists who facilitated western development. Similarly, some colonial models diminish the ability of local entrepreneurs to initially exercise control through superior access to information. Biographer Maury Klein argues that Gould was a "developmental" investor interested in long-term economic returns based on regional growth rather than an "opportunistic" investor only interested in quick profits. Nonetheless, Gerald Berk reminds us that Gould preferred autarchy. While the capitalist fostered properties that supported his lines, he crushed competition, utilizing tools afforded through the control of many territorial systems and concentrated capital.[16]

Whether Gould possessed developmental or opportunistic motives, the implications for regional railroad men remained the same. Evans and Palmer feared that power would slip from their hands. Gould wanted to create an interterritorial system, and the Union Pacific soon extended into or acquired branch lines in Colorado and Utah. Regional railroaders cried foul and petitioned the Secretary of the Interior for assistance. They claimed that Gould forced their Kansas Pacific "to default on its first-mortgage bonds, thereby impairing the security of the United States . . . [because] the Union Pacific Railroad Company . . . has persistently refused to transport passengers and freight in connection with Kansas Pacific Railway and the Denver Pacific Railway and Telegraphy Company at their point of intersection at Cheyenne, on the terms and in the manner required by the several acts of Congress." The government took no action against Gould, and he persisted in his quest, acquiring Kansas Pacific stock and assuming part of its debt. Through various mechanisms, Gould gained control of the Kansas Pacific, the Denver Pacific, and the Colorado Central by 1880, the very railroads that secured Denver's hegemony ten years earlier. Local entrepreneurs refused to acknowledge how their poor financial choices contributed to the loss of the Kansas Pacific. When the 1873 panic slowed land sales and prices dropped, the directors continued to expand through mortgages on land grant property. Consolidation with the Colorado Central in 1875 increased maintenance and construction costs, but brought insufficient returns to cover them.[17]

Gould then turned his attention to the leading regional railroad. The Denver & Rio Grande was the center of the empire that Palmer envisioned, but the 1873 depression left it in dire straits, unable to pay interest on its bonds. Given the road's importance to the region and since it had netted almost 360,000 dollars in profit in 1877, federal Judge Moses Hallett placed it in a friendly receivership, allowing Palmer to focus on his battle for Leadville with the Santa Fe in southern Colorado. At the same time, Gould hoped to eliminate the Santa Fe from meaningful competition for transcontinental traffic. Recognizing a common enemy, Gould and Palmer reached an agreement in September 1879. Gould bought almost forty thousand shares of Denver & Rio Grande stock and advanced 400,000 dollars toward the line's debt. Palmer agreed to forego traffic agreements with Union Pacific's competitors. When Gould joined Palmer's board, however, the wolf entered the chicken coop. At the board's November 1881 meeting, Palmer still controlled enough stock to maintain his leadership, but Gould began applying pressure, arguing that stock prices had fallen due to Palmer's mismanagement. Gould soon gobbled up Evans's Denver & South Park line and supported the former governor when Evans challenged Palmer with the Denver & New Orleans line from Denver to Pueblo. Palmer tried to hold off Gould by extending his empire into Utah. William Bell and he negotiated privately with Salt Lake City businessmen to form small railway and construction companies that would build from Utah, and then absorbed them within their new corporation, the Denver & Rio Grande Western Railway ("the Western"). As the new company's president, and although it was not legally a subsidiary, Palmer leased the Western to the older line, the Denver & Rio Grande, for thirty years. Steep cliffs between Utah and Colorado complicated construction and forced the line through southern Colorado, but in 1883, the Salt Lake connection finally opened.[18]

In his fight with Gould, Palmer gained little help from the region's other entrepreneurs due to his own aggressive tactics. He built cities at the expense of more established communities, and in platting the Denver & Rio Grande, gained control of much of the area's coal. Evans, among others, believed Palmer as guilty as Gould in imposing noncompetitive rates that undermined other regional railroads. At the same time, Denver & Rio Grande board members associated with

Gould complained that Palmer's free-spending construction strategies depleted limited cash stores. In letters to stockholders, Palmer blamed the problems on Gould and the Union Pacific, those who "are threatened by the new and better line to Salt Lake and to the Central Pacific connection, and who, with its confederates, is at the bottom of many of the attacks and rumors about the Denver and Rio Grande Railway Company." Nonetheless, as the Denver & Rio Grande teetered near bankruptcy in August 1883, and uncertain of whether he possessed shareholder support, Palmer resigned the presidency of his "little railroad," the Denver & Rio Grande.[19] William Jackson, Palmer's old associate, became the receiver and president, but Gould held the real power. After some litigation, they dissolved the lease between the Denver & Rio Grande and the Western. Denver's David Moffat assumed the presidency of the older line in 1887, but had little success in his efforts to extend the railroad directly from Denver to Salt Lake City or El Paso. Distant investors held all but five hundred shares of Denver & Rio Grande stock, and few shared Moffat's interest in expanding Denver's influence. Facing increasing criticism from eastern board members, Moffat resigned in 1891. A Gould man, Edward T. Jeffery of Chicago, replaced him. Ten years later, Gould's son bought Palmer out of the Western.[20]

The usurpation of these railroads is but one example of how the Denver region shifted from a peripheral frontier area to a full-fledged membership in the national and international economies and, at the same time, became susceptible to monopolistic takeover. Distant events could either enervate or energize regional industries. The 1893 depression clobbered silver mining, but also impacted seemingly unrelated enterprises. Corporate ditch companies had stopped investing in the region following losses and unfavorable court decisions, while farmers in eastern Colorado and western Kansas and Nebraska finished four years of drought and found themselves deep in debt. Senator Teller blamed the agricultural depression on dishonest railroad practices and federal laws that favored eastern capital. His comments revealed the extensive integration of the regional economy. He explained the cause of the farmers' plight to *The Colorado Farmer's* editor:

> The demonetization of silver has been the direct and
> immediate cause of the shrinkage in the volume of the
> world's money and therefore it may be truthfully said
> that this depression is the result of that great folly. . . .
> I am in favor of a general control by the Government of
> the United States of all railroad corporations engaged in
> international commerce so as to secure just and fair
> rates to all persons and all communities engaged in
> such commerce without unjust discrimination.[21]

In response to cash shortages and climatic crises, many farmers temporarily relied on private charity from Denver and Colorado Springs, while a few left surreptitiously to avoid creditors. Others in areas more distant from water shifted to livestock production or tried dry-farming techniques that foretold environmental catastrophe in the 1930s. Significantly, the farmers, who eagerly wrested control from outside carriers for their mutual stock companies, rethought issues of water conservation. They looked to the federal government to finance elaborate systems that guaranteed a regular flow. Western historians have discussed the Reclamation Act of 1902 at great length. Whether it was the savior of western farming and society, as Norris Hundley, Jr. contends, or the ruin of western environments through the enhancement of hydraulic productive power, as Worster argues, one thing remains clear. Regional agriculturalists acknowledged their inability to manage an essential natural element and willingly ceded power to the government to stabilize and enhance production.[22]

The shift to sugar-beet cultivation influenced the new perspective of many farmers. Sugar beets required precise and extensive irrigation, and the new industry demanded more and larger reservoirs. Europe provided the biggest competition in the refined sugar industry, and the fortunes of regional farmers depended on national tariffs. Tenets of localism and the regulated society that initially shaped regional agricultural communities faded away. By 1905, the Great Western Sugar Corporation, part of the American Sugar and Refining Company trust, consolidated the Platte River plants, while the Holly Sugar Corporation merged the Arkansas River Valley facilities. While a few local entrepreneurs such as Charles Boettcher succeeded, the trusts established prices. Beets remained among the more profitable cash crops, but farmers lost their negotiating leverage. Their laborers, initially German-Russian immigrants and later Mexican and Mexican-American migrant workers, possessed even less power in the international economy.[23]

By this time, the region had been fully integrated into worldwide markets. The British decision to stop minting rupees combined with the United States' commitment to the gold standard to lower the price of silver almost 25 percent in the early 1890s. Aspen's David Hyman observed that "the effect was that all the smelters and mines all over the U.S. were closed down and the mining section of the country which had been prosperous beyond anything ever known, was suddenly thrown into utter despair and apparently hopeless bankruptcy." Despite claims from the Denver Chamber of Commerce that the smeltermen "did not let the panic of 1893 get them down," many found themselves in trouble. They acquired substantial debt during intensive construction in the 1880s, and with the depression outside capital investments dried up. Some plants returned to production to service Cripple Creek; others closely tied to silver mines stayed closed. Regional smelters remained ripe for monopolistic takeover. August Meyer, who had managed the Harrison Reduction Works in Leadville and became president of Consolidated Kansas City Smelting and Refining, argued that western smelters must combine their resources or be absorbed by larger interests like the Guggenheim brothers who, from their New York office, directed four smelters in Pueblo, Perth Amboy, and Mexico.[24]

Yet the first threat to local entrepreneurs came from the nation's richest man, not the Guggenheims. In 1899, John D. Rockefeller backed the American Smelting and Refining Company, a new monopoly that quickly acquired six plants in Colorado and a dozen more in other states. One Guggenheim biographer suggests that the new trust set out to destroy the brothers because they were Jewish and they initially refused to participate. Possessing holdings equal to only one-fourth of the trust's properties, the Guggenheims offered substantial competition. Within two years, the ambitious brothers traded their smelters for a third of the trust's stock and gained control of American

Smelting and Refining. Mine operators and smelter workers worried that in the absence of competition, the monopoly would set prices as high and wages as low as it pleased. As was frequently the case, however, the concerns of local entrepreneurs remained ambiguous. Hyman bemoaned the deleterious impact of outsiders on silver mining, but as a major stockholder in Denver's Omaha & Grant smelter, happily accepted the trust's initial overture in 1901 and later purchased mines for it in Coeur d'Alene, Idaho. As an owner of mines at Aspen, Hyman became an intermediary between other proprietors and the trust, although no one was certain where his sympathies lay.[25]

While the Guggenheims seized the smelting trust, Rockefeller set his sights on the Colorado Fuel & Iron, the region's largest enterprise. By 1900, the company produced the bulk of the coal and coke from Colorado and the surrounding states, operated the only steel plant in the West, and employed more than fifteen thousand men. Pooling agreements with some eastern steel firms seemed to protect it, but despite net profits in various years during the 1890s, Colorado Fuel & Iron failed to repay obligations incurred while updating its Bessemer facilities. When the company issued new stock to finance repayment, it too became ripe for a takeover. John Osgood, Colorado Fuel & Iron's president, turned to Rockefeller and George Gould in 1901 to forestall the first bid from Chicago's newly organized United States Steel Corporation. However, disruptions caused by U.S. Steel's failed attempt and the corporation's lingering debts allowed Rockefeller and his son, John Jr., to become the principal shareholders in 1903. That same year, Denver attracted a small steel-casting plant, a manufacturer of boilers, a rubber-tire company, a gauge-saw manufacturer, a coal-mining machinery company, and a can company. Their combined production remained immeasurably small compared to that of the Pueblo colos-

Figure 19 (opposite). Sugar Beet Stacks in Greeley, Colorado.
Mounds of sugar beets fill the grade between Union Pacific tracks
just outside the Great Western Sugar Company plant, revealing
the predominant shift to this cash crop and the concentrated
capital of the sugar trust. Photograph by A. E. Dickerson.
Courtesy of Denver Public Library, Western History Collection.

sus that now belonged to the Rockefellers.[26] Supplanted by outsiders in the consolidation of the industries that underwrote economic growth and extended the influence of the region's cities, local entrepreneurs learned that the authority they initially enjoyed because of their business acumen and superior access to investment information diminished as they created more complicated trade linkages. Outside investments propelled the region from the periphery, but as it became more intimately connected to the core of the country's economy, the advantages that local businessmen exercised became equally available to the national capitalist class that usurped their leadership.

Other challenges to urban entrepreneurial control emerged earlier from within the region from participants who believed that their share of the wealth failed to match the contribution of their labors. Byers and other Denverites guided the extension of the agricultural hinterland through sales of land grant properties and established their city as the distribution center for its products. Some farmers, however, almost immediately demonstrated an entrenched resistance to urban and corporate control and the diffusion of market values. The agriculturalists continued a commitment to a well-ordered society with more equitable notions of property distribution. The Patrons of Husbandry formed its first grange at Greeley in February 1873. Fifteen years later, there were eighty-five lodges with almost twenty-four hundred members spread across Colorado, with more in the surrounding states. In addition to advancing their members' moral character and developing synergy through economic cooperatives, the Grange conveyed a strong anticorporate sentiment. It lobbied for a reduction of freight rates at the Colorado constitutional convention, although Denver railroad men, including five convention members, blocked the proposal. In a compromise, the constitution declared that railroads were common carriers and thus subject to the state's police powers, although the state only established an underfunded commission to govern them in 1885. The farmers garnered sufficient political power to organize the 1879 irrigation conference that eventually secured favorable changes in land and water laws and defeated large ditch corporations with the aid of Colorado's supreme court. As historian Richard Hogan observes, regional farmers developed a class consciousness in opposition to the entrepreneurs and the power of concentrated capital, but geographic distance, the renitency of stockgrowers, and a lack of empathy for wage workers sharply circumscribed their political influence in the final decades of the nineteenth century. Many farmers increasingly committed to beet production found themselves answering to the sugar trust as well as the railroads.[27]

Laborers contested entrepreneurial leadership with similarly mixed results. Colorado's constitution was among the first in the nation to call for healthier working environments and prevent the employment of children under age twelve, but the state failed to appoint inspectors in the major industries until the 1880s. Once in place, agencies closely aligned with management did little to improve the financial status of workers. The Denver Chamber of Commerce "confined [membership] to personal and individual owners." It extended opportunities to businessmen who invested capital instead of workers who produced it. And property gave entrepreneurs greater access to political capital. In addition to lobbying politicians, they pursued government offices. Gilpin, Evans, A. C. Hunt, and Samuel Elbert (Evans's son-in-law) became territorial governors. State executives included James Grant (smelting), Benjamin Eaton (agriculture), and Alva Adams (mining). Chaffee, Teller, Hill, Tabor, and Simon Guggenheim held U.S. Senate seats.[28]

Many laborers shared the entrepreneurs' goals for regional autonomy and personal wealth, but experienced less success in their individual efforts. Prospectors arrived in each new district seeking their own fortunes, but with the high costs of lode mining, most found themselves working for others. The corporate structure of Rocky Mountain mining imposed distinct divisions. Colorado Springs and its hinterland illustrated this social order. Refined people, capitalists with mining investments, wealthy invalids, and tourism entrepreneurs, called the front-range community home. The city's working class remained small. Few investors lived in the camps. Managers and supervisors entrusted with development of the mines formed one stratum in those communities. Miners who offered their sweat for daily wages composed the other. With frequent surpluses of labor, employees benefited less proportionately from booms at Leadville, Aspen, or Cripple Creek. Low wages, long hours, and limited opportunities left workers mired in poverty and the environmental muck of the camps.[29]

Entrepreneurs who celebrated their cities enjoyed the profits from regional growth, according to historian David Brundage, while the working people experienced the exploitation that accompanied industrial development. Americans rarely partook equally in the consumption, or degradation, of nature. Hard-rock miners, for example, faced explosions, collapses, floods, equipment malfunctions, and gas leaks. They received higher wages than other laborers, although barely enough to support their families. Workers in mining and other heavy manufactories suffered firsthand the health consequences of industrial pollution, such as those bemoaned by Helen Hunt Jackson at Crested Butte, while Colorado Fuel & Iron's directors and officers lived faraway in Colorado Springs, Denver, or New York City.[30] In response to such conditions, laborers began to organize, first with small efforts, such as the enrollment of Boulder coal miners in the 1870s. Local unions in different hard-rock and coal camps successfully preserved or increased wages on thirty occasions during the following decade, but others experienced setbacks at Leadville, Central City, and Caribou. Workers increasingly fought the limitations imposed through the social order and the corporate structure, regardless of whether regional entrepreneurs or distant capitalists exercised the authority. Disconnected local efforts, however, offered no guarantee that concessions gained in one dispute would carry over to the next or be enforced by state and federal officials who usually backed management. For example, Denver railroad workers from the local Knights of Labor assembly prevented wage decreases and job cutbacks by the Union Pacific in 1884. Having observed events, the Denver & Rio Grande prepared to thwart a similar effort by its employees. The vexed social problems that Palmer once thought his railroad might avoid were at hand. Management lobbied Judge Moses Hallett to send federal marshals and arrest the strike leaders. When Judge David Brewer later sentenced them to six months, he lectured them on the principles of supply and demand. The railroads permanently blackballed the defeated workers.[31]

Like most entrepreneurs and corporate officers, Judge Brewer viewed unions and their strikes as un-American. He believed that an

Figure 20. *Aspen Miners and Mule. This interior of the Bushwacker Mine illustrates the dangerous conditions hard-rock miners experienced, as well as the exploitation of timber and animal resources that accompanied regional mining. Photograph by Harry Buckwalter. Courtesy of Colorado Historical Society, Denver, Colorado.*

individual should negotiate a wage based on his own abilities, ignoring how industrialization usurped the workers' bargaining power. With the support of courts across the nation, ruling classes rejected unions and broke up strikes to both protect their business interests and regenerate their moral prerogatives. Given the united power of capital and government, workers often saw unions as their only chance to attain decent wages and safer conditions and to express their independence within the emerging urban-industrial system.[32] As the Denver region moved closer to a modern capitalist society, the state supreme court might support yeoman farmers against canal corporations, but judges such as Brewer rarely made such allowances for wage earners. As the United States and the Denver region adjusted to wide-scale industrialization and its inherent social problems, organized labor seemed to threaten the ability of the mine operator, the railroad, or the smelter to put resources to their most productive uses and thus supposedly undermined the community.

As market principles cemented in the 1890s, class tensions and labor unrest increased with some seventy strikes by organized labor. Delegates from Colorado, Idaho, Montana, Utah, and South Dakota met in Butte to form the Western Federation of Miners (WFM), to secure wages compatible with the dangers of their workplace, and to introduce safety measures that minimized them. The WFM promised to seek cooperative relations with employers, but the owners remained openly hostile. Responses by management and government confirmed the entrenchment of the capitalist ethic. In Idaho and Montana, at the fringe of the Denver region, miners generally demonstrated greater radicalism, but the most significant tests of the WFM occurred in Denver's backyard.[33]

In 1893, thousands of unemployed silver miners flooded Cripple Creek where the gold mines remained in production. In response to a labor surplus, mine owners tried to reduce the daily three-dollar wage by fifty cents, or alternatively to increase the work day to ten hours. With the support of WFM miners across the Rockies, Cripple Creek workers walked out and in February 1894, seized the mines for 130 days. While the strikers attempted to stake their share of wealth and power, Colorado Springs mining entrepreneur Irving Howbert charged that "by their actions [they] brought about a condition of anarchy." With Moffat, James Hagerman, and other proprietors, he organized the Cripple Creek Mine Owners' Association, and since many of the workers were Irish, contacted the anti-Catholic American Protective Association about strike-breaking tactics like the use of brass knuckles. The owners obtained an injunction, hired twelve hundred local sheriffs and Pinkertons as security guards, and prepared to prosecute the leaders. Due to unique political and economic circumstances, these usual methods failed to defeat the union. Virtually all district workers remained united, while some owners wanted to accept the union's terms and resume production given the strength of the gold economy. More important, Populist Davis Waite held the governor's office. He dispatched the National Guard to Cripple Creek as neutral monitors following a few violent episodes. Waite acted as the miners' representative in negotiations, and the owners agreed to maintain established wages and hours. The Populist-dominated legislature even mandated an eight-hour day in 1894, although the state supreme court ruled it unconstitutional four years later.[34]

In seeking concessions from both sides at Cripple Creek, Waite argued for a return to "good fellowship," with neither labor nor management asserting rights antagonistic to the welfare of the larger community. He sought a balancing of interests that benefited all. With the increasing entrenchment of the capitalist ethic and facing solid opposition from the mine owners and other entrepreneurs, Waite and the Populists found themselves out of office following the 1894 election. The owners prepared to stop the WFM in Leadville in 1896 when the union demanded a three-dollar daily wage and called a strike. Many of the same entrepreneurs owned properties in Leadville and Cripple Creek. Led by Eben Smith, Moffat, and Hyman, they formed the Colorado Mining Association "for the purpose of cooperation and mutual protection" because "the quiet, peaceable and legal operation of the properties belonging to [them] and under [their] charge, is liable to be interfered with by persons and organizations having no legal nor equitable right to so interfere."[35] The united owners refused to bargain and brought in strikebreakers and private security guards. After violence erupted, the new governor sent the National Guard in support of management rather than as neutral observers. As silver prices lagged, the owners experienced only minimal losses during the strike. Possessing little leverage to force negotiations, the miners returned without the wage increase.[36]

The greatest blow to the WFM, however, came later at the site of its earlier victory. The federation faced internal tension when it began to include in its ranks unskilled laborers from western mills and smelters, and called a poorly organized, local strike at the Colorado City mills in 1903. The national organization, which had relocated to Denver, supported the strikers by ordering a work stoppage at Cripple Creek. The mine-owners' association employed scab labor and openly sought the destruction of the WFM. Middle-class merchants backed the earlier Cripple Creek walkout, but had grown suspicious of WFM radicalism. When a dynamite explosion killed thirteen nonunion workers in June 1904, Governor James Peabody, an avowed union hater, blamed the strikers and declared martial law. The National Guard deported strikers, destroyed the union hall, and removed supportive county officials. The strike collapsed. Soon thereafter, the Guard and the owners' private security force broke up another WFM action in Telluride. By the end of the year, both districts employed card systems through which only approved miners received jobs.[37]

The United Mine Workers also faced Peabody's guardsmen. Although they won some concessions in northern Colorado coal fields, violence broke out in the southern areas with the employment of strikebreakers. The State Inspector of Coal Mines supported the owners and tried to diminish the impact of the strike.

> Nominally the strike is still on, although nearly all the mines are working at full capacity with non-union men, and the output is approaching the maximum mark it had prior to the strike. What has been remarkable is the fact that despite the strike, which usually paralyzes business and development, a greater activity has been manifested in coal mining than has been evident in the past.

Union coal miners had little success over the next ten years, until the negative publicity from the infamous "Ludlow Massacre" in 1914 prompted the Rockefellers to improve wages and working conditions.[38]

Figure 21. Guarding Emmett Mine, Leadville. With mine buildings and tailing piles visible in the background, a heavily armed man stands guard at Leadville's Emmett Mine, probably during the labor disputes of 1896. He embodies the state-supported power of the mining entrepreneurs. Photograph by O'Keefe and Stockdorf. Courtesy of Denver Public Library, Western History Collection.

With few exceptions, mine operators and other industrialists maintained a firm grip on workers throughout the nineteenth century, although labor unrest and the Grange's campaigns illustrated that some regional residents resisted the singular march toward a modern capitalist society. Innumerable, far-reaching, and permanent transformations followed the discovery of gold in 1858, permeating every aspect of human life and touching every element of the diverse ecosystems that made up Denver's tributary spheres. The metropolis emerged from early urban competition to dominate the region's control exchange functions and thus to define its character and the extent of its influence. Entrepreneurial counterparts in Colorado Springs and Pueblo guided important, albeit smaller hinterlands. Identifying and commodifying natural resources with market value, they integrated the mountains and plains into an expansive economy, often along the arc of the Rocky Mountains and the valley of the Rio Grande. Initially located on the periphery of the nation's economy, tenets of localism and a regulated society persisted in an odd mixture, sometimes as a means of tempering rapid advances that seemed to endanger the welfare of the local community, and at other times as the means by which local visions of a regional empire might be realized.

Workers and farmers, who frequently contested urban entrepreneurial control, joined leading businessmen in their development of hinterlands and contributed through their labor to the permanence and stability of the urban system. The Americans who arrived after 1858 worked together to remove perceived obstacles to growth. Undergirded by racist philosophies, they killed or exiled Native Americans whose societies and economies seemed ill suited to the new order. With superior capital and better access to American courts, entrepreneurs obtained large Mexican land grants and marginalized the Hispano communities of southern Colorado.

Whether driven by the values of the marketplace or communitarian principles, these new arrivals also shared an anthropocentric belief in the utility of nature. Farmers and ranchers filled the plains, competing for its limited water resources. Miners and tourists swarmed over the mountains seeking golden nuggets and sublime wilderness. Guiding the investment of outsiders' capital, entrepreneurs made Denver and Pueblo home to heavy manufacturing, and extended their influence across the West and into Mexico. In purposeful and unanticipated ways, they imposed a new human geography and reshaped the plains and the mountains, prompting environmental changes that inhibited their own future activities and permanently damaged indigenous flora and fauna.

As the Denver region moved closer to the center of the nation's economy, both physically through improved transportation and communication systems and more abstractly through financial institutions and capital investments, its entrepreneurs discovered that the control they initially exercised had dissipated. Changes in the nation's legal and financial structures facilitated the monopolistic concentration of capital near the end of the nineteenth century, and the industries so central to the region's extractive economy and its residents' sense of autonomy fell prey. Henry Porter, Palmer, Byers, Evans, and others promulgated an exclusionary vision of empire that drew upon the contributions of Hispanos, laborers, and farmers, but offered these participants few of its benefits. In the end, their dependence upon outside capital proved their undoing as the Goulds, Guggenheims, and Rockefellers supplanted them at the helm. Yet, while these entrepreneurs failed to fully realize their vision of an autonomous, competitive regional economy, with the help of these other participants they left a permanent legacy. A complex, integrated, diversified, urban-based economy remained in place. Over the twentieth century, their successors responded to internal events and external developments to expand and revise their hinterlands. Denver, Colorado Springs, and Pueblo led the development of new tourist areas for skiing, the extraction of new fuels, and the recruitment of the federal dollars that flowed westward with World War Two. Unfortunately, like their predecessors, these new urban leaders infrequently considered the implications of their activities for the marginalized members of society or the consequences for the environment.

ABBREVIATIONS

The following abbreviations are used to identify frequently cited archives, collections, and companies.

AVL&CC	Arkansas Valley Land & Cattle Company
CC&I	Colorado Coal & Iron Company
CCRC	Colorado Central Railroad Company
CF&I	Colorado Fuel & Iron Company
CHS	Colorado Historical Society
COC&PP	Central Overland, California & Pike's Peak Express Company
CSA	Colorado State Archives
D&RG	Denver & Rio Grande Railway
DBOT	Denver Board of Trade
DCOC	Denver Chamber of Commerce
DPL	Denver Public Library
DPRY	Denver Pacific Railway
DTFW	Denver, Texas & Fort Worth Railroad
FNBD	First National Bank of Denver
KPRY	Kansas Pacific Railway
RMN	*Rocky Mountain News*
UPED	Union Pacific Eastern Division

NOTES

Introduction

1. Henry M. Porter, *Autobiography of Henry M. Porter* (Denver: World Press, 1932); *Pencilings of an Early Pioneer* (Denver: World Press, 1929); and Mark S. Foster, *Henry M. Porter, Rocky Mountain Empire Builder* (Niwot: University Press of Colorado, 1991).

2. New western historians recognize this urban imperative, but it receives little attention in much western and environmental history. Exceptions include Richard Wade, *The Urban Frontier: The Rise of Western Cities, 1790–1830* (Cambridge: Harvard University Press, 1959; repr., *The Urban Frontier: Pioneer Life in Early Pittsburgh, Cincinnati, Lexington, Louisville, and St. Louis* [Chicago: University of Chicago Press, Phoenix Books, 1964]); Gunther Barth, *Instant Cities: Urbanization and the Rise of San Francisco and Denver* (New York: Oxford University Press, 1965); William Cronon, *Nature's Metropolis: Chicago and the Great West* (New York: W. W. Norton, 1991); and Gray Brechin, *Imperial San Francisco: Urban Power, Earthly Ruin* (Berkeley: University of California Press, 1999). On the cities' importance and the lack of study, see Gerald Thompson, "Another Look at Frontier/Western Historiography," 95, and Michael P. Malone, "The 'New Western History,' an Assessment," 98–99, in Patricia Nelson Limerick, Clyde A. Milner II, and Charles E. Rankin, eds., *Trails toward a New Western History* (Lawrence: University Press of Kansas, 1991). The index to this anthology contains no listings for "cities" or "urbanization" and only one each for "Denver" and "San Francisco."

3. Regarding interurban relations, Eugene Moehring, "The Comstock Urban Network," *Pacific Historical Review* 66 (August 1997): 337–62; Timothy R. Mahoney, *River Towns in the Great West: The Structure of Provincial Urbanization in the American Midwest, 1820–1870* (Cambridge: Cambridge University Press, 1990); and Michael P. Conzen, "The Progress of American Urbanism, 1860–1930," in Robert D. Mitchell and Paul A. Groves, eds., *North America: The Historical Geography of a Changing Continent* (Totowa, N.J.: Rowman and Littlefield, 1987).

4. In examining urban systems, this book differs from good histories of Denver, Colorado, and the Rockies, including Stephen J. Leonard and Thomas J. Noel, *Denver: Mining Camp to Metropolis* (Niwot: University Press of Colorado, 1990); Carl Ubbelohde, Maxine Benson, and Duane A. Smith, *A Colorado History*, 6th ed. (Boulder: Pruett Publishing Co., 1988; Carl Abbott,

Colorado: A History of the Centennial State (Boulder: Colorado Associated University Press, 1976); Robert Athearn, *The Coloradans* (Albuquerque: University of New Mexico Press, 1976); and Duane A. Smith, *Rocky Mountain West: Colorado, Wyoming, and Montana, 1859–1915* (Albuquerque: University of New Mexico Press, 1992).

5. Cronon, *Nature's Metropolis,* xvi. Regarding pre-1858 activity, see Elliott West, *The Contested Plains: Indians, Goldseekers, and the Rush to Colorado* (Lawrence: University of Kansas Press, 1998), 63–93 passim; Mark J. Stegmaier and David H. Miller, eds., *James F. Milligan: His Journal of Fremont's Fifth Expedition, 1853–1854; His Adventurous Life on Land and Sea* (Glendale, Calif.: Arthur H. Clark Co., 1988); and Howard Roberts Lamar, *The Far Southwest, 1846–1912: A Territorial History* (New Haven: Yale University Press, 1966; repr., New York: W. W. Norton and Co., 1970).

6. D. W. Meinig observes that "any landscape is composed of not only what lies before our eyes but what lies within our hearts." *The Interpretation of Ordinary Landscapes* (New York: Oxford University Press, 1979), 34.

7. "These many human visions of nature are always jostling against each other, each claiming to be universal and each soon making the unhappy discovery that even its nearest neighbors refuse to acknowledge that claim." William Cronon, "Introduction," in Cronon, ed., *Uncommon Ground: Toward Reinventing Nature* (New York: W. W. Norton and Co., 1995), 51. William Wyckoff and Larry M. Dilsaver discuss mountains as "barriers" in "Defining the Mountainous West," in Wyckoff and Dilsaver, eds., *The Mountainous West: Explorations in Historical Geography* (Lincoln and London: University of Nebraska Press, 1995), 29.

8. William G. Robbins, *Colony and Empire: The Capitalist Transformation of the American West* (Lawrence: University Press of Kansas, 1994), 167. Robert Athearn discussed a north-south axis for regional railroads; this book considers its expansion via other industries as well. *Rebel of the Rockies: A History of the Denver and Rio Grande Western Railroad* (New Haven and London: Yale University Press, 1962).

9. Timothy R. Mahoney, "Urban History in a Regional Context: River Towns on the Upper Mississippi, 1840–1860," *Journal of American History* 72 (September 1985): 318–20.

10. D. W. Meinig suggests a geographical construction of the West as dynamic regions anchored by six cities, including Denver. "American Wests: Preface to a Geographical Interpretation," *Annals of the Association of American Geographers* 62 (1972): 159–84. Also, see Michael C. Steiner and David M. Wrobel, "Many Wests: Discovering a Dynamic Western Regionalism," in Wrobel and Steiner, eds., *Many Wests: Place, Culture and Regional Identity* (Lawrence: University Press of Kansas, 1997), 11; and on transformative processes, William G. Robbins, "Western History: A Dialectic on the Modern Conditions," *Western Historical Quarterly* 20 (November 1989): 429–49.

11. Cronon, *Nature's Metropolis,* 282–83. Among others, my model draws from Meinig, "American Wests," 169–74; Mahoney, "Urban History in a Regional

Context," 320; David Meyer, "A Dynamic Model of the Integration of Frontier Urban Places into the United States System of Cities," *Economic Geography* 56 (September 1980): 135; William Wyckoff, "Incorporation as a Factor in the Formation of an Urban System," *Geographical Review* 77 (1987): 279–92, and "Revising the Meyer Model: Denver and the National Urban System, 1859–1879," *Urban Geography* 9 (1988): 11–15.

12. David R. Meyer, "The National Integration of Regional Economies, 1860–1920," in Mitchell and Groves, *North America,* 321–46; Wyckoff, "Incorporation," 284; Robbins, *Colony and Empire,* xi, 3, 7; Donald Worster, *The Wealth of Nature: Environmental History and the Ecological Imagination* (New York: Oxford University Press, 1993), 9–11; and James Sherow, "Utopia, Reality, and Irrigation: The Plight of the Fort Lyon Canal Company in the Arkansas River Valley," *Western Historical Quarterly* 20 (May 1989): 170.

13. Morton Horwitz argues that by 1860, judges directed social change by instrumentally channeling control of the means of production to dynamic actors. *The Transformation of American Law, 1780–1860* (Cambridge: Harvard University Press, 1977), 1, 30. William J. Novak alternatively uncovers persistent regulation into the 1870s and concludes that the law released Willard Hurst's creative energies only when they would not be antagonistic to the community. *The People's Welfare: Law and Regulation in Nineteenth-Century America* (Chapel Hill and London: University of North Carolina Press, 1996), 6–7, 32–42, 239–40; and James Willard Hurst, *Law and the Conditions of Freedom in the Nineteenth-Century United States* (Madison: University of Wisconsin Press, 1956), Chap. 1, 53–66 passim. Also, see Donald J. Pisani, *To Reclaim a Divided West: Water, Law, and Public Policy, 1848–1902* (Albuquerque: University of New Mexico Press, 1992).

14. Theodore Steinberg, *Slide Mountain: Or, the Folly of Owning Nature* (Berkeley and Los Angeles: University of California Press, 1995), 10; and Arthur F. McEvoy, *The Fisherman's Problem: Ecology and Law in the California Fisheries, 1850–1950* (Cambridge University Press, 1986), 14–16.

15. Richard Hogan discusses this "national capitalist class." *Class and Community in Frontier Colorado* (Lawrence: University Press of Kansas, 1990), 4.

Chapter 1

The epigraph is from William Pierson, Denver, to Richard, 30 January 1860, in Duane Smith, *Rocky Mountain West,* 19.

1. Carl Abbott, "Frontiers and Sections: Cities and Regions in American Growth," *American Quarterly* 37 (1985): 406–7.

2. In 1859, W. A. H. Loveland founded Golden, diggers settled Boulder and Colorado City, and towns appeared at abandoned outposts near Pueblo and Cañon City. Recordbook, Mechanics' Mining and Trading Company, CHS; West, *Contested Plains,* 174; Barth, *Instant Cities,* xxi; Peter Wiley and

Robert Gottlieb, *Empires in the Sun: The Rise of the New American West* (New York: G. P. Putnam's Sons, 1982), 121; Robbins, *Colony and Empire,* 175; Keith L. Bryant, Jr., "Entering the Global Economy," in Clyde A. Milner II, Carol A. O'Connor, and Martha A. Sandweiss, eds., *The Oxford History of the American West* (New York: Oxford University Press, 1994), 198; and Duane Smith, *Mining America: The Industry and the Environment, 1800–1980* (Lawrence: University Press of Kansas, 1987), 2.

3. *Eighth Annual Report of the Denver Chamber of Commerce and Board of Trade* (Denver: New Printing Company, 1890), 9; Wade, *Urban Frontier,* 39–42; Thomas Huber, *Colorado: The Place of Nature, the Nature of Place* (Niwot: University Press of Colorado, 1993), 5–6; and Clifford C. Hill, "Wagon Roads in Colorado, 1858–1876," (Master's thesis, University of Colorado, 1949), 9–14, in Athearn, *Coloradans,* 8–10.

4. Neither Spain nor Mexico sent mineral expeditions, but Zebulon Pike in 1807 and William Gilpin in the 1840s reported about gold. Donald Jackson, ed., *The Journals of Zebulon Montgomery Pike, with Letters and Related Documents* (Norman: University of Oklahoma Press, 1966), 89; Gilpin, *The Central Gold Region: The Grain, Pastoral and Gold Region of North America* (1859; repr., St. Louis: E. K. Woodward, 1860), 3; Col. R. B. Marcy, *Thirty Years of Army Life on the Border* (New York: Harper and Bros., 1866), 260–63; Henry Villard, *The Past and Present of the Pike's Peak Gold Regions* (St. Louis: Sutherland and McEvoy, 1860), 22–23; Nolie Mumey, *History of the Early Settlements of Denver (1599–1860)* (Glendale, Calif.: Arthur H. Clark Company, 1942); Oakah L. Jones, *Los Paisanos: Spanish Settlers on the Northern Frontier of New Spain* (Norman: University of Oklahoma Press, 1979), 135; and Earl Pomeroy, *The Pacific Slope: A History of California, Oregon, Washington, Idaho, Utah, and Nevada* (New York: Alfred A. Knopf, 1966), 124.

5. James H. Pierce, "With the Green Russell Party," *The Trail* 13 (May 1921): 11 (quote), also in Leonard and Noel, *Denver,* 8. Northern Colorado initially was in Kansas Territory; southern Colorado was New Mexican. Also Ovando J. Hollister, *The Mines of Colorado* (Springfield, Mass., 1867), 127; Jerome Smiley, *History of Denver* (Denver: Sun Publishing, 1901), 149–55; Junius Wharton, *History of the City of Denver from Its Earliest Times* (Denver: Byers and Dailey, 1866), 23–29; and William Henry Harrison Larimer, *Reminiscences of General William Larimer and His Son William H. H. Larimer* (Lancaster, Penn.: New Era Printing, 1918), 34.

6. Edward W. Wynkoop, "Unfinished Colorado History," typescript, 9, Edward W. Wynkoop Collection, CHS; Carol A. O'Connor, "A Region of Cities," in Milner, O'Connor, and Sandweiss, *Oxford History,* 540; Cronon, *Nature's Metropolis,* 32; Novak, *People's Welfare,* 9–10, 115–17; and Lyle W. Dorsett, *The Queen City: A History of Denver,* Western Urban Series (Boulder: Pruett Publishing Company, 1977), 5–10.

7. R. E. Whitsitt, to Daniel Witter, 16 May 1859, in Mumey, *History of the Early Settlements,* 192; Thomas Wildman, Denver, to Augustus Wildman, 20 June

1859, in LeRoy R. Hafen and Ann W. Hafen, eds., *Reports from Colorado: The Wildman Letters, 1859–1865* (Glendale, Calif.: Arthur H. Clark Company, 1961), 39; and Leonard and Noel, *Denver,* 12. When Eastern newspapers contested Denver's population, migration stalled until three journalists celebrated the city. The *Cincinnati Commercial's* Villard, *Past and Present of the Pike's Peak Gold Regions;* the New York Tribune's Horace Greeley, *An Overland Journey: From New York to San Francisco in the Summer of 1859* (New York: C. M. Saxon, Barker, 1860); and the *Boston Journal's* Albert D. Richardson, *Beyond the Mississippi: From the Great River to the Great Ocean* (Hartford, Conn.: Times Press, 1867).

8. *RMN,* 7 April 1860; Novak, *People's Welfare,* 10, 115–17; and Leonard and Noel, *Denver,* 8–9.

9. When the Leavenworth & Pike's Peak reneged on debts, the Central Overland, California & Pike's Peak Express Company bought it. This overextended company sold to Holladay in 1861. Holladay sold to Wells Fargo in 1867 for a profit. In 1860, Denver received twenty million pounds of freight; by 1866, over one hundred million. Map, William Henry Brewer Papers, DPL; *RMN,* 7 May 1859; Porter, *Autobiography,* 23; Alexander Majors, *Seventy Years on the Frontier* (Chicago and New York: Rand, McNally and Co., 1893), 160–65; Hill, "Wagon Roads," 9–20; and Huber, *Colorado,* 5.

10. *First Annual Report of the Officers of the Denver Pacific Railway and Telegraph Company, December 1868* (Chicago: Rand McNally and Co., 1869), 9; Governor John Evans Private Papers, CHS; Memorial for Road to Snake River by Various Parties in Summit County to the Denver Board of Trade, 10 December 1867, DBOT Records, DPL; and J. Valerie Fifer, *American Progress: The Growth of the Transport, Tourist, and Information Industries in the Nineteenth-Century West seen through The Life and Times of George A. Crofutt, Pioneer and Publicist of the Transcontinental Age* (Chester, Conn.: Globe Pequot Press, 1988), 17–20, 101–8, 127. Crofutt worked in eastern publishing before bankruptcy in 1857. After mining unsuccessfully, he began long-distance freighting.

11. Denver telegraph lines reached Santa Fe in 1868 and Cheyenne in 1869, connecting Colorado, New Mexico, and Wyoming with the nation. Porter, *Autobiography,* 31; Articles of Incorporation, United States and Mexico Telegraph Company, 28 November 1867, Henry Miller Porter Papers, CHS; Foster, *Henry M. Porter,* 45–46; *RMN,* 23 April 1859; and Mumey, *History of the Early Settlements,* 119–25.

12. Kassler, Denver, to Maria Stebbens, New York City, 11 April 1864, George Washington Kassler Collection, CHS; Randall Rohe, "Environment and Mining in the Mountainous West," in Wyckoff and Dilsaver, *Mountainous West,* 169–70; Otis Young, *Western Mining* (Norman: University of Oklahoma Press, 1970), 30; and James E. Fell, Jr., *Ores to Metals: The Rocky Mountain Smelting Industry* (Lincoln: University of Nebraska, 1979), 6.

13. When a miner violated rules, however, harsh and speedy justice included whippings, hangings, and banishment. Henry James Hawley, Diary, CHS;

Hogan, *Class and Community,* 52; Gordon Bakken, "The Influence of the West on the Development of Law," *Journal of the West* 24 (January 1985): 66–67; Margaret R. Somers, "Rights, Relationality, and Membership: Rethinking the Making and Meaning of Citizenship," *Law and Social Inquiry* 19 (winter 1994): 63–112; and Novak, *People's Welfare,* 10–11. For different perspectives on federal appointees' importance, see Rodman Paul, *The Far West and the Great Plains in Transition, 1859–1900* (New York: Harper and Row, 1988), 97.

14. Hollister, *Mines of Colorado,* 360–63; Laws of the Territory of Colorado, 1861, 249, and Laws of the Territory of Colorado, 1862, 69, in Lawrence M. Friedman, *A History of American Law,* 2nd ed. (New York: Simon and Schuster, 1985), 367; Robert W. Swenson, "Legal Aspects of Mineral Resources Exploitation," in Paul W. Gates, *History of Public Land Law Development* (Washington, D.C.: U.S. Government Printing Office, 1968), 716–23; Donald J. Pisani, "Promotion and Regulation: Constitutionalism and the American Economy," *Journal of American History* 74 (December 1987): 768; and regarding liberalism, Christopher McGrory Klyza, *Who Controls Public Lands? Mining, Forestry, and Grazing Policies, 1870–1990* (Chapel Hill: University of North Carolina Press, 1996), 31.

15. Rodman Paul, *Mining Frontiers of the Far West* (New York: Holt, Rinehart and Winston, 1963), 6, 168–75; and Rohe, "Environment and Mining," 169–70.

16. Frank Hall, Spanish Bar, Colorado, to Captain Low, Syracuse, 14 April 1864?, Frank Hall Collection, CHS. Hall abandoned prospecting, worked for Denver newspapers over thirty years, and wrote *The History of Colorado,* 4 vols. (Chicago: Blakely Printing Co., 1889–1895).

17. Samuel Mallory, Nevada City, Colorado, to *The Jeffersonian* (Danbury, Conn.), 24 June 1860, Samuel Mallory Collection, CHS; and Fell, *Ores to Metals,* 10–20. A New York-based corporation owned the Bobtail, but Chaffee guided its operations. With over one hundred mines, Chaffee became a leading investor in the West. Journal, Bobtail Gold Mining Company Records, DPL; and O. L. Baskin, *History of the City of Denver, Arapahoe County and Colorado* (Chicago: O. L. Baskin & Co., 1880), 361.

18. *Western Mountaineer* (Denver) 26 July 1860 (quote); and *RMN,* 8 March 1859, 25 July 1860.

19. Charles Holly, Speaker of the House, and Edward A. Arnold, President of the Council, Joint Memorial to the Senate and the House, 4 November 1861, signed by William Gilpin, Territorial Governor, FNBD Records, CHS; Smiley, *History of Denver,* 814; and Robert S. Pulcipher, First of Denver . . . A History (Denver: Robert S. Pulcipher and the First National Bank of Denver, 1971), 21–23.

20. *Miner's Register* (Central City), 20 August 1864; *RMN,* 17 March 1864; Organization Certificate, FNBD Records; and inquiries to Comptroller of Currency, Pulcipher, *First of Denver,* 25, 34.

21. Original advertisement, December 1862, and Inventory of Estate Property, Last Will and Testament, Charles B. Kountze, filed in probate, 23 November 1911, Kountze Family Collection, DPL; Lists of Shareholders, 1868 and 1870 and Minute Book, 3, 10, 16, 19, 43, Rocky Mountain National Bank Records, DPL; "History of the First National Bank of Central City and Joseph A. Thatcher," manuscript, Harry Lake Notes, 1924, DPL; *New York Financier,* 1 November 1897; and Larry Schweikart, "Frontier Banking in Colorado: A New Perspective on Public Confidence and Regulation, 1862–1907," *Essays and Monographs in Colorado History* 8 (1988), 18–19.

22. *RMN,* 9 May 1865; Stock ledger Number One, FNBD records; Baskin, *History of the City of Denver,* 361; and Steven F. Mehls, "Success on the Mining Frontier: David H. Moffat and Eben Smith—A Case Study" *Essays and Monographs in Colorado History* 1 (1981): 92. Moffat partnered in a Denver stationery and insurance business with Kassler.

23. William Gilpin, *The Cosmopolitan Railway: Compacting and Fusing Together All the World's Continents* (San Francisco: The History Company, 1890), 108; *RMN,* 24 November 1859; and Gilbert Stelter, "The City and Westward Expansion: A Western Case Study," *Western Historical Quarterly* 4 (1973): 187–202. Cheyenne's 1870 population was 1,450; Denver's 4,800. Riley Moffat, *Population History of Western U.S. Cities and Towns, 1850–1990* (Lanham, Md., and London: Scarecrow Press, 1996), 69, 338.

24. The Colorado Central succeeded the Colorado and Clear Creek Railroad, which never laid tracks. Boston investors dominated its shareholders. Minutes, 10 July 1865, 3, and 10 July 1867, 1, and By-laws, 16 June 1867, CCRC Collection, CHS; *Daily Mining Journal* (Black Hawk), 12 July 1867; and *RMN,* 4 December 1867.

25. Minutes, 10 July 1867, and Resolution, Denver Meeting of Directors, 4 January 1868, CCRC Collection; *Miner's Register,* 6 November 1868; "Memorial of H. M. Teller Remonstrating against the Admission of Colorado as a State into the Union," 40th Congress, 20 February 1868, DPL; and Elmer Ellis, *Henry Moore Teller, Defender of the West* (Caldwell, Idaho: The Caxton Printers, 1941), 62–77; and Paul, *Far West,* 98–99.

26. *First Report,* DPRY, 8 (quote); *RMN,* 20 November 1867; and Porter, *Autobiography,* 29, 31. Local investors took DPRY shares, in part, so the Board could "lay before our eastern friends correct statistics of the vast mineral, agriculture and pastoral advantages of what I trust may soon become the state of Colorado." George Crater, New York City, to Henry C. Leach, Secretary, DBOT, Denver, 16 June 1868, DBOT Records. Physician John Evans prospered in Chicago real estate and railroads, and established Evanston and Northwestern University. Evans replaced Gilpin in 1862. Harry E. Kelsey, Jr., *Frontier Capitalist: The Life of John Evans* (Denver: Pruett Publishing Co., 1969).

27. *Second Annual Report of the Board of Directors of the Kansas Pacific Railway Company* (New York: Baker and Golden Printers, 1869), 17–21 (quote), KPRY Collection, CHS; *RMN,* 18 May 1868, 22 June 1870; *First Report,*

DPRY, 32; John Evans, Washington, to Mrs. Evans, Denver, 5 July 1868, Evans Private Papers; and Abbott, *Colorado,* 9, 86–87.

28. Rossiter Raymond, Denver, to wife Sarah, Brooklyn, New York, 1 October 1870 (quote), Rossiter Worthington Raymond Collection, CHS; and Resolution, Board of Directors, 21 February 1868, CCRC Collection. Raymond edited the *American Journal of Mining.*

29. Cheyenne lacked comparable leadership. Stelter, "City and Westward Expansion," 202.

30. Porter, *Autobiography,* 31.

31. Hall to Captain Low 14 April 1867 (quote); Thomas Eggleston, *The Boston and Colorado Smelting Works* (Philadelphia: Sherman and Co., 1877), 1–5; and Clark C. Spence, *Mining Engineers and the American West: The Lace-Boot Brigade, 1849–1933* (New Haven and London: Yale University Press, 1970), Chap. 2 passim.

32. A mining engineer wrote to investors: "everyone here is anxious to aid us because they think our unbiased opinions may have weight in the east." Alfred Rockwell, Georgetown, Colorado, to Kate Rockwell, Boston, 20 July 1871, Alfred Rockwell Papers, DPL. Also, see Duane Smith, *Silver Saga: The Story of Caribou Colorado* (Boulder: Pruett Publishing, 1974), xii; Moehring, "Comstock Urban Network," 352–53; Hurst, *Law and the Conditions of Freedom,* 17; Alan Trachtenberg, *The Incorporation of America: Culture and Society in the Gilded Age* (New York: Hill and Wang, 1982), 4; Jared Warner Mills, *Mills' Constitutional Annotations* (Chicago: E. B. Myers and Co., 1890), 74–78; and Wyckoff, "Incorporation," 284–87.

33. Robert H. Wiebe, *The Search for Order, 1877–1920* (New York: Hill & Wang, 1967), 1; Paul Sibley Barnett, "Colorado Domestic Business Corporations, 1859–1900" (Ph.D. diss., University of Illinois, Urbana, 1966), 107, 110; and Leonard and Noel, *Denver,* 44.

34. *The Natural Resources and Industrial Development and Condition of Colorado* (Denver: State Bureau of Immigration and Statistics, 1889), 7; *Report of the State Bureau of Mines, Colorado, for the year 1897* (Denver: Smith-Brooking Printing Company, 1897), 160–62; and Wiebe, *Search for Order,* 1. Before 1876, half of the stock needed to be paid within two years. After 1876, only 25 percent was paid within 1 year. *General Laws and Joint Resolutions, Memorials and Private Acts,* 3d session, Territorial Legislative Assembly of Colorado (Denver: Byers and Dailey, RMN Office, 1864), 52; and *General Laws, and Joint Resolutions, Memorials and Private Acts,* 11th session, Territorial Legislative Assembly of Colorado (Denver: William N. Byers, Public Printer, 1876), 47.

35. *Eighth Report,* DCOC, 12; *Statistical History of Clear Creek County from 1859–1881* (Georgetown: Miners Printing Co., [1882]), 1; *"Official Information: Colorado"* (Denver: Rocky Mountain News Steam Printing House, 1872), 20–25; J. W. Nesmith, *The Interests of Colorado in the Iron and Steel Manufacture* (Denver: Press of C. J. Kelly, 1890); and Estate Inventory, Kountze Collection.

36. Henry Wolcott, Argo, Colorado, to Will Wolcott, undated letter, in Edward Oliver Wolcott Papers, DPL; Prospectus, Bald Mountain Mining Company, Leadville, DPL; Stock lists, Alma Pool Association, James Dexter Papers, CHS; Pooling Agreement, 28 May 1888, Hubert Mining Company Records, 1895, DPL; Denver Stockholder Proxies, Quartz Hill Mining and Tunneling Company Records, DPL; *Biennial Report of the Secretary of State of Colorado for the Fiscal Years ending November 30, 1883 and November 30, 1884* (Denver: Times Printing Co., 1884), 10–43; and *Biennial Report of the Secretary of State of Colorado, for the Fiscal Years Ending November 30, 1885 and November 1886* (Denver: Times Printing Co., 1886), 9–44.

37. Smith, *Silver Saga,* 45–46, 63–81; and Mehls, "Success," 92–93.

38. Tabor divorced Augusta to marry the younger Elizabeth "Baby Doe" McCourt. Augusta died wealthy; Baby Doe froze to death in 1935 at the Matchless Mine. Tabor told her to keep this property, convinced it would be profitable again. It never was. Duane Smith, *Horace Tabor: His Life and the Legend* (Boulder: Colorado Associated University Press, 1973); and Inventory, Tabor's indebtedness, FNBD records.

39. Warranty Deed, Riche to Chaffee, 5 November 1878, Little Pittsburgh Lode, Lewis C. Rockwell Papers, CHS; Mehls, "Success," 94; Smith, *Horace Tabor,* 70–75, 110–29; and R. G. Dun reports in Dorsett, *Queen City,* 65–67.

40. F. Andrews, London, to shareholders, La Plata Company, 3 October 1882 (quote), Memorandum of Agreement, 26 February 1891, the London and Amsterdam General Investment Company and Moffat, and Articles of Association, 16 May 1891, Maid of Erin Silver Mines, Limited, London, FNBD Records; and Moffat Estate Company Report, David H. Moffat Papers, DPL. Britain's western mining investments dipped only during depressions. Clark C. Spence, *British Investments and the American Mining Frontier, 1860–1901* (Ithaca, N.Y.: Cornell University Press, 1958), 1–22.

41. Documents for holdings in Eben Smith Papers, DPL. Also Moffat Estate Company Report; and Charles J. Moore, *Leadville, Up-to-Date Literature concerning the "Greatest Mining Camp on Earth"* (Leadville: Press of the Herald Democrat, [1895]), 3.

42. Moffat and Chaffee agreed to buy half the Durant for 120,000 dollars, but backed out. "The Romance of a Mining Venture," 40, unpublished manuscript, David M. Hyman Collection, CHS; Declaration of Trust, 24 January 1885, by David Hyman, Jerome Chaffee and David Moffat, FNBD Records; Malcolm Rohrbough, *Aspen: The History of a Silver-Mining Town, 1879–1893* (New York: Oxford University Press, 1986), 94–100; and 17 Stat. 91 (10 May 1872).

43. *Rocky Mountain Sun* (Aspen), 4 December 1886 (quote), in Rohrbough, *Aspen,* 103–4; Hyman Manuscript, passim; and "Jerome B. Wheeler and Pitkin County," *Frank Leslie's Illustrated Newspaper* 68 (22 February 1890): 68.

44. Hyman manuscript, 39–46. Regarding liberalism, see Klyza, *Who Controls Public Lands?,* 64. Others do not address the verdict. Swenson, "Legal

Aspects," 723–24; and Richard H. Jackson, "Federal Lands in the Mountainous West," in Wyckoff and Dilsaver, *Mountainous West,* 260–66.

45. *Aspen Times* 16 April 1891; and undated clipping, E. Dunbar Wright Collection, CHS.

46. *First Annual Report to the Stockholders of the Denver & Rio Grande Railroad* (Denver, 1872), 5–6, 10. Also, see *Denver and Rio Grande Railway* (Philadelphia: 1870), 7, 12, 19; Athearn, *Rebel of the Rockies,* 140, 160–61; and Robbins, *Colony and Empire,* 75.

47. Evans, Denver, to Maggie, London, 8 February and 6 March 1876, respectively; Articles of Association of the Denver, South Park & Pacific Railroad Company, 14 June 1873, Evans Private Papers; and John Evans, Denver, to Edwin Harrison, St. Louis, 4 February 1878, Edwin Harrison Collection, CHS. Other investors included Kountze, Moffat, and Governor Samuel Elbert.

48. Mary Hallock Foote to Helena Gilder, 12 May 1879 (on difficult Leadville journey), in Rodman Paul, ed., *A Victorian Gentlewoman in the Far West: Reminiscences of Mary Hallock Foote* (San Marino, Calif.: Huntington Library, 1972), 171; Duane Smith, "'A Country of Tremendous Mountains': Opening the Colorado San Juans, 1870–1910," in Wyckoff and Dilsaver, *Mountainous West,* 101; and Novak, *People's Welfare,* 125.

49. Robert Edmund Strahorn, *Gunnison and San Juan* (Omaha: The New West Publishing Co., 1881), 6; and Smith, "'A Country of Tremendous Mountains,'" 113. Robbins argues that railroads were the catalysts. *Colony and Empire,* 171.

50. *Engineering and Mining Journal,* 29 September 1877; *Historical and Descriptive Review of Colorado's Enterprising Cities: Their Leading Business Houses and Progressive Men* (Denver: Jno. Lethem, 1893), 73–95; Rohe, "Environment and Mining," 179; and Moehring, "Comstock Urban Network," 350. Failed prospectors rarely left records. One who spent fifty unsuccessful years in Boulder and Summit counties, abandoning claims and selling others for taxes, left the Frank S. Reardon Papers, CHS.

51. Barnett, "Colorado Business Corporations," 107, 120–22; Smith, *Rocky Mountain West,* 151–59; and Ubbelohde, Benson, and Smith, *Colorado History,* 217–20.

52. Pulcipher, *First of Denver,* 124; and Wiebe, *Search for Order,* 22. Moffat's wealth was estimated between eight million dollars and twenty-five million dollars. Moffat's obituary, *Denver News,* n.d., Hall Collection.

53. Florence Construction Company, Trial Balance, 31 May 1897, and Accounting of the Cripple Creek State Bank and the Bank of Victor, M. M. Hammas, CPA, to J. C. Helm, Attorney, Estate of David Moffat, 15 August 1911, Moffat Papers; Eben Smith to William Lennox, 27 September 1894, and to W. K. Gillett, 31 October 1895, Smith Papers; Mehls, "Success," 97–98; and *Biennial Report of the Secretary of State of Colorado for the Fiscal Years Ending November 30, 1891 and November 30, 1892* (Colorado Springs:

Gazette Printing Co., 1893), 10–41. Smith Papers and Moffat Papers contain various company documents including, among others, Anaconda Mining Company, Colorado Gold Reduction Company, Gold Exploration and Tunnel Company of Cripple Creek, and Victor Milling Company.

54. Smith to C. J. Hughes, Jr., 5 November 1895, William Brevoort, Boston, to Smith, Denver, 22 February, 1 September 1898, and Smith to Moffat, 24 September 1900, Smith Papers; and Mehls, "Success," 98–100.

55. Mining Deeds, 29 May 1878, 13 August 1881, Smuggler Consolidated Mining Company Records, CHS. Also, from the Walter Scott Cheesman Papers, CHS: correspondence on Eagle Bird, Little Nellie, and Commodore Mines, Leadville; Agreement of the Deep Mining and Drainage Company, Aspen, 20 February 1891; Moffat, Denver, to N. C. Creede, Los Angeles, 29 August 1894, regarding Amethyst Mining Company, Creede, Colorado; and Journal, Amos Bissell, Receiver, District Court, Arapahoe County, Cheesman and George Clayton v. David D. Belden. Also, see H. Lee Scamehorn, *Albert Eugene Reynolds: Colorado's Mining King* (Norman and Lincoln: University of Oklahoma Press, 1995), 25, 83–84, 92. Albert Eugene Reynolds Papers, CHS, include documents for his three hundred mines.

56. Ferdinand S. Winslow of the Scandinavian Bank, Chicago, to James Dexter, Denver, 22 April 1872 (Central City investments managed by Dexter); Harry Allen, President of the Climax Mining Company, New York City, to Stockholders of the company, 7 January 1881 (Dexter managed Leadville property); George P. Armstrong, London, to Dexter, Denver, 2 April 1884 (Armstrong sold Dexter's stock); and Oliver Wolcott, Denver, to Dexter, Denver, 21 January 1896 (Dexter recommended drilling for Pittsburgh investors), Dexter Papers.

57. Pooling Agreement, Rocky Mountain Bank, Central City, 28 May 1888; Stock Certificate Book, Bill-Jim Mining Company Collection, CHS; Sullivan, Denver, to Has. A. Hall, Mesa, Arizona, 13 November 1896, Dennis Sullivan Letters, DPL; and John Dietz and Albert Larson, "Colorado's San Luis Valley," in Wyckoff and Dilsaver, *Mountainous West,* 357.

58. Porter, *Autobiography,* 42–59; A. A. Hayes, Jr., *New Colorado and the Santa Fe Trail* (London: C. Kegan Paul and Co., 1881); and Diary, 17–20 May 1889, A. G. Bowes & Sons, Inc., Realtors Collection, CHS. Also, see Herman Kountze, Omaha, to Charles, Denver, 19 January 1888; G. G. Symes, Helena, Montana, to Charles, Denver, 4 June 1890; A. T. Smith, Sec., Kountze Brothers, New York, to W. H. Hollister, East Texas Land and Improvement Co., New York City, 4 June 1892; and stocks of forty-eight mines owned by Charles at his death, Kountze Collection.

59. The Mexican National Coal, Timber and the Iron Company and the Maritime Canal Company of Nicaragua incorporated in Denver with capital of one million dollars and ten million dollars, respectively. *Secretary of State, 1883,* 24, 33; Stock, Mines of Mexico Company, Kountze Collection; and Brechin, *Imperial City,* 217–21.

60. *Denver Tribune,* 29 March 1884; Evans, President, Denver & New Orleans, to stockholders, 20 July 1881, and "Third Address on Crisis of Denver before the Denver Chamber of Commerce and Board of Trade," 12 August 1886, Evans Private Papers; and Report to the Interstate Commerce Commission, 1888, DTFW Collection, CHS.

61. *Eighth Report,* DCOC, 12–13; Pulcipher, *First of Denver,* 91–92; Smith, *Horace Tabor,* 269–70; and Lamar, *Far Southwest,* 301.

Chapter 2

Epigraph is from an interview with John Evans, 1884, manuscript, 20, Bancroft Library, University of California.

1. For a similar discussion, see Moehring, "Comstock Urban Network," 354–60. Historians use the misnomer "Indian" because it is difficult to translate names used by some indigenous people to describe themselves. Some like the Cheyenne used the ethnocentric "the People." "Native Americans" or "indigenous people" appear periodically here, but, as Gregory Nobles observed, these are often awkward writing tools. *American Frontiers: Cultural Encounters and Continental Conquest* (New York: Hill and Wang, 1997), 391.

2. Jackson, *Journals of Zebulon Montgomery Pike,* 297–98; Edwin James, *"Account of an Expedition from Pittsburgh to the Rocky Mountains Under the Command of Maj. S. H. Long, of the U.S. Topographical Engineers,"* in Reuben G. Thwaites, ed., *Early Western Travels, 1748–1846* (New York: Ams Press, 1966), 15:232–51; Unpublished Diary, 19 August 1870, Peter G. Scott Collection, CHS; Hall, Black Hawk, Colorado, to Emma Skidmore Low, Syracuse, New York, 19 June 1864, Hall Collection; Hill, Denver City, to Alice Hale Hill, Providence, Rhode Island, 14 June and 10 July 1864, Nathaniel Peter Hill Collection, CHS; and William N. Byers, Circular, National Land Company, May 1871, DPL. Also, see Martin J. Bowden, "The Great American Desert and the American Frontier, 1800–1882: Popular Images of the Plains," in Tamara K. Harevan, ed., *Anonymous Explorations in Nineteenth-Century Social History* (Englewood Cliffs, N.J.: Prentice-Hall, 1971), 48–79.

3. *RMN,* 11 July 1866 (quotes); Thomas Jefferson, *"Notes on the State of Virginia"* (1781), in Merrill Peterson, *Thomas Jefferson and the New Nation, A Biography* (New York: Oxford University Press, 1970), 256–57; Jack Temple Kirby, "Rural Culture in the American Middle West: Jefferson to Jane Smiley," *Agricultural History* 70 (fall 1996): 583–89; and Willard Wesley Cochrane, *The Development of American Agriculture: A Historical Analysis,* 2d ed. (Minneapolis: University of Minnesota Press, 1993), 54–58.

4. Ray Allen Billington, "Foreword," in Gilbert C. Fite, *The Farmers' Frontier, 1865–1900* (New York: Holt, Rinehart and Winston, 1966), vi. Billington echoes Frederick Jackson Turner, who converted Jefferson's idealized farmer into the forge of democracy and American identity.

5. Elliott West, *Growing Up with the Country: Childhood on the Far Western Frontier* (Albuquerque: University of New Mexico Press, 1989), 18; Kirby, "Rural Culture," 597; West, *Contested Plains,* 240; and Leonard and Noel, *Denver,* 12.

6. David T. Courtwright, *Violent Land: Single Men and Social Disorder from the Frontier to the Inner City* (Cambridge: Harvard University Press, 1996), 66–92; Leonard and Noel, *Denver,* 8–9; and Novak, *People's Welfare,* 153. Western saloons also provided space for church services, elections, and financial transactions. Thomas J. Noel, *The City and the Saloon: Denver, 1858–1916* (Lincoln and London: University of Nebraska Press, 1982), 11–20; and Elliott West, *The Saloon on the Rocky Mountain Mining Frontier* (Lincoln and London: University of Nebraska Press, 1979), 73–96.

7. Intertwined motives were common. Eugene Moehring found that the "pull of gold" and "push of war" drove Idaho town-making. "The Civil War and Town Founding in the Intermountain West," *Western Historical Quarterly* 28 (autumn 1997): 318, 323. Also, see Courtwright, *Violent Land,* 142–51.

8. Reminiscences, George Hodgson, unpublished manuscript, 1932 (?), 2, CHS; Villard, *Past and Present of the Pike's Peak Gold Regions,* 111–12; Warranty Deeds, Thomas Skerritt Papers, CHS; Irving Howbert, *Memories of a Lifetime in the Pike's Peak Region* (New York and London: G. P. Putnam's Sons, 1925), 51, 59; Edward Bliss, *A Brief History of the New Gold Regions of Colorado Territory* (Denver, 1864), 10–12; Charles V. Barton, "Colorado: Its Resources, Advantages and Prospects," in *Colorado as an Agricultural State, the Progress of Irrigation* (Denver: The Local Committee of Arrangements for the National Irrigation Congress, 1894), 1; Alvin T. Steinel, *History of Agriculture in Colorado* (Fort Collins, Colo.: State Agricultural College, 1926), 50–51; and West, *Contested Plains,* 251–53.

9. *Resources of Colorado* (Brooklyn, N.Y.: The Union Steam Presses, 1868), 2 (quote). Regarding booster literature, see Hollister, *Mines of Colorado;* Villard, *Past and Present of the Pike's Peak Gold Regions;* and Frank Fossett, *Colorado: Its Gold and Silver Mines* (New York: C. G. Crawford, 1879).

10. Hall to Skidmore Low, 19 June 1864.

11. Frontier towns played major roles in subjugating indigenous peoples across the globe. Moehring, "Civil War and Town Founding," 323; and David Hamer, *New Towns in the New World: Images and Perceptions of the Nineteenth-Century Urban Frontier* (New York: Columbia University Press, 1990), 11–12.

12. There were seven Ute bands, discussed in greater detail in Charles S. Marsh, *People of the Shining Mountain* (Boulder: Pruett Publishing Co., 1982), 24–36; and Nancy Wood, *When Buffalo Free the Mountains* (Garden City, N.Y.: Doubleday & Co., 1990), 1–10. Also Huber, *Colorado,* 2–9, 17–20, 64–68, 77, 80, 117, 151, 166, 197–204; and Depue Falck, E. R. Greenslet, and R. E. Morgan, "Land Classification of the Central Great Plains: Eastern Colorado," *United States Department of the Interior Geological Survey* (Washington, D.C.: Government Printing Office, 1931), 8–12.

13. Carl Sweezy, *The Arapaho Way*, ed. Althea Bass (New York: Clarkson N. Potter, 1966), 3 (quote); Margaret Coel, *Chief Left Hand: Southern Arapaho* (Norman: University of Oklahoma Press, 1981), 28; West, *Contested Plains*, 67–80; Dan Flores, "Bison Ecology and Bison Diplomacy: The Southern Plains from 1800 to 1850," *Journal of American History* 78 (September 1991): 466, 474–76, 483; Virginia Cole Trenholm, *The Arapaho, Our People* (Norman: University of Oklahoma Press, 1970), 163; and Richard H. Hart and James A. Hart, "Rangelands of the Great Plains before European Settlement," *Rangelands* 19 (February 1997): 4–11.

14. Diary, 27 December 1853, 3 January, 13 January, February 23, 1854, Milligan, 150, 153, 168; Donald J. Hughes, *American Indians in Colorado* (Boulder, Colo.: Pruett Publishing Co., 1977), 48; and *Report of the Commissioner of Indian Affairs, 1849–1850,* 139, in West, *Contested Plains,* 82 (quote), 92.

15. Flores, "Bison Ecology," 479, 483–85; Andrew Isenberg, "The Return of the Bison: Nostalgia, Profit and Preservation," *Environmental History* 2 (April 1997): 179, and "Toward a Policy of Destruction: Buffaloes, Law, and the Market, 1803–1883," *Great Plains Quarterly* 12 (1992): 235–37; and Elliott West, *The Way to the West: Essays on the Central Plains* (Albuquerque: University of New Mexico Press, 1995), 58–82.

16. George Bent, Colony, Oklahoma, to George E. Hyde, Omaha, Nebraska, 15 October 1904, George Bent Letters, CHS; Donald J. Berthrong, *The Southern Cheyenne* (Norman: University of Oklahoma Press, 1963), 127; Charles J. Kappler, ed., *Indian Affairs Laws and Treaties,* Vol. 2 (Washington, D.C.: Government Printing Office, 1904), 595, 623; Francis Paul Prucha, *American Indian Treaties: The History of a Political Anomaly* (Berkeley: University of California Press, 1994), 238–40; and Hughes, *American Indians in Colorado,* 54.

17. "Hispano" identifies the subgroup of Mexicanos, or subsequently Mexican Americans, who settled in the Upper Rio Grande and adjacent regions of northern New Mexico and southern Colorado. Sylvia Rodriguez, "Land, Water, and Ethnic Identity in Taos," in Charles L. Briggs and John R. Van Ness, eds., *Land, Water, and Culture: New Perspectives on Hispanic Land Grants* (Albuquerque: University of New Mexico Press, 1987), 391.

18. Janet Lecompte concludes that from the Utes' perspective, the "massacre" was the "culmination of eight years of frustration and misunderstanding in their dealings with the United States government and its contradictory agents." *Pueblo, Hardscrabble, Greenhorn: The Upper Arkansas, 1832–1856* (Norman: University of Oklahoma Press, 1978), 253 (quote), 216–61; and Marsh, *People of the Shining Mountain,* 52–53, 67–70.

19. *Report of Commissioner of Indian Affairs, 1859,* 137–39, in West, *Contested Plains,* 192–93, 257–60.

20. *RMN,* 2 May 1860.

21. Charles Caldwell, *Thoughts on the Original Unity of the Human Race*

(Cincinnati: J. A. and U. P. James, 1852); and Samuel George Morton, *Crania Americana or, a Comparative View of the Skulls of Various Aboriginal Nations of North and South America. To Which is Prefixed an Essay on the Varieties of the Human Species* (Philadelphia: J. Dobson, London, Simpkin, Marshall, 1839), in Isenberg, "Toward a Policy of Destruction," 234; Robert E. Bieder, *Contemplating Others: Cultural Contacts in Red and White America: An Annotated Bibliography on the North American Indian* (Berlin: John F. Kennedy-Institut fur Nordamerikastudien, Freie Universitat Berlin, 1990), 3–7, and *Science Encounters the Indian, 1820–1880: The Early Years of American Ethnology* (Norman: University of Oklahoma Press, 1986), 12–15; and Robert F. Berkhofer, Jr., *The White Man's Indian: Images of the American Indian from Columbus to the Present* (New York: Alfred A. Knopf, 1978), 86–90.

22. Nancy Shoemaker, "How Indians Got to Be Red," *American Historical Review* 102 (June 1997): 625; Audrey Smedley, *Race in North America: Origin and Evolution of a Worldview* (Boulder: University of Colorado Press, 1993), 22–25; Berkhofer, *White Man's Indian*, 3–20; Reginald Horsman, *Race and Manifest Destiny: The Origins of American Racial Anglo-Saxism* (Cambridge: Harvard University Press, 1981), 130; and Alexander Saxton, *The Rise and Fall of the White Republic: Class Politics and Mass Culture in Nineteenth-Century America* (London and New York: Verso, 1990), 1.

23. Gilpin, *Cosmopolitan Railway,* 125. Also, see West, *Contested Plains,* 82, 185–88, and *Way to the West,* 85–125 passim; Kathleen Neils Conzen, "A Saga of Families," in Milner, O'Connor, and Sandweiss, *Oxford History,* 327–29; Vron Ware, *Beyond the Pale: White Women, Racism and History* (London: Verso, 1992), 253; and Ruth Frankenberg, *White Women, Race Matters: The Social Construction of Whiteness* (Minneapolis: University of Minnesota Press, 1993), 1.

24. *RMN,* 23 April 1861, in David Svaldi, *Sand Creek and the Rhetoric of Extermination* (Latham, Md.: University Press of America, 1989), 137; and Diary, 15 June 1860 and Letter No. 5, Mallory Collection.

25. *RMN,* 23 April 1861, August 1860 and 9 May 1861, in Svaldi, *Sand Creek and the Rhetoric of Extermination,* 139; and undated 1862 report, Fort Lyon Colorado Papers, CHS.

26. *RMN,* 19 August 1861; Alvin M. Josephy, Jr., *The Civil War in the American West* (New York: Alfred A. Knopf, 1991), 292–94; Lamar, *Far Southwest,* 226–27; and Moehring, "Civil War and Town Founding," 320.

27. RMN, 2 September 1861; Donald E. Alberts, *The Battle of Glorieta* (College Station: Texas A&M University Press, 1998), passim; and Reginald Craig, *The Fighting Parson, the Biography of Colonel John M. Chivington* (Los Angeles: Westernlore Press, 1959), passim. Byers campaigned for Gilpin's removal because Gilpin awarded his competitor the territorial printing contract. Evans became Byers's silent partner. Kelsey, *Frontier Capitalist,* chaps. 3–5 passim.

28. Bent, Colony, Oklahoma, to George E. Hyde, Omaha, 16 November 1904, Bent Letters; and J. S. Hoy Manuscript, typescript copy, CHS, 10–24.

29. Regarding extraregional depredations, *RMN,* 26 March, 26 April, 28 May, 24 June, 24 July 1862, and regarding "vagabonds," 17 July 1862, in Svaldi, *Sand Creek and the Rhetoric of Extermination,* 146; and Josephy, *Civil War,* 297.

30. *RMN,* 19 July 1862 (Evans's Message), 24 March 1863 (Pueblos), and 4 April 1863 (Colorado Indians).

31. *RMN,* 27 April 1863, in Svaldi, *Sand Creek and the Rhetoric of Extermination,* 150.

32. U.S. Department of the Interior, Bureau of the Census, *Eighth Census of the United States, 1860 Population* (Washington, D.C.: Government Printing Office, 1864), 549, and *Ninth Census of the United States, 1870 Population* (Washington, D.C.: Government Printing Office, 1871), 603; Lamar, *Far Southwest,* 45–47, 250–51; and Berthrong, *Southern Cheyenne,* 195–200.

33. *RMN,* 13 June and 22 September 1863; George Hyde, *Life of George Bent, Written from his Letters,* ed. Savoie Lottinville (Norman: University of Oklahoma Press, 1968), 106; and Berthrong, *Southern Cheyenne,* 198.

34. John Evans, Denver, to Commissioner Dole, Washington, D.C., 10 November 1863, in *The War of the Rebellion: A Compilation of the Official Records of the Union and Confederate Armies,* Series I, Volume 24, Part 4 (Washington, D.C.: Government Printing Office, 1891), 100, in Svaldi, *Sand Creek and the Rhetoric of Extermination,* 155; and Ovando J. Hollister, *Colorado Volunteers in New Mexico* (1863; repr., Chicago: Lakeside Press, 1962), 31.

35. *Daily Mining Journal,* 22 August and 30 August 1864 (quote; emphasis in original); and Svaldi, *Sand Creek and the Rhetoric of Extermination,* 6, 157.

36. Speech in Kelsey, *Frontier Capitalist,* 155–60.

37. Samuel Colley to William P. Dole, Report of Commissioner of Indian Affairs, 1863, in West, *Contested Plains,* 285–90.

38. *Denver Daily Commonwealth and Republican,* 16 June 1864. The flood destroyed the *RMN* office. Byers worked from the Commonwealth before purchasing it, with Evans's assistance. The *RMN* resurfaced 26 June 1864.

39. Richard White, "Frederick Jackson Turner and Buffalo Bill," in James R. Grossman, ed., *The Frontier in American Culture* (Berkeley: University of California Press, 1994), 27.

40. Hill, Denver City, to Hattie Hale, 17 June 1864, Hill Collection.

41. *RMN,* 17 July to 20 July and 5 August 1864; Hill, Denver, to Alice Hale Hill, Providence, Rhode Island, 11 August 1864, Hill Collection; West, *Contested Plains,* 290; and Moehring, "Comstock Urban Network," 357.

42. *RMN,* 27 June, 10 August, 12 August (quote), and 13 August 1864; and John Evans's Letterbook, Executive Papers, 1861–1870, Governor's Office, Executive Record, 1:174–177, CSA.

43. *RMN,* 30 September and 1 October 1864; Testimony of Edward W. Wynkoop, United States Senate, Report, Joint Committee on the Conduct of the War, 'Massacre of the Cheyenne Indians,' 38th Cong., 2d Sess., Senate Report 142 Serial 1241, and 'Report of the Secretary of War, in compliance with a resolution of the Senate of February 4, 1867, evidence taken at Denver and Fort Lyon, Colorado Territory, by military commission ordered to inquire into the Sand Creek massacre, November 1864,' 39th Cong., 2d Sess., 1867, Ex. Doc. No. 26, 90–91, in Svaldi, *Sand Creek and the Rhetoric of Extermination,* 175; and Stan Hoig, *The Sand Creek Massacre* (Norman: University of Oklahoma Press, 1961), 109–12.

44. *Black Hawk Journal,* 28 November 1864; and *RMN,* 1 October 1864.

45. "Some Bent County History: George Bent, Son of Col. Bent, pioneer fur trader, Indian agent, and the builder and owner of Bent's Fort on the Arkansas River," Article, n.d., Bent Letters; *RMN,* 17 December 1864; Kassler, Denver, to Maria Stebbins, New York City, 21 December 1864, Kassler Collection; Samuel F. Tappan Diary, n.d., transcribed by Thomas Goertner, 1959, Samuel F. Tappan Collection, CHS, 21; and West, *Contested Plains,* 301.

46. Tappan Diary, 1 January 1865, and Testimony, Military Commission, 867.

47. Affidavit, James Clancy, 21 April 1865, Wynkoop Collection; and C. A. Prentice, "Captain Silas S. Soule, A Pioneer Martyr," *Colorado Magazine* 12 (November 1935): 224. Denver remained under martial law after Sand Creek, with Soule as commander. An unknown assailant killed him in 1865.

48. Senate Report, Joint Commission, 'Massacre of the Cheyenne Indians,' Wynkoop's Testimony, 82, and conclusion, 1123–24 (quote); and William Seward, Department of State, Washington, D.C., to John Evans, Denver City, 18 July 1865 (seeking Evans's resignation), Evans Private Papers. Evans alleged Dog Soldiers were at Sand Creek. Reply of Governor Evans to report of the "Committee on the Conduct of the War," (6 August 1865), 6–7. Chivington later served as Arapaho County undersheriff and coroner. Craig, *Fighting Parson,* 125–40.

49. Howbert, *Memories of a Lifetime,* 134, and *The Indians of the Pike's Peak Region* (New York: The Knickerbocker Press, 1914); and Morse H. Coffin, *The Battle of Sand Creek* (Waco, Tex.: Wm. Morrison, 1965), 9–10, 89. (Coffin wrote this around 1890.) Historians who agree with the commission are too numerous to list, but include Hoig, *Sand Creek Massacre,* and West, *Contested Plains,* 295–303. The few who disagree include Craig, *Fighting Parson;* William R. Dunn, *"I Stand by Sand Creek"* (Fort Collins, Colo.: Old Army Press, 1985); and Bob Scott, *Blood at Sand Creek: The Massacre Revisited* (Caldwell, Idaho: The Caxton Printers, 1994).

50. On continuing conflicts and Wynkoop's search for an honorable solution, Frank Hall, Central City, to Emma Skidmore Low, Syracuse, New York, 30 June 1867, Hall Collection; J. H. Leavenworth, United States Indian Agent, Cow Creek Ranch, to Senator James Rood Doolittle (Indian Affairs Committee), Washington, D.C., 23 August 1865, Treaty with Arapahos and

Cheyennes, 18 August 1865, and D. N. Cooley, Indian Commissioner, to Doolittle, 15 December 1865, James Rood Doolittle Collection, CHS; *Denver Times,* 18 January 1865; and *RMN,* 12 February 1865. On Sand Creek as a failure, see Athearn, *Coloradans,* 75; and Ubbelohde, *Colorado History,* 109.

51. The reservation forced profound changes. "Cheyennes and Arapahos still live in Lodges, they move about visiting one another, they all have wagons now and do not use pack animals any more. They do not go hunting any more, nothing for them to hunt." Bent, Colony, Oklahoma, to George Hyde, Omaha, 24 July 1905, Bent Letters.

52. Official Information: Colorado, 10; Wood, *When Buffalo Free the Mountains,* 43; and Prucha, *American Indian Treaties,* 277. Ouray negotiated for most Utes, but U.S. officials mistakenly assumed he spoke for all. Marsh, *People of the Shining Mountain,* 20–25, 51–53, 85–90.

53. *Summer in Colorado* (Denver: Richards and Co., 1874), n.p. (Quote); F. V. Hayden, *Annual Report to the United States Geographical and Geological Survey of the Territories, Embracing Colorado, Being a Report of Progress of the Expedition of the Year 1873* (Washington, D.C.: Government Printing Office, 1874), 78–80; Frederic Enlich Report in F. V. Hayden, *Annual Report of the United States Geographical and Geological Survey* (Washington, D.C.: Government Printing Office, 1876), 185–86; and Prucha, *American Indian Treaties,* 315–16.

54. *Denver Tribune,* 16 September 1876, and 25 May 1877; Byers, Hot Sulphur Springs, to Wife, Denver, 15 September 1878, William Newton Byers Papers, DPL; O. L. Matthews, Ouray, Colorado, to Senator Henry Moore Teller, Denver, 25 November 1877, and Governor John L. Routt, Denver, to Teller, 15 April 1878, Henry Moore Teller Letters, DPL; and Jo Lea Wetherilt Behrens, "'The Utes Must Go'—with Dignity: Alfred B. Meachams's Role on Colorado's Ute Commission, 1880–1881," *Essays and Monographs in Colorado History* 14 (1994): 40–41.

55. "Population and Social Statistics," *Statistics of the Population of the United States at the Tenth Census* (June 1, 1880), xx (quote); Hall, *History of Colorado,* 4:272–73; *Aspen, Pitkin County, Colorado: Her Mines and Mineral Resources* (Aspen: Aspen Daily Ledger, 1892), 2; and R. J. McNutt, Del Norte, Colorado, to Teller, Denver, 18 March 1878, and Routt to Teller, 15 April 1878, Teller Letters.

56. Meeker, White River Agency, Colorado, to Teller, Denver, 27 May 1878, Teller Letters; *The Ute War: A History of the White River Massacre and the Privations and Hardships of the Captive White Women among the Hostiles on Grand River* (Denver: Denver Tribune Printing Co., 1879); and Behrens, "'The Utes Must Go,'" 39.

57. *Council Fire* 4 (December 1881): 177–78, in Behrens, "'The Utes Must Go,'" 37–71; Steven F. Mehls, *Valley of Opportunity: A History of West-Central Colorado* (Denver: Bureau of Land Management, 1982), 42; and Kathleen Underwood, *Town Building on the Colorado Frontier* (Albuquerque: University of New Mexico Press, 1987), 1–5.

58. Frank Hall, *The Early Seekers for Gold in Colorado: The Exploration of "The Louisiana Purchase," Pamphlet of Historical Information for the Prospector* (repr., Denver: Mineral Department of the State Board of Land Commissioners, 1934), 10.

Chapter 3

Epigraph is from Hodgson, Reminiscences, 1

1. *RMN,* 11 July 1866 (first quote), in Abbott, *Colorado,* 143; and Alva Adams, Pueblo, to Frank Hall, 8 May 1909, Hall Collection. Historians emphasizing capitalist modes of production include Worster, *Wealth of Nature,* 45–63, 114; and Frieda Knobloch, *The Culture of Wilderness: Agriculture as Colonization in the American West,* Studies in Rural Culture, (Chapel Hill: University of North Carolina Press, 1996), 3–7, 143–44.

2. Intertwined ideologies engendered disparate western agrarian societies in Idaho, Utah and Oregon, according to Dean L. May, *Three Frontiers: Family, Land and Society in the American West, 1850–1900* (New York: Cambridge University Press, 1994), 105–23. Allan Kulikoff asserts that contested capitalist traditions continued on different agricultural frontiers into the 1930s. *The Agrarian Origins of American Capitalism* (Charlottesville and London: University Press of Virginia, 1992), 17–18, 264–66.

3. *RMN,* 4 December 1859, 31 July 1861 (quote); *Resources of Colorado,* 2; and Cronon, *Nature's Metropolis,* 50–54, 267–80.

4. *Resources of Colorado,* 2 (quote); *Second Report,* KPRY, 20–21; Handdrawn Map, Gregory Diggings, DPL; Reminiscences, Hodgson, 13; Ora Brooks Peake, *The Colorado Range Cattle Industry* (Glendale, Calif.: Arthur H. Clark Company, 1937), 22; and Edward Everett Dale, *The Range Cattle Industry* (Norman: University of Oklahoma Press, 1930), 28–31.

5. Letter from George, Greeley, to Rhoda, Michigan City, Indiana, 10 July 1871 (quote), DPL. Also, see Gene M. Gressley, *Bankers and Cattlemen* (New York: Alfred A. Knopf, 1966), 24; and Richard Goff and Robert H. McCaffree, *A Century in the Saddle* (Denver: Colorado Cattleman's Centennial Commission, 1967), 6.

6. Luke Cahill, "Recollections of a Plainsman," Manuscript, 40 (quote), CHS. Also, see Paul W. Gates, "An Overview of American Land Policy," *Agricultural History* 50 (January 1976): 213; and John Opie, *The Law of the Land: Two Hundred Years of American Farmland Policy* (Lincoln: University of Nebraska Press, 1987), 56.

7. Clifford Westermeier, "The Legal Status of the Colorado Cattleman, 1867–1887," *Colorado Magazine* 25 (July 1948): 159 (quote); and Gates, *History of Public Land Law Development,* 393–99, 466–68, 470, 474, and "The Homestead Act: Free Land Policy in Operation, 1862–1935," in Allan G. and Margaret Beattie Bogue, eds., *The Jeffersonian Dream: Studies in the History of American Land Policy and Development* (Albuquerque: University of New Mexico Press, 1996), 46–47.

8. Minutes, Colorado Cattleman's Association, 7 December 1867, 18 January 1868 (quote), CHS; *Denver Tribune*, 1 December 1867; and Goff and McCaffree, *Century in the Saddle*, 17–18, 23–26. Holly and Sullivan, for example, managed ranches from Denver. Dennis Sullivan, Denver, to J. A. Thatcher, 9 June 1882, AVL&CC, DPL.

9. Unpublished article, Scott Collection; Lewis Atherton, *The Cattle Kings* (Bloomington: Indiana University Press, 1961), 36–47; Peake, *Colorado Range*, 56–58; Goff and McCaffree, *Century in the Saddle*, 35, 54–59; and West, *Contested Plains*, 250.

10. *Tameling v. U.S. Freehold & Emigration Co.*, 93 U.S. 644 (1874) (confirming the Sangre de Cristo grant); Porter, *Pencilings*, 17–18; *Trinchera Estate*, n.d. (after 1892), 6, and Articles of the Trinchera Estate Company, 1886, William Gilpin Papers, CHS; *Fourth Report of The Trinchera Estate Company to the Stockholders, January 1, 1892* (Colorado Springs: Gazette Printing Co., 1892), William A. Bell Papers, CHS; *The Great San Luis Valley, Colorado: Sunshine, Irrigation, Independence* (Denver: C. F. Hoeckel, Printer, 1892), 1; Malcolm Ebright, *Land Grants and Lawsuits in Northern New Mexico* (Albuquerque: University of New Mexico Press, 1994), 27; Lamar, *Far Southwest*, 266–67; Herbert O. Brayer, *William Blackmore*, Vol. 1, *The Spanish-Mexican Land Grants of New Mexico and Colorado, 1863–1878* (Denver: Bradford-Robinson, 1949), 59–123, 314–18; and Marianne L. Stoller, "Grants of Desperation, Lands of Speculation: Mexican Period Land Grants in Colorado," in John R. Van Ness and Christine M. Van Ness, eds., *Spanish and Mexican Land Grants in New Mexico and Colorado* (Manhattan, Kans.: Sunflower University Press, 1980), 25, 35.

11. *Maxwell Land Grant* (London: Taylor and Co., 1870); Prospectus, Maxwell Land Grant Company (in Dutch), 1870; Wilson Waddingham, Santa Fe, to Jerome Chaffee, Washington, D.C., 12 December 1872; and M. P. Pels, Maxwell Land Grant Company, to George E. Ross-Lewin, Cashier, FNBD, 28 August 1889, FNBD Records. Also, see *Springer News* (New Mexico), 1 July 1880 in Lamar, *Far Southwest*, 142–46.

12. Margaret McBride Manuscript, 1, DPL; Affidavit, Henry Whigham, Receiver, Maxwell Land Grant, *Wright, et al. v. Maxwell Land Grant Co.*, 27 September 1886, Colfax County, New Mexico, and *U.S. v. Maxwell Land Grant Company, et al.*, United States Supreme Court, No. 974, Appellees' Brief, 5, T. A. Schomburg Collection, CHS; Robert J. Rosenbaum and Robert W. Larson, "Mexicano Resistance to the Expropriation of Grant Lands in New Mexico," in Briggs and Van Ness, *Land, Water, and Culture*, 277–86; and Morris F. Taylor, *O. P. McMains and the Maxwell Land Grant Conflict* (Tucson: University of Arizona Press, 1979), 35–36.

13. J. M. Waldron, Catskill, New Mexico, to M. P. Pels, Raton, New Mexico, 27 October 1892, Schomburg Collection; *U.S. v. Maxwell Land Grant Company*, 121 U.S. 325 (1887); and Ebright, *Grants and Lawsuits*, 39–40, 45.

14. Jim Berry Pearson, *The Maxwell Land Grant* (Norman: University of Oklahoma Press, 1961), 112–43; Morris F. Taylor, "The Leitensdorfer Claim

in the Vigil & St. Vrain Grant," in Van Ness and Van Ness, *Spanish and Mexican Land Grants*, 92–99; and Ebright, *Land Grants and Lawsuits*, 249–62.

15. *Colorado Chieftain* (Pueblo), 10 June 1869; William E. Pabor, *Colorado as an Agricultural State* (New York: Orange Judd Company, 1889), 13; Porter, Denver to J. M. Cunningham, East Las Vegas, New Mexico, 20 August 1893, Porter Papers; and Porter, *Pencilings*, 19–22. Other Denverites invested. Tabor, for example purchased one-fourth of the St. Vrain. Deed, George W. Thompson, Trinidad, to Horace Tabor, Denver, 3 May 1881, Lewis Rockwell Papers.

16. *Second Annual Report of the Officers of the Denver Pacific Railway and Telegraph Company* (Denver, 1869), 6, DPRY Collection; Circular, National Land Company; James F. Willard and Colin B. Goodykoontz, eds., *Experiments in Colorado Colonization, 1869–1872: Selected Company Records Relating to the German Colonization Company and the Chicago-Colorado, St. Louis-Western and Southwestern Colonies* (Boulder: University of Colorado Press, 1926), xiv–xx; and Pisani, *To Reclaim a Divided West*, 77.

17. Richard L. Nostrand, *The Hispano Homeland* (Norman: University of Oklahoma Press, 1992), 82; and Willard and Goodykoontz, *Experiments*, xvii–xxiv, German Colonization Society, 27–133, passim.

18. Greeley in Richard White, *"It's Your Misfortune and None of My Own": A New History of the American West* (Norman: University of Oklahoma Press, 1991), 143; Peterson, *Thomas Jefferson*, 256; and Carl Abbott, "New West, New South, New Region: The Discovery of the Sunbelt," in Raymond Mohl, ed., *Searching for the Sunbelt: Historical Perspectives on the Region* (Knoxville: University of Tennessee Press, 1990), 14.

19. James F. Willard, *The Union Colony at Greeley, 1869–1871* (Boulder: University of Colorado Press, 1918), xx–xxiii; David Boyd, *A History: Greeley and the Union Colony of Colorado* (Greeley: Greeley Tribune Co., 1890), 11–25, 54–57; *RMN*, 20 May, 29 May, 17 June 1868; Steinel, *History of Agriculture in Colorado*, 64–66; and Circular, National Land Company.

20. Constitution, Union Colony Papers, CHS; Membership applications, Letterbook, Nathan Cook Meeker Papers, DPL; and Boyd, *History*, 54–65, 294.

21. Circular, National Land Company; *RMN*, 29 April 1871; *First Annual Report of the Union Colony of Colorado, including a History of the Town of Greeley, from its Date of Settlement to the Present Time* (New York: George W. Southwick, 1871), 16; *Prospectus, Articles of Incorporation and By-Laws of the Cache La Poudre Irrigating Company* (Greeley: Greeley Tribune Book and Job Printing, 1878); and Fite, *Farmers' Frontier*, 182.

22. *Chicago Tribune* in *Chicago-Colorado Colony* (Chicago: Republican Printing and Engraving Company, [1871]), 2; Chicago-Colorado Colony Charter, 1 March 1871, DPL, and Minutes, 30 May and 28 August 1871,

DPL; Holly, Denver, to George Bowen, Chicago, 4 May and 13 May 1871, George S. Bowen Papers, DPL.

23. Willard and Goodykoontz, *Experiments,* xxiv–xxx, 135–200; and Report Summarizing 1871 and Chicago-Colorado Colony's Accomplishments, 16 February 1872, 1, Seth Terry Papers, DPL.

24. Boyd, *History,* 180; Willard and Goodykoontz, *Experiments,* xxi–xxiii, 331–96; and Paul, *Far West,* 103.

25. Novak, *People's Welfare,* 10 (quote),187–89; Boyd, *History,* 75–77; and James Willard Hurst, *Law and Economic Growth: The Legal History of the Lumber Industry in Wisconsin, 1836–1915* (Cambridge: Harvard University Press, 1964), passim.

26. Willard and Goodykoontz, *Experiments,* 397–449, passim; *Fountain Colony* (Denver, 1871), Bell Papers; and Steinel, *History of Agriculture in Colorado,* 384–90.

27. Seventeen hundred farms in 1870 grew to forty-five hundred in 1880. Hall, *History of Colorado,* 1:518; Fite, *Farmers' Frontier,* 183; and Moffat, *Population History,* 69.

28. Pabor, *Colorado as an Agricultural State,* 4; David Boyd, "Greeley's Irrigation Methods," *Irrigation Age* (January 1, 1892): 353; Boyd, *History,* 59–60; Willard and Goodykoontz, *Experiments,* 120–29; Pisani, *To Reclaim a Divided West,* 77–81; and Fite, *Farmers' Frontier,* 182.

29. *Proceedings of the Constitutional Convention of Colorado, 1875 and 1876* (Denver, 1906), 44 ; and *Yunker v. Nichols,* 1 Colo. 551, 553 (1872). Also, see Robert G. Dunbar, *Forging New Rights in Western Waters* (Lincoln and London: University of Nebraska Press, 1983), 78, and "The Adaptability of Water Law to the Aridity of the West," *Journal of the West* 24 (January 1985): 57; John D. W. Guice, *The Rocky Mountain Bench: The Territorial Supreme Courts of Colorado, Montana, and Wyoming, 1861–1890* (New Haven: Yale University Press, 1972), 124; Norris Hundley, *Water and the West: The Colorado River Compact and the Politics of Water in the American West* (Berkeley and Los Angeles: University of California Press, 1966), 66–73; and Bakken, "Influence of the West," 67.

30. *Coffin v. Left Hand Ditch Co.,* 6 Colo. 443, 446 (1882); Pisani, *To Reclaim a Divided West,* 335, and "Enterprise and Equity: A Critique of Western Water Law in the Nineteenth Century" *Western Historical Quarterly* 18 (January 1987), 20–23; Sam S. Kepfield, "Great Plains Legal Culture and Irrigation Development: The Minitare (Mutual) Irrigation Company, 1887–1896" *Environmental History Review* 19 (winter 1995): 49, 63; Webb, *The Great Plains* (Boston: Ginn and Co., 1931), 2–9; and Powell, *Report on the Lands of the Arid Regions of the United States, with a More Detailed Account of the Lands of Utah* (Washington: Government Printing Office, 1879).

31. Colorado Mortgage and Investment Company, *Farmlands in Colorado* (Denver: Rocky Mountain News Printing Co., 1879), 1–3, 7; Dunbar, *Forging New Rights,* 78–90; and Kepfield, "Great Plains Legal Culture," 51.

32. Gilpin captured these tensions: "To bring from abroad money, intelligence, and experience, and expend the same in working agricultural lands, in stock-raising, mining, or manufactures, must surely have a tendency not only to add to the wealth of the country, but to elevate and improve both industries and people." But he added, "Nor is it to be expected that a nation which found one king too many for it, will long endure the yoke of a number of kings, in the shape of foreign land monopolists . . ." *Cosmopolitan Railway,* 251, 276. Also, see Pisani, *To Reclaim a Divided West,* 57; Dunbar, *Forging New Rights,* 91, 98; and Jane E. Norris and Lee G. Norris, *Written in Water: The Life of Benjamin Harrison Eaton* (Athens: University of Ohio Press, 1990), 119–22, 138–39.

33. *Irwin v. Phillips,* 5 Cal. 140 (1855), discussed in Douglas R. Littlefield, "Water Rights during the California Gold Rush: Conflicts over Economic Points of View," *Western Historical Quarterly* 14 (October 1983): 417.

34. Colorado Mortgage and Investment Company, *Farmlands,* 1–7; Prospectus, Loveland & Greeley Irrigation and Land Company, Denver, 1 October 1889, DPL; *Secretary of State, 1883,* 10–43; Barnett, "Colorado Business Corporations," 106–7; and Kepfield, "Great Plains Legal Culture," 51.

35. *Farmers' H.L.C. & R. Co. v. Southworth,* 13 Colo. 111, 121 (1889); *Proceedings of Constitutional Convention,* 44; *Wheeler v. Northern Colorado Irrigation Co.,* 10 Colo. 582, 588 (1887); Historical Sketch of the Jackson or Dry Creek Ditch, Larimer County, Unpublished transcript, n.d., B. K. Howard Papers, DPL; and Kepfield, "Great Plains Legal Culture," 63. Mutual stock companies formed by farmers could hold water rights. Lower courts occasionally attempted to extend proprietorship to canal companies, but the supreme court reversed them. *Wyatt v. Larimer and Weld Irrigation Co.,* 18 Colo. 298, 308 (1893), reversing 1 Colo. App. 480, 502–6 (1892).

36. Pabor, *Colorado as an Agricultural State,* 12; Historical Sketch, Dry Creek; *RMN,* 7 January, 26 February, 3 March 1887; Steinel, *History of Agriculture in Colorado,* 199–201; Pisani, "Equity and Enterprise," 37; and James E. Sherow, "Watering the Plains: An Early History of Denver's High Line Canal," *Colorado Heritage* 4 (1988): 3–13.

37. Chicago-Colorado Accomplishments (quote); and Pisani, "Equity and Enterprise," 37. Water-rights owners formed the Cache La Poudre Irrigating Company to purchase Union Colony's Canal Two when the colony failed to maintain it. Prospectus, Cache la Poudre Irrigating. Also, see By-laws, Baca Irrigating Ditch Company, Records, Meetings of the Board of Directors, 1885–1903, CHS; Barnett, "Colorado Business Corporations," 106–7; and Sherow, "Utopia, Reality, and Irrigation," 175.

38. *Immigrant's Guide to the Great San Luis Park* (Denver: Republican Publishing Co., 1884); *About Colorado Farming; Agriculture by Irrigation in Colorado* (Denver: Colorado Land and Loan Co., 1884), 13; and T. C. Henry, Denver, to Scott, 18 December 1864, Colorado Land and Immigration Company Records, CHS.

39. L. P. Brockett, *Our Western Empire: Or the New West beyond the Mississippi* (Philadelphia: Bradley, Garretson and Co., 1881), 706; letters from William Byers, Hot Sulphur Springs, to wife, Denver, June 1883, Byers Papers; and Underwood, *Town Building*, 25–50.

40. *By-Laws of the Grand Junction Fruit Growers Association* (Grand Junction: Sentinel Book and Job Print, 1894), 9; Minutes, 24 July 1898, Grand Junction Fruit Growers Association Collection, CHS; and *Annual Reports of the Colorado State Horticultural and Forestry Association for the Years 1887–1888* (Denver: Collier and Cleaveland Lith. Co., 1888), 6–8, 11. From 1883 to 1893, apple production increased from 4,257 bushels to 70,420; and peaches from 37 to 11,529. *Agricultural Statistics of the State of Colorado, 1883* (Denver: Times Steam Publishing House, 1884), 8–9, and *Agricultural Statistics of the State of Colorado, 1893,* Secretary of the State Board of Agriculture (Denver: Smith-Brooks Printing Co., 1895), 14–15.

41. *Seventh Annual Report, Denver Chamber of Commerce* (Denver: New Printing Co., 1890), 5, 33, 34, 52. John Mullen formed Colorado Milling and Elevator Company with facilities in Denver, Golden, Longmont, Fort Collins, and Greeley, marketing flour from the Pacific to the Mississippi. "Statement for D. W. Mullen and Wife Concerning the Individual Business of J. K. Mullen," 28 May 1902, John Kernan Mullen Collection, CHS.

42. *Agricultural Statistics of the State of Colorado, 1887* (Denver: Collier and Cleaveland Lith. Co., 1889), 9–10; *Seventh Report,* DCOC, 33–34, 50; Greeley Farmer's Club, Minutes, 13 March 1872, DPL; *Cattle Canning* (Denver: Chamber of Commerce and Board of Trade, 1884); and *Bulletin on Fruit Growing in Colorado* (Denver: Chamber of Commerce and Board of Trade, [1908], 4.

43. Address, John Campion, President, *The Fifteenth Annual Report of the Denver Chamber of Commerce and Board of Trade, 1898* (Denver: News Printing Co., 1899), 22; *Biennial Report of the Bureau of Labor Statistics, 1901–1902* (Denver: Smith Brooks Printing Co., 1902), 404; *Twentieth Annual Report of the State Board of Agriculture and the State Agricultural College* (Denver: Smith-Brooks Printing Co., 1899), 143; *RMN*, 22 June 1866; and Hodgson, Reminiscences, 13–24.

44. *Secretary of State, 1883,* 10–43; and Gressley, *Bankers and Cattlemen,* 97.

45. Porter, Denver, to Asa Middaugh, Del Norte, Colorado, 11 May 1885; Porter, Denver, to Anderson Brothers, Eagle Rock, Idaho, 12 April 1887; Porter, Denver, to J. M. Cunningham, 24 July 1893; Porter, Denver to T. W. Henderson, Grafton, New Mexico, 10 July 1893, Porter Papers. Also, see Porter, *Autobiography,* 50–53. Albert Reynolds added 160,000 Texas panhandle acres to Arkansas River Valley land he acquired after the Cheyennes' departure. Records, Reynolds Land and Cattle Company, Reynolds Papers. John Campion, Denver National vice-president and mining entrepreneur, invested in the Big Horn Mining and Cattle Company. Records in John F. Campion Collection, CHS.

46. E. L. Lomax, *Colorado: Resources of the State, Population, Industries, Opportunities, Climate, Etc.* (Omaha: Union Pacific Railroad Company, 1906), 80 (quote); Articles of Association and tax schedules, Prairie Cattle Company Collection, CHS; Agreement, 15 September 1882, AVL&CC Papers; W. M. Pearce, *The Matador Land and Cattle Company* (Norman: University of Oklahoma, 1964), 39, 64; and Peake, *Colorado Range,* 237–39.

47. Patterson in Henry Nash Smith, *Virgin Land: The American West as Symbol and Myth* (1950; repr., Cambridge: Harvard University Press, 1970), 232; *Laramie Sentinel,* 8 January 1887, in David M. Emmons, *Garden in the Grasslands* (Lincoln: University of Nebraska Press, 1971), 191; and Webb, *Great Plains,* 424.

48. Quit Claim Deed, Bent County, Colorado, 11 July 1882, AVL&CC Papers; 13 March 1872, Greeley Farmer's Club, Minutes; and Chicago Colorado Accomplishments, 1.

49. *About Colorado Farming,* 30; Fite, *Farmers' Frontier,* 124, 186; Norris and Norris, *Written in Water,* 186–89; and Gates, *History of Public Land Law Development,* 401.

50. William Sommerville, Denver, to Alexander Mackay, Dundee, Scotland, 30 November 1886, Records, Matador Land and Cattle Company, CHS. Cattle grazed for three to five years before shipment, allowing a cow to produce one to three calves. Goff and McCaffree, *Century in the Saddle,* 9–11; and *Agricultural Statistics, 1887* (Denver: Collier and Cleaveland Lith. Co., 1889), 22.

51. *Resources and Attractions of Colorado for the Home Seeker, Capitalist, and Tourist* (Chicago: Rand, McNally and Co., Printers, 1889), 19 (first quote); Lomax, *Colorado,* 408 (second quote); *Agricultural Statistics, 1893,* 18–19; *Seventh Report,* DCOC, 52; *Ninth Report,* DCOC, 30; and Inventory, Ballantine and Rockwell Ranch, 1 March 1899, Fred S. Rockwell Collection, CHS.

52. *Ninth Report,* DCOC, 42; and S. K. Hooper, *The Fertile Lands of Colorado* (Denver: Denver & Rio Grande Railroad, 1899), 7, 68.

53. Barton, "Colorado: Resources," 4, 9.

Chapter 4

Epigraph is from Adams, 1887 Inaugural Address, in William Jackson Palmer, Address, White Night Club, Colorado Springs, 4 July 1903, William Jackson Palmer Papers, CHS.

1. Richard Price, "*Observations on the Importance of the American Revolution*" (Dublin: L. White, 1785), 69, in Thomas Bender, *Toward an Urban Vision: Ideas and Institutions in Nineteenth-Century America* (Lexington: University Press of Kentucky, 1975), 7.

2. Frederick Jackson Turner, "The Significance of the Frontier in American History" *Annual Report of the American Historical Association for the Year*

1893 (1894): 200–201; Dean MacCannell, *The Tourist: A New Theory of the Leisure Class* (New York: Schocken Books, 1976), 97, 106; John F. Sears, *Sacred Places: American Tourist Attractions in the Nineteenth Century* (New York: Oxford University Press, 1989), 4–5; Susan Rhoades Neel, "Tourism and the American West: New Departures," *Pacific Historical Review* (November 1996): 518–19; and Earl Pomeroy, *In Search of the Golden West: The Tourist in Western America* (New York: Alfred A. Knopf, 1957), vii. Americans believed that greatness lay in cities, but worried about the deleteriousness of rapid urbanization and industrialization. Wiebe, *Search for Order,* 149–54, 166–78.

3. *Eighth Report,* DCOC, 29–30; and *In Summer, Fall or Winter, Go Visit the Great Rocky Mountain Resorts of Colorado Via the Kansas Pacific Railway* (Chicago: Rand McNally and Co., 1875).

4. Richard Harding Davis, *The West from a Car Window* (New York: Harper and Brothers, 1892), 270.

5. William Jackson Palmer, Salina, Kansas, to Queen Mellen, Flushing, Long Island, 17 January 1870, Palmer Papers. In 1871, Palmer married this daughter of investor and attorney William Proctor Mellen.

6. Ibid.; *Historical and Descriptive Review of Colorado's Enterprising Cities,* 232; and *Denver & Rio Grande Railway* (Philadelphia, 1870), 12. Born in 1836 in Philadelphia, Palmer began on a railroad-surveyor's crew. In 1855, he studied railroads and mining in England and France and investigated coal-burning coal methods for the Pennsylvania Railroad as its president's assistant. Fighting for the Union, he was wounded, captured, and released, and discharged as a brigadier general. Palmer was the UPED's secretary and treasurer and surveyed its Colorado routes and construction into Denver. George L. Anderson, *General William J. Palmer: A Decade of Colorado Railroad Building, 1870–1880* (Colorado Springs: Colorado College, 1936).

7. Palmer, Denver, to Queen Mellen, Flushing, 21 May 1870, and Palmer, Denver, to William Mellen, Flushing, 25 October 1870, Palmer Papers; *Denver and Rio Grande,* 7, 19; and Brayer, *William Blackmore,* Vol. 2, *Early Financing of the Denver and Rio Grande Railway,* 43. Educated as a physician in England, Bell met Palmer when he joined a UPED survey. Returning home, Bell penned *New Tracks in North America: A Journal of Travel and Adventures Whilst Engaged in the Survey of a Southern Railroad to the Pacific Ocean, 1867–1868,* 2 vols. (London: Chapman and Hall, 1869), which prominently associated Bell with the West.

8. *The Denver and Rio Grande Railway of Colorado and New Mexico* (London, 1871), 14–18; Bell, London, to Blackmore, London, 3 January 1871, Bell Papers; Argument of J. B. Chaffee, Application for Survey of Beaubien and Miranda Land Grant in New Mexico, to Hon. J. D. Cox, Secretary of the Interior, Washington, D.C., FNBD Records; and Robbins, *Colony and Empire,* 171–72.

9. *First Report,* D&RG, 5–10; and Map, Mexican National Railway, Palmer Papers.

10. Palmer, Colorado Springs, to Robert A. Cameron, Denver, 16 December 1871 (quote); and Palmer, Salina, Kansas to Queen Mellen, 17 January 1870, Palmer Papers.

11. Palmer, Fort Sheridan, to Queen Mellon, 18 December 1869, and Palmer, Santa Fe, to Queen Mellon Palmer, 15 October 1874, Palmer Papers. Bell aligned with Gilpin and Blackmore. *Trinchera Estate*. Also, see Robbins, *Colony and Empire*, 173; and Gates, *History of Public Land Law Development*, 364–69.

12. Palmer, Denver, to Queen Mellen, Flushing, 29 July 1869 (quote); Palmer, Denver, to Queen Mellen, Flushing, 9 March 1870, Palmer Papers; and Howbert, *Memories of a Lifetime*, 220–22. Howbert took shares in the Colorado Springs Company. With dividends, he invested in other local railroads.

13. *The Heart of the Continent* (Chicago: Rand McNally and Co., 1892), 28–29 (quote); Rossiter Raymond, Denver, to Wife, New Braintree, Massachusetts, 19 June 1869, Raymond Collection; Samuel Bowles, *The Switzerland of America* (Springfield, Mass.: Samuel Bowles, 1869); Anne Farrar Hyde, *An American Vision: Far Western Landscape and National Culture, 1820–1920* (New York and London: New York University Press, 1990), 109–15; MacCannell, *Tourist*, 3; and Thomas K. Hafen, "City of Saints, City of Sinners: The Development of Salt Lake City as a Tourist Attraction 1869–1900," *Western Historical Quarterly* 28 (autumn 1997): 345.

14. Unidentified D&RG passenger quoted in A. M. Morrison, "An Excursion to Alamosa in 1878," *Colorado Magazine* 19 (January 1942): 29; and *When in Colorado* (Denver: C. J. Kelly Printer and Bookbinder, 1894). Niagara Falls power plants were popular attractions. William Irwin, *The New Niagara: Tourism, Technology, and the Landscape of Niagara Falls, 1776–1917* (University Park: Pennsylvania State University Press, 1996), 153–62.

15. *Historical and Descriptive Review of Colorado's Enterprising Cities*, 233; *An Emigrant's Guide to Pike's Peak* (Kansas Herald, 1859); and Daniel Blue, *Thrilling Narrative of the Adventures, Sufferings and Starvation of Pike's Peak GoldSeekers* (Chicago, 1860); and LeRoy R. Hafen, ed., *Pike's Peak Gold Rush Guidebooks of 1859*, Vol. 9, Southwest Historical Series (Glendale, Calif.: Arthur H. Clark Company, 1941).

16. Robert Cameron, Colorado Springs, to Edward Adams, Greeley, 12 November 1871, Bell Papers; and Marshall Sprague, *Newport in the Rockies: The Life and Good Times of Colorado Springs* (1961, repr., 1971), 34–35.

17. Palmer, Colorado Springs, to Cameron, Denver, 16 December 1871, Palmer Papers (quote); *Fountain Colony* (Denver, 1871), Bell Papers; and John F. Kasson, *Rudeness and Civility: Manners in Nineteenth-Century Urban America* (New York: Hill and Wang, 1990), 34–54.

18. *Colorado Springs Gazette,* 19 January 1872; *Our New Saratoga: Colorado Springs and La Font* (Denver, 1871); and *Villa La Font: The Fountain Colony* (Denver, 1871).

19. R. B. Townsend, *A Tenderfoot in Colorado* (London: Chapman and Hall, 1873), 18; A. C. Hunt, Denver, to Palmer, Colorado Springs, 18 November 1871, Bell Papers; Lewis Iddings, "Life in the Altitudes: The Colorado Health Plateau," *Scribner's* 19 (1896): 143–47; and Fifer, *American Progress,* 254.

20. *Greeley Tribune,* 4 August 1874, in Athearn, *Coloradans,* 97; *Colorado Springs Gazette,* 14 June 1873; *Denver Tribune,* 16 August 1871; and Iddings, "Life in the Altitudes," 142. Also, see Marguerite S. Shaffer, "'See America First': Re-Envisioning Nation and Region through Western Tourism," *Pacific Historical Review* 65 (November 1996): 578.

21. Fossett, *Colorado,* 155. The Denver Public Library has six volumes of D&RG brochures over four decades, such as *Colorado Springs, Colorado: Saratoga of the West* (1872); *Rhymes of the Rockies, or What the Poets Have Found to Say of the Beautiful Scenery on the Denver and Rio Grande* (1887); or *Sights, Places and Resorts in the Rockies* (1900). Also regarding railroads promoting tourism in national parks, see Stephen Pyne, *How the Canyon Became Grand: A Short History* (New York: Penguin Books, 1998), 112–13; and Mark Spence, *Dispossessing the Wilderness: Indian Removal and the Making of the National Parks* (New York: Oxford University Press, 1999), 79–80.

22. Fossett, *Colorado,* 155.

23. Pomeroy, *In Search of the Golden West,* 20–27; Tom Zimmerman, "Paradise Promoted: Boosterism and the Los Angeles Chamber of Commerce," *California History* 64 (winter 1985): 22–23; and Hafen, "City of Saints," 344.

24. S. Anna Gordon, *Camping in Colorado* (New York: W. B. Smith and Co., 1879), 141–56; Ernest Ingersoll, *Knocking Round the Rockies* (New York: Harper and Brothers, 1883); MacCannell, *Tourist,* 128; Dona Brown, *Inventing New England: Regional Tourism in the Nineteenth Century* (Washington: Smithsonian Institution Press, 1995), 1–5; Karl Jacoby, "Class and Environmental History: Lessons from the 'War in the Adirondacks,'" *Environmental History* 2 (July 1997): 325; and Sears, *Sacred Places,* 5.

25. Such phrases appear in Eliza Greatorex, *Summer Etchings in Colorado* (New York, 1873); Summer in Colorado; John H. Tice, *Over the Plains and on the Mountains* (St. Louis: Industrial Age Printing Co., 1872); James Russling, *Across America: Or the Great West and the Pacific Coast* (New York: Sheldon, 1874); Samuel Nugent Townshend, *Colorado: Its Agriculture, Stockfeeding, Scenery and Shooting* (London, 1879); and James Burnley, *Two Sides of the Atlantic* (London: Simpkin, Marshall, 1880). Also, see Athearn, *Coloradans,* 98.

26. Samuel S. Wallihan and T. O. Bigney, eds., *The Rocky Mountain Directory and Colorado Gazetteer for 1871* (Denver: S. S. Wallihan and Co., 1870), 248.

27. Helen Hunt Jackson, "Colorado Springs," 233 (quote), and "Cheyenne Canyon," 234, in *Bits of Travel at Home* (Cambridge, Mass.: Roberts

Brothers, 1878); *A Century of Dishonor: A Sketch of the United States Government's Dealings with Some of the Indian Tribes* (New York: Harpers, 1881); *Ramona* (1884; repr., Boston: Little, Brown and Co., 1903); and Valerie Sherer Mathes, *Helen Hunt Jackson and Her Indian Reform Legacy* (Austin: University of Texas Press, 1990). Thoreau's wilderness, Walden, was a short walk from Concord. Henry David Thoreau, "Walking," *The Works of Thoreau,* ed. Henry S. Camby (Boston: Houghton Mifflin, 1937), 672; and Sears, *Sacred Places,* 6–7, 15.

28. William Cronon, "The Trouble with Wilderness or, Getting Back to the Wrong Nature," *Environmental History* 1 (January 1996): 10–15; William M. Denevan, "The Pristine Myth: The Landscape of the Americas in 1492," *Annals of the Association of American Geographers* 82 (1992): 369–85; and Nicholas Green, *The Spectacle of Nature* (Manchester: Manchester University Press, 1990), 3.

29. Bowles, *Switzerland of America,* 19; and Robert E. Strahorn, *To the Rockies and Beyond, or a Summer on the Union Pacific Railroad and Branches, Sauntering in the Popular Health, Pleasure and Hunting Resorts of Nebraska, Dakota, Wyoming, Colorado, New Mexico, Utah, and Idaho* (Omaha: Omaha Republican Press, 1881), 25; and Fossett, *Colorado,* 151. Also, see Susan Jane Edwards, "Nature as Healer: Denver, Colorado's Social and Built Landscapes of Health, 1880–1930" (Ph.D. diss, University of Colorado, 1994), 32–33; and Sears, *Sacred Places,* 37–38.

30. Pomeroy, *In Search of the Golden West,* 55–57; Katherine Ott, *Fevered Lives: Tuberculosis in American Culture since 1870* (Cambridge: Harvard University Press, 1997), 18–30; Sheila M. Rothman, *Living in the Shadow of Death: Tuberculosis and the Social Experience of Illness in America* (New York: BasicBooks, 1994), 3–6, 14, 142; and Barbara Bates, *Bargaining for Life: A Social History of Tuberculosis, 1876–1938* (Philadelphia: University of Pennsylvania Press, 1992), 1–8. Tuberculosis eventually became a civic issue and a stigma of the poor.

31. Edward Roberts, *Colorado Springs and Manitou* (Colorado Springs: Gazette Publishing Co., 1883), 7–10; and Edwards, "Nature as Healer," 11.

32. Samuel Edwin Solly, *Manitou, Colorado, U.S.A., its Mineral Waters and Climate* (St. Louis: Jno. McKittrick and Co., 1875), and *Colorado for Invalids* (Colorado Springs: Gazette Pub. Co., 1880); and Sprague, *Newport in the Rockies,* 103.

33. Charles Denison, *The Influence of the Climate of Colorado on the Nervous System* (Denver: Richards, 1874)(quote), 6, and *Rocky Mountain Health Resorts, An Analytical Study of High Altitudes in Relation to the Arrest of Chronic Pulmonary Disease* (Boston: Houghton Mifflin, 1881); and Gilpin, *Cosmopolitan Railway,* 207.

34. F. J. Bancroft, Territorial Board of Immigration pamphlet, 1872, in Carl Ubbelohde, *A Colorado Reader* (Boulder: Pruett Publishing Co., 1962), 131; and S. A. Fiske, "Colorado for Invalids," *Popular Science Monthly* 25 (July 1884): 313.

(quote); Fossett, *Colorado,* 107–11;
and Edwards, "Nature as Healer," chap. 2 passim.

36. *Health, Wealth and Recreation: Idaho Springs, Colorado* (Denver: Smith-Brooks
Printing Co., [1902]; *Glenwood Springs, Colorado: A Health and Pleasure Resort*
(Glenwood Springs: Glenwood Hot Springs Co., [1891]), 3; *The Colorado,
Glenwood Springs, Colorado: In the Heart of the Rocky Mountains* (n.p.,
[1893]); and Brochure, Inter-Laken Hotel, Twin Lakes, Colorado, Dexter
Papers, CHS. On a failed resort near Pueblo, *Beulah, A Summer Resort,* John J.
Burns Papers, CHS.

37. Anonymous quote in Fifer, *American Progress,* 368; and Pomeroy, *In Search of
the Golden West,* 22–23. Other local areas only challenged Colorado Springs's
hegemony in the 1920s, with improved highways, motoring tourists, and
skiing. *Colorado Springs Gazette-Telegraph,* 10 November 1940.

38. *A Few Words about Colorado Springs and its New Hotel, the Antlers* (Chicago:
R. R. Donnelly and Sons, Printers, [1883])(quote); *Colorado Springs Gazette,*
18 April 1871; Shaffer, "'See America First,'" 569; and Fifer, *American
Progress,* 255–70, 315–27. When the city failed to meet the loan, Hanson
Risley, Palmer's official receiver, became trustee for it. Sprague, *Newport in the
Rockies,* 103.

39. *Harper's Weekly,* 20 November 1886; and Richard Hamilton, "The Hotel
Marketing Phenomenon: Souvenirs, Mementos, Advertising, and Promotional
Materials," *Historical New Hampshire* 50 (spring/summer 1995): 104–5.

40. Letter to "English Investors," 25 July 1875 (quote)(presumably written by
Bell); George H. Parsons, Secretary and Treasurer of the Colorado Springs
Company, Colorado Springs, to William Bell, Kent, England, 28 October
1891; List of Personal Assets of William Bell, 7 January 1906; and Prospectus,
Manitou Mineral Water, Bath and Parks Company, Bell Papers. Also, see
Articles of Incorporation, Manitou Mineral Water, Bath and Parks Company,
15 September 1882, Manitou Mineral Water Company Collection, CHS; and
Sears, *Sacred Places,* 176–77.

41. *Colorado Resources and Industries* (Denver: Colorado Midland Railroad
Company, 1906), 3; inventories and letterbooks, Edward Nicholson
Collection, CHS, regarding local ranching; and Wyckoff, "Incorporation,"
288–89.

42. John Lipsey, *The Lives of James John Hagerman: Builder of the Colorado Midland
Railway* (Denver: Golden Bell Press, 1968), 27–88 passim.

43. Colorado Midland Railroad Time Table, 1887, Colorado Midland Collection;
The Gold Fields of Colorado (Denver: Denver & Rio Grande Railway, 1896);
and Lipsey, *Lives of James John Hagerman,* 117, 156.

44. Henry Lee Jacques Warren, *Cripple Creek and Colorado Springs; A Review and
Panorama of an Unique Gold Field, with Geologic Features and Achievements of
Five Eventful Years, Including Outlines of Numerous Companies* (Colorado
Springs: Warren and Stride, 1896), 1–10, 57; Edgar C. McMechan, "The

228

Founding of Cripple Creek," *Colorado Magazine* 12 (January 1935): 13, 28–35; and Smith, *Rocky Mountain West,* 191. When gold played out, Cripple Creek and Victor faded, and by 1950 both towns had fewer than one thousand people. Moffat, *Population History,* 69, 81.

45. Palmer, Address, White Night Club.

46. By 1900, the Exchange listed 496 mining ventures and 236,000,000 shares of stock valued at thirty-four million dollars. *Official Manual of the Cripple Creek District* (Colorado Springs: Fred Hills, 1902); *Constitution of the Colorado Springs Mining Exchange* (Colorado Springs: Telegraph Printing Company, 1894), 3–5; George Buckman, *Colorado Springs, Colorado at the Foot of Pike's Peak, Its Manifold Attractions as a Health Resort, a Pleasure Resort, A Scenic Center and a Residence City, Together with a Collection of Medical Facts Concerning Colorado Springs* (Colorado Springs: Gazette Printing Co., 1892); and Smith, *Rocky Mountain West,* 191.

47. By contrast, 311 new incorporations in 1883–84 listed Denver as their head-quarters, with 70 percent of the capitalization. *Secretary of State,* 188, 10–43; and *Biennial Report of the Secretary of State for Colorado, for the Fiscal Years Ending November 30, 1895 and November 30, 1896* (Denver: Smith-Brooks Printing Co., 1896), 9–44.

48. Address, Crocker, 9 January 1896, *Eleventh Report,* DCOC, 12–13; Mehls, "Success," 97–100; and Smith, *Rocky Mountain West,* 190–91. In 1891, for example, 34 percent of the new corporations with almost 40 percent of authorized capital in Denver. *Secretary of State 1891,* 11–43.

49. Jackson, "Colorado Springs," 226 (quote); Fountain Colony, *Prospectus,* 1873; *Trees Native to the Forests of Colorado and Wyoming* (Washington, D.C.: Department of Agriculture, 1908); Ivo E. Lindauer, "A Comparison of the Plant Communities of the South Platte and Arkansas River Drainages in Eastern Colorado," *Southwestern Naturalist* 28 (August 1983): 249–58; and John W. Reps, *The Making of Urban America: A History of City Planning in the United States* (Princeton, N.J.: Princeton University Press, 1965), 403–4.

50. *The Broadmoor, Colorado Springs, Colorado: European Luxury in the Rockies* (Colorado Springs: Colorado Springs Gazette Printing Co., 1896); and Sprague, *Newport in the Rockies,* 121–26.

51. Judith L. Hamilton, "Restoration of Springs and Artesian Wells, Manitou Springs, Colorado," Report, 1990, Mineral Springs Foundation, CHS.

52. *Pike's Peak By Rail* (Manitou: Manitou and Pike's Peak Railway, 1893), CHS (quote); and Crofutt, *Crofutt's Grip-Sack Guide of Colorado* (Omaha: The Overland Publishing Co.; Denver: Alvord and Co., 1881). Simmons developed wooden insulators for Western Union; one stood atop Pike's Peak. He assigned stock to Moffat, Wheeler, and others, but mostly financed the project with his money. Sprague, *Newport in the Rockies,* 108–12, 132–34.

53. Sprague, *Newport in the Rockies,* 150–51. "Tourism required that the Niagara reservation function as a park rather than a realm of wild nature." Irwin, *New Niagara,* 85.

54. Palmer, Philadelphia, to Queen Mellen, Flushing, 2 July 1869, Palmer Papers.

Chapter 5

Epigraph is from *Sketch of the Pueblos and Pueblo County, Colorado* (Pueblo: Board of Trade, Chieftain Steam Print, 1883), 41.

1. Mahoney, "Urban History in a Regional Context," 320.

2. Lecompte, *Pueblo,* 10–12, 35, 45, 198–227, 237–53.

3. Wyckoff, "Incorporation," 283; Mahoney, "Urban History in a Regional Context," 319–22; Conzen, "The Progress of American Urbanism," 352–54; Virginia McConnell Simmons, *The Upper Arkansas: A Mountain River Valley* (Boulder: Pruett Press, 1990), 44, 48, 65; and Ubbelohde, *Colorado History,* 63, 76, 94.

4. Hill, Denver, to Alice Hale Hill, Providence, Rhode Island, 31 July 1864, Hill Collection; *History of the Arkansas Valley, Colorado* (Chicago: O. L. Baskin and Co., 1881), 550, 776; Howbert, *Memories of a Lifetime,* 45–48; Porter, *Autobiography,* 31; and Ubbelohde, *Colorado History,* 63, 74.

5. Wolfe Londoner, "Western Experiences and Colorado Mining Camps," *Colorado Magazine* 6 (March 1929): 69–70; Paul, *Mining Frontiers,* 127; Athearn, *Coloradans,* 130; Stephen M. Voynick, *Leadville: A Miner's Epic* (Missoula, Mont.: Mountain Press, 1984), 20–25; and Webster D. Anthony, "Journal of a Trip from Denver to Oro City in 1860," cited in Simmons, *Upper Arkansas,* 49–50; and Wyckoff, "Incorporation," 285.

6. John Evans, Washington, D.C., to his wife, Denver, 5 July 1868, Evans Private Papers; and *Fourth Report,* KPRY, 12.

7. Peter Scott, Las Animas, to Donald Aschermann, Rocky Ford, Colorado, 1 September 1870, Scott Collection; *RMN,* 12 June, 17 June, and 26 June 1868; Mark L. Blunt, Pueblo, to mother, 19 August 1864, Mark L. Blunt Collection, CHS; and Mahoney, "Urban History in a Regional Context," 320.

8. *Colorado Chieftain,* 4 June and 1 December 1871, 31 January, 2 February, and 20 June 1872; and Milo L. Whittaker, *Pathbreakers and Pioneers of the Pueblo Region* (Philadelphia: Milo L. Whittaker, 1917), 101–8; Anderson, *General William J. Palmer,* 54–55; and Athearn, *Rebel of the Rockies,* 15, 22.

9. *The Central Colorado Improvement Company, Second Report of the Board of Directors to the Stockholders and Bondholders, 1874* (Colorado Springs: "Out West" Printing and Publishing Co., 1875), 3, CF&I Collection, CHS. Gervacio Nolan received the last two major Mexican grants in 1843, which Congress reduced from 3,500,000 to 48,695 acres. Brayer, *William Blackmore,* Vol. 1, *Land Grants,* 190, 217, and Vol. 2, *Financing,* 86–87, 95; H. Lee Scamehorn, *Pioneer Steelmaker of the West: The Colorado Fuel and Iron Company, 1872–1903* (Boulder: Pruett Publishing Company, 1974), 12; Moffat, *Population History,* 78; Athearn, *Rebel of the Rockies,* 20–22, 43; and Whittaker, *Pathbreakers,* 110.

10. *Colorado Chieftain*, 11 January, 9 February, 27 March, and 30 December 1873; *The Pueblo Colony of Southern Colorado* (Lancaster, Pa.: Enquirer Printing and Publishing Co., 1879); Hall, *History of Colorado*, 3:469; Lamar, *Far Southwest*, 280–84; Athearn, *Rebel of the Rockies*, 23–25; and Scamehorn, *Pioneer Steelmaker*, 10, 103–4. On the importance of railroads to western cities, see Cronon, *Nature's Metropolis*, 72, 74.

11. *Improvement Company, Second Report*, 4 (quote), 13–14, 34; and 13 Stat. 343 (1864) and 13 Stat. 529 (1865), in Swenson, "Legal Aspects," 724.

12. Dr. William Bell's Address, 28 January 1920, Denver, to D&RG employees, 6, Robert F. Weitbrec Collection, CHS; Articles of Association, 11 November 1871, Central Colorado Improvement Company, and Central Colorado Improvement Company Minute Book, 37–40, CF&I Collection; "Agreement of the Denver and Rio Grande Railway Company with the Central Colorado Improvement Company," D&RG Collection, CHS; and 17 Stat. 607 (1873), in Swenson, "Legal Aspects," 707, 724–25.

13. National Land and Improvement Company, *Annual Report, 1873* (Philadelphia, 1874), Bell Papers, 16–19; *Improvement Company, Second Report*, 9–12; and Scamehorn, *Pioneer Steelmaker*, 12.

14. *Pueblo Colony*, 8 (quote); *Improvement Company, Second Report*, 7–9; Report of R. Nielson Clark, 10 February 1874, D&RG, *Annual Report, 1874* (Colorado Springs, 1874), 68–73, 83–84, D&RG Collection; *Central Colorado Improvement Company* ("*Central Colorado*") (Colorado Springs: "Out West" Printing and Publishing Co. 1875), 9–22, and "Predecessor Companies of The Colorado Coal & Iron Co.: The Central Colorado Improvement Co., The Southern Colorado Coal & Town Co., The Colorado Coal & Steel Works Co.," statistical study of the predecessor companies in the CF&I Steel Corporation's Comptroller's Office, Pueblo," CF&I Collection; and Scamehorn, *Pioneer Steelmaker*, 187.

15. *Central Colorado*, 22 (quote); Prospectus, Trinidad Extension, and William A. Bell, *Progress of the Denver and Rio Grande Railway* (London, 10 March 1877), Palmer Papers; and William S. Jackson, *Trinidad Pool* (20 October 1876), William S. Jackson Papers.

16. Evans, Denver, to Maggie Evans, London, 20 December 1876 (first quote), and 6 March 1876 (second quote), Evans Private Papers; and James Marshall, *Santa Fe: The Railroad That Built an Empire* (New York: Random House, 1945), 91–93.

17. Athearn, *Rebel of the Rockies*, 53–56; and Marshall, *Santa Fe*, 144–58.

18. *Historical and Descriptive Review of Colorado's Enterprising Cities*, 73–76, 193–200; Elmer R. Burkey, "The Georgetown-Leadville Stage," *Colorado Magazine* 14 (September 1937): 177–87; and Donald L. Griswold and Jean Harvey Griswold, *The Carbonate Camp Called Leadville* (Denver: Denver University Press, 1951), 23.

19. William Palmer, Leadville, to Charles Lamborn, D&RG vice president, Colorado Springs, 15 September 1877, and *Leadville and Oro, a Confidential Pamphlet* (New York, 1878), 6–19, Bell Papers.

20. William Palmer, Colorado Springs, to William Bell, New York City, 18 December 1878, Bell Papers; *Report, 1881,* 3, D&RG Collection; Athearn, *Rebel of the Rockies,* 58–69; and Ubbelohde, *Colorado History,* 159–60.

21. Paul, *Mining Frontiers,* 126–27; and Fell, *Ores to Metals,* 63–40, 177. A similar phenomenon occurred along the Mississippi. "The location of manufacturing was rearranged as the critical variable shifted from location to transportation access, to access to capital and labor, and finally to the ability to generate economies of scale and agglomeration advantages. The effect of that process was the gradual centralization of large-scale manufacturing at the entrepot." Mahoney, "Urban History in a Regional Context," 335.

22. Kountze Brothers, New York City, to Charles Kountze, Denver, 27 December 1893, Kountze Collection; Fell, *Ores to Metals,* 143–64; Lawrence H. Larsen and Barbara J. Cottrell, *The Gate City: A History of Omaha* (Boulder: Pruett Publishing Co., 1982), 62. Guggenheim emigrated from Switzerland in the 1840s. He imported lace and spice, operated a wholesale grocery firm, and started in Leadville when a merchant offered half interest in two mines to settle an obligation. He invested in more, but dissatisfied with refining, started the Globe. Of Meyer's seven sons, Benjamin, who died on the *Titanic,* managed the smelters, and Simon, who later Colorado's senator, managed ore purchases. John H. Davis, *The Guggenheims: An American Epic* (New York: William Morrow and Company, 1978); and Edwin P. Hoyt, Jr., *The Guggenheims and the American Dream* (New York: Funk and Wagnalls, [1967]).

23. *Sketch of Pueblos,* 41 (quote); and Fell, *Ores to Metals,* 166.

24. *Engineering and Mining Journal,* 43 (March 1887): 227, 47 (May 1889): 485, and 50 (December 1890): 723, in Fell, *Ores to Metals,* 167–77. Thatcher worked with brother Joseph in Central City. Joseph moved to the Denver National Bank, and Mahlon to Pueblo. "History of the First National Bank of Central City," 1–3.

25. *Pueblo Daily Chieftain,* 10 April 1888; Fell, *Ores to Metals,* 182–84; Wyckoff, "Incorporation," 288; and Davis, *Guggenheims,* 58–62, 69.

26. Ruter, Pueblo, to William Lawson, New York, 4 August 1889, Charles Ruter Collection, CHS. Ruter wrote to an Ohio foundry owner: "I understand that you are corresponding with the Denver Chamber of Commerce . . . Allow me to suggest to you, before deciding to locate there to investigate the resources and advantages of this city [Pueblo] for any kind of manufacturing enterprise, but more especially for a stove foundry." The Board lost the foundry, but recruited from Iowa Merchant's Union Barb Wire Company, in which Ruter invested. Ruter to Mr. Kibler, Newark, Ohio, 14 December 1888, and Ruter, to Mr. J. Ree, Lincoln, 9 December 1889.

27. *Labor Statistics, 1891,* 40; *Biennial Report of the Bureau of Labor Statistics of the State of Colorado, 1895–1896* (Denver: Smith-Brooks Printing Co., 1896), 25; *Sketch of Pueblos; Eleventh Report,* DCOC, 51; David Stradling, "Civilized Air: Coal, Smoke, and Environmentalism in America, 1880–1920" (Ph.D. diss., University of Wisconsin, Madison, 1996), 29; Duane A. Smith, *Rocky*

Mountain Mining Camps: The Urban Frontier (Bloomington: Indiana University Press, 1967), 76; and Moffat, *Population History*, 78.

28. Shareholders List, CC&I, 1884, and *First Report of The Colorado Coal and Iron Company*, December 31, 1879 (Colorado Springs: Daily Gazette Publishing Co., 1880), 3, 12, CF&I Collection; Scamehorn, *Pioneer Steelmaker*, 45; and Robbins, *Colony and Empire*, 93. New Yorkers and other easterners held 83,000 of 100,000 shares. 6,900 were placed in Britain and Europe. Of 1,418 shares owned by Coloradans, Jackson held 600, Palmer 253, and Bell 194.

29. A. H. Danforth, General Manager, CC&I, South Pueblo, to William J. Palmer, President, 1 February 1882, Palmer Papers; CC&I Report, 1879, 9; *Pueblo Daily Chieftain*, 8 September 1881; *Colorado Coal and Iron Annual Report, 1880* (Colorado Springs: Daily Gazette Publishing Co., 1881), 5, 10–11, and "Predecessor Companies," 25, CF&I Collection.

30. Manufacturing capital grew from $9,030 in 1881 to $2,000,000 in 1883. Reports, Assessor of Pueblo County, *Sketch of the Pueblos*. Pueblo had greater total capitalization because of steel, but Denver had six times as many manufacturing firms. Nesmith, *Interests of Colorado: First Biennial Report of the Bureau of Labor Statistics of the State of Colorado, 1887–1888* (Denver: Collier and Cleaveland Lith. Co., 1888), 387; *Labor Statistics, 1891*, 78–80; and Cronon, *Nature's Metropolis*, 269–79.

31. Charles Rolker, "Report on the Property of The Colorado Coal & Iron Co.," 27 June 1884 (New York: Jno. C. Rankin, Jr., 1884), 44, and *CC&I Annual Report, 1885* (New York, 1886), 16, CF&I Collection; and William S. Jackson, Colorado Springs, to William J. Palmer, Colorado Springs, 23 October 1882, Bell Papers.

32. *Report of the State Inspector of Coal Mines of the State of Colorado for the Year 1884* (Denver: Times Steam Publishing House, 1884), 10, 57–58, 64, 68, 72, 79, 83, 87; *Fourth Biennial Report of the State Inspector of Coal Mines of the State of Colorado for the Years of 1889–90* (Denver: Collier and Cleaveland Lith. Co., 1890), 7–8; *Labor Statistics, 1891*, 43; Danforth to Palmer, 1 February 1882; and Map, Colorado Coal and Iron properties, ca. 1885, in Scamehorn, *Pioneer Steelmaker*, 21. Regarding Durango, see William Palmer, New York City, to William Bell, London, 15 November and 20 November 1890, and James Porter, Durango, to William Bell, 18 February 1892 and 21 February 1893, Bell Papers.

33. Osgood bought coal for the Burlington railroad in Iowa, moved to Denver to locate new sources, and formed the Denver Fuel Company in 1882. In 1889, Osgood incorporated Colorado Fuel Company, with all but two directors from Denver. Section A, "A Statement of Business and Personal Relations— John C. Osgood and John L. Jerome—August 1882 to August 1903," a legal Brief by John L. Jerome, n.d., John Lathrop Jerome Papers, CHS; J. A. Kebler, Denver, to J. C. Osgood, President, New York, "Report: Grand River Coal & Coke Co. Property," 21 May 1892, Jerome B. Wheeler Collection, CHS; *Colorado Fuel Company, Annual Report, 1889* (New York, 1889), 5, *Colorado*

Fuel Company, Annual Report, 1892 (New York, 1892), 1, and Denver Fuel Company Minute Book, 1, 7, CF&I Collection; and Scamehorn, *Pioneer Steelmaker,* 70–71.

34. *Colorado Fuel Company, Annual Report, 1892,* 10, and *Thirteenth Annual Report of the Colorado Coal and Iron Co. for the Year Ending December 31, 1891* (Colorado Springs: Daily Gazette Publishing Co., 1892), 13, CF&I Collection; *Daily Chieftain,* 18 July, 14 August 1892; and Scamehorn, *Pioneer Steelmaker,* 71. In *The Interests of Colorado in Iron and Steel Manufacture,* J. S. Nesmith, vice-president of the Denver Manufacturing and Mercantile Bureau, proposed a Denver works.

35. *Colorado Fuel and Iron Company, Annual Report, 1893* (New York, 1893), 1–3, CF&I Collection; and *Historical and Descriptive Review of Colorado's Enterprising Cities,* 197. Pueblo facilities employed twenty-two hundred men. CF&I also received financing from New York trust companies. Section A, "Statement—Osgood and Jerome."

36. *Labor Statistics, 1891,* 41; Frederick E. Saward, *The Coal Trade: A Compendium of Valuable Information Relative to Coal Production, Prices, Transportation, Etc., at Home and Abroad* (New York: Coal Trade Journal, 1894), 11, 31–32, Palmer Papers; and CF&I Report, 1893, 18–33. Also, see Scamehorn, *Pioneer Steelmaker,* 92–93; Robbins, *Colony and Empire,* 95; and Abbott, *Colorado,* 121.

37. By 1906, CF&I employed one out of ten Coloradans. Duane A. Smith, *When Coal Was King: A History of Crested Butte, Colorado, 1880–1952* (Golden: Colorado School of Mines Press, 1984), 51. The CF&I Collection contains materials on properties in Wyoming, Utah, New Mexico, Nevada, Arizona, California and Missouri. See reports to Osgood dated 20 August 1892, 12 December 1892, 28 February 1895, 13 July 1895, 15 July 1896, 18 September 1899, 12 June 1900, and 10 September 1900.

38. Section B, "Statement—Osgood and Jerome"; and Scamehorn, *Pioneer Steelmaker,* 95–97.

39. *Historical and Descriptive Review of Colorado's Enterprising Cities,* 197.

40. "Report of the Durango Trust to the Subscribers," 1 September 1884, William A. Bell, Trustee, and the "First Report of the Durango Land and Coal Company to the Stockholders," 1 September 1884 to 1 June 1886, Bell Papers; Bell's Address by Bell, 28 January 1920, and William A. Bell, trustee for the Durango Trust, Colorado Springs, to Robert F. Weitbrec, 14 September 1880 and 15 March 1881, Weitbrec Collection; *Great San Luis Valley, Colorado,* 10; Cathy E. Kindquist, "Communication in the Colorado High Country" in Wyckoff and Dilsaver, *Mountainous West,* 114–17; Athearn, *Rebel of the Rockies,* 104–5, 134, 145 ; and Duane A. Smith, *Rocky Mountain Boom Town: History of Durango, Colorado* (Boulder: Pruett Publishing Co., 1980), 5–10, 28, 33–34.

41. *Crested Butte, Gunnison County, Colorado: The Great Coal, Coke and Ore Centre of the Gunnison County, Depot for the Only Anthracite Coal West of*

Pennsylvania (Pueblo(?): Denver and Rio Grande Railroad, 1881), 1, 7; and Smith, *When Coal Was King,* 12–38, 51.

42. *Pueblo Colony,* 1–5, 13, 25; *Improvement Company, Second Report, 1874,* 7–9; Press Release, CC&I (n.d.; prior to 1892), Bessemer Town Collection, CHS; Porter, *Pencilings,* 22; and James Earl Sherow, *Watering the Valley: Development along the High Plains Arkansas River, 1870–1950* (Lawrence: University Press of Kansas, 1990), 8–27, 46–47.

43. *Colorado as an Agricultural State* (emphasis added), 47; Hayes, *New Colorado,* 27; and Reports, Pueblo County Assessor, *Sketch of Pueblos.*

44. *Historical and Descriptive Review of Colorado's Enterprising Cities,* 199 (quote); and Sherow, *Watering the Valley,* 9–11, 166.

45. *Great San Luis Valley,* 1; Dietz and Larson, "Colorado's San Luis Valley," 355; and Athearn, *Coloradans,* 60, 107, 113.

46. United States Army Corps of Engineers, *Report of the Exploring Expedition from Santa Fe, New Mexico to the Junction of the Grand and Green Rivers of the Great Colorado of the West, in 1859* (Washington, D.C.: Government Printing Office, 1876), 53; *Central Colorado,* 15; and Athearn, *Coloradans,* 111–12, 122–26.

47. *$30,000. 1,200 Acres. A Bargain,* pamphlet, Colorado Land and Immigration Company Collection, CHS; *Great San Luis Valley,* 2; *Colorado as an Agricultural State,* 51; Articles, Trinchera Estate Company; *Trinchera Estate Report,* 1892; and Lamar, *Far Southwest,* 266–67.

48. W. B. Vickers, "History of Colorado," in *History of the Arkansas Valley,* 35–38.

49. Manuscript (quote), J. S. Hoy Collection, CHS; Sarah Deutsch, *No Separate Refuge: Culture, Class, and Gender on an Anglo-Hispanic Frontier in the American Southwest, 1880–1940* (New York: Oxford University Press, 1987), 19–20; Nostrand, *Hispano Homeland,* 193; Lecompte, *Pueblo,* 35, 47–56; Rosenbaum and Larson, "Mexicano Resistance," 277–79, 286; and Ebright, *Land Grants and Lawsuits,* 249–62.

50. Hill, Costilla, to Alice Hale Hill, Providence, Rhode Island, 19 July 1864, Hill Collection.

51. Hill, Costilla, to his mother, Mrs. M. C. Hill, 13 July 1864 (quote); and Hill, Culebra, to Alice Hale Hill, Providence, 12 July 1864, Hill Collection.

52. Even when small Hispano landholders won, they frequently lost their land because of high litigation expenses. The sugar-beet industry was an important source of seasonal wage labor after 1900. Ebright, *Land Grants and Lawsuits,* 268–69; Stoller, "Grants of Desperation," 37; and Deutsch, *No Separate Refuge,* 20–21, 27–29.

53. *Central Colorado,* 7–8 and 9, respectively.

54. *Sketch of Pueblos,* 9.

Chapter 6

Epigraph is from William Gilpin, *Cosmopolitan Railway,* iv.

1. Donald Worster, *Under Western Skies: Nature and History in the American West* (New York: Oxford University Press, 1992), 13; William Cronon, "The Uses of Environmental History," *Environmental History Review* 17 (fall 1993): 10; and Richard White, *The Organic Machine: The Remaking of the Columbia River* (New York: Hill and Wang, 1995), 65–69.

2. Flores, "Bison Ecology," 472; Douglas J. Buege, "The Ecologically Noble Savage Revisited," *Environmental Ethics* 18 (spring 1996): 71–72; and Kent Redford, "The Ecologically Noble Savage," *Cultural Survival Quarterly* 15 (1991): 46–48.

3. Gilpin, *Cosmopolitan Railway,* iv; Bender, *Toward an Urban Vision,* 7; Steinberg, *Slide Mountain,* 10–11; and McEvoy, *Fisherman's Problem,* 15–16.

4. Porter, *Pencilings,* 45. Some Americans worried about resource exhaustion, including George Perkins Marsh, *Man and Nature: or, Physical Geography as Modified by Human Action,* ed. David Lowenthal (Cambridge, Mass.: Belknap Press of Harvard University Press, 1965); and Powell, *Report on the Lands of the Arid Region.*

5. "Comparative statement of rainfall," *Horticultural and Forestry, 1887,* 251; and Sherow, *Watering the Valley,* 9–10, 82.

6. Mormons changed Utah pasturage under similar communal schemes. Elizabeth Raymond, "When the Desert Won't Bloom: Environmental Limitation and the Great Basin," in Wrobel and Steiner, *Many Wests,* 71–92; and Dan L. Flores, "Zion in Eden: Phases of the Environmental History of Utah," *Environmental Review* 7 (1983): 325–44.

7. *Denver & Rio Grande Railway,* 12.

8. Map, *First Report,* DPRY; and Map, Pearson, *Maxwell Land Grant.* Regarding Maxwell timber, see Inventories of Saw Timber; and J. M. Waldron, Catskill, New Mexico, to M. P. Pels, Raton, New Mexico, 27 October 1892, Schomburg Collection.

9. Samuel Mallory, Nevada City, to *The Jeffersonian* (Danbury, Connecticut), 16 July 1861, Mallory Collection; Journal of Daily Operations, 1879, Silver Reduction Works Collection, CHS; and Michael Williams, *Americans and their Forests: A Historical Geography* (New York: Cambridge University Press, 1990), chap. 1 passim. Regarding Leadville timber, see *Leadville: A Silver Setting in a Sea of Silver* (Leadville: John Nowland and Company, 1890), 11; regarding Cripple Creek, see *Colorado Springs Gazette-Telegraph,* 14 January 1946; and regarding Golden, see Captain Edward L. Berthoud, Mayor, Golden, to Edgar T. Ensign, Forest Commissioner of the State of Colorado, 1 October 1890, printed in *Biennial Report of the Forest Commissioner of the State of Colorado for the Years 1889 and 1890* (Denver: Collier and Cleaveland Lith. Co., Printers, 1891), 24–26.

10. Hoy Manuscript, 33. Duane Smith found only four articles from 1802 to 1906 regarding environmental impacts. *Mining America,* 42.

11. Rockwell, Central City, to Kate Rockwell, Boston, 25 June 1871, and Rockwell, Georgetown, to Kate, 23 July 1871, Alfred Rockwell Papers.

12. Blunt, Golden, to Frances Blunt, Boston, 3 November 1861, Blunt Collection.

13. Ibid.; Rockwell, 23 July 1871; *1896 Report of the Bureau of Mines, Colorado* (Denver: Smith-Brooks Printing Company, 1896), 10–12; and William Wyckoff, *Creating Colorado: The Making of a Western Landscape, 1860–1940* (New Haven: Yale University Press, 1999), 68–69.

14. Stuart Lindley, Leadville, to Father, 9 October 1879, Stuart Lindley Collection, CHS; *Leadville: A Silver Setting,* 14; Pilot Knob Lode, Journal, Lewis Rockwell Papers; and Rohe, "Environment and Mining," 178. The counties are Boulder, Chaffee, Clear Creek, El Paso, Fremont, Lake, Pitkin, and San Juan. *Bureau of Mines, 1896,* 12, 18, 21, 37, 45, 68, 96, 112.

15. *First Report, Union Colony,* 28; *Colorado Springs Gazette-Telegraph,* 14 January 1946 (quote); Berthoud letter, *Biennial Report of the Forest Commissioner, 1889,* 24–26; Elinor G. K. Melville, *A Plague of Sheep: Environmental Consequences of the Conquest of Mexico* (Cambridge: Cambridge University Press, 1994), chap. 1 passim; and Fifer, *American Progress,* 101. Lacking higher quality trees, the region shipped in fine lumber from around the nation. J. L. Wilson, Sugar Loaf, to Henry M. Teller, Washington, D.C., 8 February 1878, Teller Letters.

16. Speech, Senate of the United States, 31 March and 2 April 1908, "The State's Control over its Waters," 32, Henry Moore Teller Papers, CHS.

17. J. L. Wilson to Teller, 8 February 1878 (quote), N. P. Hill, Black Hawk, to Teller, 2 January 1878, A. W. Brazee, Denver, to Teller, 3 April 1878, and R. J. McNutt, Del Norte, to Teller, 18 March 1878, Teller Letters; *Horticultural and Forestry, 1887,* 156–67; and *Seventeenth Annual Report of the State Board of Agriculture, including the Eighth Annual Report of the Agricultural Experiment Station, Fort Collins* (Denver: Smith-Brooks Printing Co., 1896), 111.

18. *Silver Plume Mines and Scenery* (Silver Plume, Colo.: Board of Mines and Trade, [1903]), 1; and Florence Construction Company, Trial Balance, 31 May 1897, Moffat Papers.

19. *Colorado as an Agricultural State,* 13 (quote); Enos A. Mills and W. G. M. Stone, *Forests and Exotic Trees of Colorado* (Denver: Colorado State Forestry Association, 1905), 5; and testimony, Louis Carpenter, Kansas v. Colorado, in Sherow, *Watering the Valley,* 33.

20. *Forestry in Colorado (First Annual Report of the State Forest Commissioner)* (Denver: Collier and Cleaveland, [1885]), 1–2.

21. Ibid.; Address, Davis H. Waite, Denver, 27 August 1893, *Semi-Annual Report of the Colorado State Board of Horticulture for the Years 1893–1894* (Denver:

Smith-Brooks Printing Co., 1894), 7:27–29; and Donald J. Pisani, *Water, Land, and Law in the West: The Limits of Public Policy, 1850–1920* (Lawrence: University Press of Kansas, 1996), 133.

22. "Act Relating to Woodlands and Forestry in Colorado," General Assembly, State of Colorado, 4 April 1885, *Forestry in Colorado,* 13–15; *Biennial Report of the Forest Commissioner, 1889,* 15–17; *Horticultural and Forestry, 1887,* 158; Mills and Stone, *Forests and Exotic Trees,* 13; and Teller, "State's Control," 32.

23. John Evans, President, Denver, to stockholders, 20 July 1881, 3, Evans Private Papers; and *Colorado Springs Gazette-Telegraph,* 14 January 1946.

24. Rohe, "Environment and Mining," in Wyckoff and Dilsaver, *The Mountainous West,* 180–87; Wyckoff, *Creating Colorado,* 69; Brechin, *Imperial San Francisco,* 34–35; and photographs of hydraulicking at X-60079, X-60105, Z-1180, WHJ.10195, and CHS.A646, and dredging at X-60124, X-60155, and MCC-68, Western History Photos, DPL.

25. Rohe, "Environment and Mining," 173, 181–183; and John W. Reps, *Cities of the American West* (Princeton, N.J.: Princeton University Press, 1974), 472–73.

26. *Gazette-Telegraph,* 14 January 1946; Blunt, 3 November 1861; Oshkosh Northwestern, 16 August 1877, in Rohe, "Environment and Mining," 184; Wilma Dunaway, "The Incorporation of Mountain Ecosystems into the Capitalist World-System," *Review: Fernand Braudel Center* 19 (fall 1996): 377; and Wyckoff, *Creating Colorado,* 72.

27. Saward, *Coal Trade,* 11; Map, 30 June 1893, *CF&I, Annual Report, 1893,* and Report of R. C. Hills, Denver, to John C. Osgood, New York, 20 August 1892, 3–6, CF&I Collection; *Crested Butte,* 1, 7; Fell, *Ores to Metals,* 134–58, 167–71; and Smith, "'A Country of Tremendous Mountains,'" 107.

28. *Coal Mines, 1884,* 4, 12–36; and Scamehorn, *Pioneer Steelmaker,* 61–62.

29. *Coal Mines, 1884,* 12–14, 25–36; *Coal Mines, 1889,* 7; and *Seventh Biennial Report of the Inspector of Coal Mines of the State of Colorado, 1895–96, to the Governor* (Denver: Smith-Brooks Printing Co., 1897), 8–9. In 1884, one explosion killed fifty-nine. There were six more fatal and forty-four non-fatal accidents.

30. Jackson, "O-Be-Joyful Creek and Poverty Gulch," *Atlantic Monthly* (December 1883), in Smith, *When Coal Was King,* 62.

31. *Elk Mountain Pilot* celebrated Crested Butte's success. "At night the place reminded us of a Pittsburgh by being illuminated with the flames of the coke ovens." 29 December 1881, in ibid., 62.

32. "Wheeler and Pitkin County," 68; and Geological Section, Newcastle, and map, White Ash & Loveland workings, *Coal Mine, 1889*; and Richard McCloud, *Durango as It Is* (Durango: Durango Board of Trade, 1892).

33. Gilpin, *Cosmopolitan Railway,* v; *Pueblo, Colorado; Colorado Resources;* and Stradling, "Civilized Air," 29.

34. *Coal Mines, 1889,* 40–41; *Mined Land Reclamation Division, Annual Report for 1988* (Denver: Department of Natural Resources, Mined Land Reclamation Division, [1989]), 15; and Hills's Report to Osgood.

35. Worster, *An Unsettled Country: Changing Landscapes of the American West* (Albuquerque: University of New Mexico Press, 1994), 11, 56.

36. Faulkner Diary, 8 April 1859, CHS; Hartzell, Denver, to Augusta Hartzell, 21 June 1859, John Hartzell Collection, DPL; and Reminiscences, Hodgson, 15.

37. Blunt, Golden, to mother, 20 August 1859, Blunt Collection; Mallory, Nevada City, to *The Jeffersonian,* 16 July 1861, and diary, 28 March 1864, Mallory Collection; Garbutt, La Porta, Colorado, to W. P. Garbutt, Greece, New York, 18 January 1874, Edward N. Garbutt Collection, CHS; and Reminiscences, Dunham Wright, DPL.

38. Diary, 18 August 1870, Scott Collection; and Diary, 17 January 1871, Terry Papers.

39. Worster, *Unsettled Country,* 70–71; and West, *Way to the West,* 82. Eugene Fleharty alternatively argues that settler alterations produced a greater diversity of species than were present in 1865. *Wild Animals and Settlers on the Great Plains* (Norman: University of Oklahoma Press, 1995), 303.

40. Blunt, 20 August 1859; and *A Look Back : A Sixty-Five-Year History of the Colorado Game and Fish Department: 1961 Annual Report of the Colorado Game and Fish Department* (Denver, 1962), 5–6.

41. Address, Governor Edward M. McCook, 3 January 1872, in *Look Back,* 6–7.

42. *Pueblo Colony,* 7 (quote), 10, 13; Diary, 1 September 1870, Scott Collection; *Resources of Colorado,* 2; and *Historical and Descriptive Review of Colorado's Enterprising Cities,* 199.

43. *First Report, Union Colony,* 16, 19, 22, 28, 34; Chicago-Colorado Accomplishments; and *Resources of Colorado,* 2.

44. Hodgson, Reminiscences, 17; Sandra F. Pritchard, "The Agricultural Landscape of Summit County, Colorado," *Pennsylvania Geographer* 13 (spring/summer 1995): 6, 12; Jackson, "Federal Lands," 273; and *Trees Native to the Forests of Colorado and Wyoming* (U.S. Department of Agriculture, Forest Service, Rocky Mountain Region, revised 1945; n.d. for original publication), 2.

45. William Cronon, George Miles, and Jay Gitlin, "Becoming West: Toward a New Meaning for Western History" in Cronon, Miles, and Gitlin, eds., *Under an Open Sky: Rethinking America's Western Past* (New York: W. W. Norton and Co., 1992), 11–13; Goff and McCaffree, *Century in the Saddle,* 25, 34, 72; "Report on Agriculture," *Tenth Census of the United States 1880 Population and Social Statistics* (Washington, D.C.: Government Printing Office, 1880), 144–45; *Agricultural Statistics, 1883,* 4–11; and *Eleventh Annual Report of the Denver Chamber of Commerce* (Denver, 1896), 41, 46. Flores estimates the pre-gold rush bison population in "Bison Ecology," 466.

46. *Fur, Fin and Feather* (Denver: Colorado Midland Railroad Company, 1897);

Brochure, Inter-Laken Hotel; Enos A. Mills, *Wild Life on the Rockies* (1909; repr., Lincoln and London: University of Nebraska Press, 1988); and G. Edward White, *The Eastern Establishment and the Western Experience: The West of Frederic Remington, Theodore Roosevelt, and Owen Wister* (New Haven: Yale University Press, 1968), chap. 1 passim.

47. *Look Back,* 5; *Biennial Report of the Fish Commissioner, State of Colorado for the Two Years, 1879 and 1880* (Denver: Tribune Printing Company, 1880), 2; and John M. Findlay, "A Fishy Proposition: Regional Identity in the Pacific Northwest," in Wrobel and Steiner, *Many Wests,* 40.

48. Faulkner Diary, 9 April 1859; *Biennal Report of the Fish Commissioner, 1879,* 3; and *Look Back,* 6.

49. *Biennial Report of the Fish Commissioner, State of Colorado, for the Two Years, 1881 and 1882* (Denver: Tribune Printing Company, 1882), 5–6.

50. *Report of the State Fish Commissioner of Colorado for 1886* (Denver: Collier and Cleaveland Lith. Co., 1886), 7.

51. *Biennial Report of the Fish Commissioner, 1879,* 5, 8, 11–12; and *In Re Casual Deficiency,* 21 Colo. 403 (1895).

52. *Biennial Report of the State Fish Commissioner and Game Warden of Colorado for 1893 and 1894* (Denver: Smith-Brooks Printing Company, 1894), 6 (quote); and *Siedler v. Seeley,* 8 Colo. App. 499 (1896).

53. *Biennial Report of the Fish Commissioner, 1893,* 5; *Biennial Report of the State Fish Commissioner of the State of Colorado for the Years 1891 and 1892* (Denver: Smith-Brooks Printing Co., 1892), 4; and Jacoby, "Class and Environmental History," 328–33.

54. *Look Back,* 8, 38–46; *Sunny Colorado: The Healthful Winter Resort* (Burlington Route, 1905), 15; and John Sebastian, *Under the Turquoise Sky in Colorado* (Rock Island-Frisco Lines, 1907), chap. 4.

55. Worster, *Unsettled Country,* 64–66; Pisani, "Promotion and Regulation," 757–58; and Hurst, *Law and the Conditions of Freedom,* 67–70.

56. 1876 statute, *Look Back,* 8.

57. *Biennial Report of the Fish Commissioner, 1893,* 24. Utes returned to the San Juans until 1914 to hunt. Dietz and Larson, "Colorado's San Luis Valley," 353.

58. *Biennial Report of the State Forest, Game and Fish Commissioner of the State of Colorado for the Years 1897 and 1898* (Denver: Smith-Brooks Printing Co., 1898), 15–18; *Biennial Report of the State Fish Commissioner, 1891,* 4; *Agricultural Statistics,* 1893, 18–19; and Worster, *Unsettled Country,* 51–57.

Epilogue

Epigraph is from "Response of Charles J. Hughes, Jr. in favor of the Benefits that Will Result to Colorado and Denver from the Building of the Denver,

Northwestern, & Pacific Railway," 17 November 1902, Address, Denver Real Estate Exchange, 8, William A. Hover Collection, CHS.

1. Moffat, *Population History,* 54, 69, 78, 90, 128, 149, 168, 310.

2. *Agricultural Possibilities of Eastern Colorado: Wonderful Opportunities for the Homeseeker or Investor; Lands in Yuma and Washington Counties, Colorado* (Denver: Colorado Board of Immigration, 1909), 15; Timothy R. Mahoney, "Down in Davenport: A Regional Perspective on Antebellum Town Economic Development" *Annals of Iowa* 50 (summer 1990): 453; Eric Monkkonen, *America Becomes Urban: The Development of U.S. Cities and Towns, 1780–1980* (Berkeley: University of California Press, 1988), 24–25; Wyckoff, "Incorporation," 284; Meinig, "American Wests," 165; and Moffat, *Population History,* 67–68, 72, 81.

3. Map, Brewer Papers, 11; *Rocky Mountain Directory, 1871,* 320; and Leonard and Noel, *Denver,* 298–302.

4. *Historical and Descriptive Review of Colorado's Enterprising Cities,* 53 (quote), 156–59; Athearn, *Coloradans,* 59, 100, 155, 257; and Leonard and Noel, *Denver,* 326–30.

5. *RMN,* 15 January and 22 January 1868, in Athearn, *Coloradans,* 174; Porter, *Autobiography,* 30–32; Bell, *New Tracks,* 1:81; Samuel Bowles, *Across the Continent: A Summer's Journey to the Rocky Mountains, the Mormons, and the Pacific States* (Springfield, Mass.: Samuel Bowles, 1865), 21; and Ubbelohde, *Colorado History,* 122, 162.

6. Agreement between John Evans, et al. and Sidney Dillon, et al. regarding the Denver, Texas & Fort Worth R.R. Co., 1 June 1888, and Report to Interstate Commerce Commission, 1888, 3, Denver, Texas & Fort Worth Railroad Collection; *Historical and Descriptive Review of Colorado's Enterprising Cities,* 38, 41; *Statement regarding the Cincinnati-Colorado Coal, Coke and Iron Company, Its Valuable Possessions, Purposes and Business Prospects* (Cincinnati: F. W. Freeman, 1882), 4–6, and Warranty Deed, Gray Creek Coal and Coking Company, 9 July 1892, Michael Beshoar Records, DPL; and Michael Beshoar, *All about Trinidad and Las Animas County, Colorado* (Denver: Times-Steam Printing House and Blank Book Manufactory, 1882).

7. Mills, *Wild Life,* 233–43; Fossett, *Colorado,* 107–11; Athearn, *Coloradans,* 230–31; and Moffat, *Population History,* 70–73.

8. *Historical and Descriptive Review of Colorado's Enterprising Cities,* 129, 144 (quote), 168; and Ubbelohde, *Colorado History,* 152–53.

9. Brochure, Alamosa Land and Canal Company, DPL; Athearn, *Rebel of the Rockies,* 57–58, 121–22; and Underwood, *Town Building,* passim.

10. Hodgson, Reminiscences, 24; Lomax, *Colorado,* 64–66; Grand Junction Chamber of Commerce, *The Valley of the Grand, the Place for You* (Denver: Smith-Brooks Press, [1906]), 38; Sherow, *Watering the Valley,* 14–15, 88–91; and Moffat, *Population History,* 66–67, 70–75, 79–80.

11. Nathaniel P. Hill, Costilla, to Alice Hale Hill, Providence, Rhode Island,

19 July 1864, Hill Collection; Athearn, *Coloradans*, 144; and Goff and McCaffree, *Century in the Saddle*, 86.

12. *Historical and Descriptive Review of Colorado's Enterprising Cities*, 187; and Moffat, *Population History*, 66–69, 71, 74, 77, 79–81.

13. *Historical and Descriptive Review of Colorado's Enterprising Cities*, 73 (quote), 98; *Legislative, Historical and Biographical Compendium of Colorado* (Denver: C. F. Coleman, 1887), 74–76; Moore, *Leadville*, 3; Harvey N. Gardiner, "Finding New Mines within Old Mines at Leadville, Colorado," *Journal of the West* 31 (October 1992): 71–79; and Rohrbough, *Aspen*, 230–31. Even with discoveries of small gold veins in 1893 and zinc in 1899, Leadville never regained the traffic of the 1880s.

14. *Ghost Towns of Colorado*, American Guide Series (New York: Hastings House, 1947), 1; Hogan, *Class and Community*, 52; and Marshall Sprague, *Money Mountain: The Story of Cripple Creek Gold* (1953; repr., Lincoln and London: University of Nebraska Press, 1979), 231.

15. Rohrbough, *Aspen*, 219; and Trachtenberg, *Incorporation of America*, 4, 21–23.

16. Gilpin, *Cosmopolitan Railway*, 31–32; Athearn, *Rebel of the Rockies*, 110–11; DeVoto is discussed in William G. Robbins, "The 'Plundered Province' Thesis and the Recent Historiography of the American West" *Pacific Historical Review* 55(November 1986): 578; Bryant, "Entering the Global Economy," 220–21; Maury Klein, *The Life and Legend of Jay Gould* (Baltimore: Johns Hopkins University Press, 1986), 181–90; and Gerald Berk, *Alternative Tracks: The Constitution of the American Industrial Order, 1865–1917* (Baltimore: Johns Hopkins University Press, 1994), 53–55, 127–30.

17. "Kansas Pacific Railway and its Relations to the Government of the United States written to the Secretary of the Interior, Washington, D.C., by a Committee of Nine of the First-Mortgage Bondholders of the Kansas Pacific Railway," 21 April 1877, 2–3 (quote), Ten Year Land Grant Mortgage, KPRY to Adolphus Meier and John A. Stewart, Trustees," 1 July 1870, and *Colorado Transcript*, 5 May 1875, KPRY Collection; Speech, J. B. Chaffee, United States Senate, 13 November 1877 (Washington, D.C.: Government Printing Office, 1877), 4, FNBD Collection; and Supplemental Mortgage, CCRC to Fred L. Ames and Jay Gould, 1 December 1877, CCRR Collection.

18. Evans Affidavit, John Evans, Complainant v. the Union Pacific, Denver & Gulf Railway Company, et al., Defendants in Equity, Circuit Court of the United States, District of Colorado, 13 November 1893, 13–14; William J. Palmer, New York, to Subscribers to the Bonds and Stock of the Denver and Rio Grande Western Railway Company, 1 February 1882, Bell Papers; Thomas G. Alexander and James B. Allen, *Mormons and Gentiles: A History of Salt Lake City* (Boulder, Colo.: Pruett Publishing Co., 1984), 91; and Athearn, *Rebel of the Rockies*, 110–17.

19. "Evans's Memorial to Congress," *Denver Daily News*, 23 December 1883; Palmer, President, Denver and Rio Grande Railway Co., Colorado Springs, to "Those Interested in the Denver and Rio Grande Railway," 10 October 1882,

and Palmer, Salinas, Kansas, to Queen Mellen, Flushing, Long Island, 17 January 1870, Palmer Papers; Athearn, *Rebel of the Rockies,* 134–35; and Sprague, *Newport in the Rockies,* 104.

20. Moffat never abandoned plans for a Denver-Salt Lake City connection, and formed the Denver, Northwestern and Pacific Railroad in 1907. Moffat almost threw the FNBD into financial ruin supporting the project, a fact revealed after his death in 1909. The intermontane tunnel was named the Moffat Road. Moffat, President, D&RG, Denver, to G. W. Meylent, President, Commercial Club of Albuquerque, New Mexico, 16 April 1891, Moffat Collection; "Response, Hughes," 9–10; Athearn, *Rebel of the Rockies,* 172–76; and Pulcipher, *First of Denver,* 223.

21. Teller, Washington, D.C., to Daniel W. Working, editor, *The Colorado Farmer,* Denver, 8 April 1890, Daniel W. Working Papers, CHS; and Bradley J. Young, "Silver, Discontent, and Conspiracy: The Ideology of the Western Republican Revolt of 1891–1901," *Pacific Historical Review* 64 (May 1995): 244, 258.

22. Byers lobbied for federal assistance in irrigation as early as 1864. Colorado's first state governor called for huge reservoirs which only the federal government could afford. *Colorado as an Agricultural State,* 12; Worster, *Rivers of Empire: Water, Aridity and the Growth of the American West* (New York: Pantheon Books, 1985); Norris Hundley, Jr., *The Great Thirst: Californians and Water, 1770s–1990s* (Berkeley: University of California Press, 1992); Fite, *Farmers' Frontier,* 129, 135, 187; and Dunbar, *Forging New Rights,* 46. Dry farming in eastern Colorado and other parts of the Great Plains set the stage for the Dust Bowl. Donald Worster, *The Dust Bowl: The Southern Plains in the 1930s* (New York: Oxford University Press, 1979), 87.

23. *Labor Statistics, 1901,* 404; Hodgson, Reminiscences, 24–25; and Ubbelohde, *Colorado History,* 257–59.

24. Hyman Manuscript, 76–78; *Eleventh Report,* DCOC, 58; Meyer, Argentine, Kansas, to Charles Francis Adams, 2 May 1895, August Meyer Collection, CHS; *The Story of Colorado: Farming, Mining and Manufacturing* (Denver: State Board of Immigration, [1918]), 4; Speeches, Henry M. Teller, U.S. Senate, "The Financial Problem and its Solution," 12 January 1895, and "Revenue Not the Remedy: Only the Free Coinage of Silver can restore the Par of Exchange and bring a Return of Prosperity," 29 April 1896, Teller Papers; and Robbins, *Colony and Empire,* 91–92.

25. *There is Gold in Colorado and Plenty of It* (Denver: Rocky Mountain News, [1894]), 3; Hyman Manuscript, 87–90; Abbott, *Colorado,* 120–21; and Davis, *Guggenheims,* 74–76.

26. *Denver Republican,* 23 November 1903; *Ninth Biennial Report of the Inspector of Coal Mines* (Denver: 1900), 119; *Annual Report of the Chamber of Commerce and Board of Trade for the Year 1903* (Denver: Carson-Harper Co., 1904), 30–31; H. Lee Scamehorn, *Mill and Mine: The CF&I in the Twentieth Century* (Lincoln and London: University of Nebraska Press, 1992), 17–20, and *Pioneer Steelmaker,* 166–67; and Abbott, *Colorado,* 122.

27. *Labor Statistics, 1887,* 97–99; Hogan, *Class and Community,* 111–13; Wiebe, *Search for Order,* 8–9; and Cochrane, *Development of American Agriculture,* 95.

28. Colorado Constitution, 1876, Article XVI, Section 2; *Chamber of Commerce, Articles of Incorporation,* Section 4, DCOC Records, DPL; Anne F. Hyde, "Round Pegs in Square Holes: The Rocky Mountains and Extractive Industry," in Wrobel and Steiner, *Many Wests,* 105; and Abbott, *Colorado,* 275–76.

29. Smith, *Rocky Mountain Mining Camps,* 39–40; and Mark Wyman, *Hard Rock Epic: Western Miners and the Industrial Revolution, 1860–1910* (Berkeley and Los Angeles: University of California Press, 1979), 149–74.

30. David Brundage, *The Making of Western Labor Radicalism: Denver's Organized Workers, 1878–1905* (Urbana and Chicago: University of Illinois Press, 1994), 7–8; Hyde, "Round Pegs," 99–100; and Alan Taylor, "Unnatural Inequalities: Social and Environmental Histories," *Environmental History* 1 (October 1996): 15.

31. *Labor Statistics, 1887,* 100–101; *Labor Statistics, 1889,* 120–28; *Labor Statistics, 1901,* Table 1; Smith, *Rocky Mountain West,* 176–77; Brundage, *Making of Western Labor Radicalism,* 56–58; Wyman, *Hard Rock Epic,* 163–65; and Hogan, *Class and Community,* 208.

32. T. J. Jackson Lears, *No Place of Grace: Antimodernism and the Transformation of American Culture, 1880–1920* (New York: Pantheon Books, 1981), 5; and Trachtenberg, *Incorporation of America,* 89–90.

33. Western Federation Constitution, in Smith, *Rocky Mountain West,* 177.

34. *In Re Morgan,* 58 Pacific 1071 (1899); Howbert, *Memories of a Lifetime,* 271; *Report on Labor Disturbances in the State of Colorado from 1880 to 1904 Inclusive* (Washington, D.C.: Government Printing Office, 1905), 75; Emma F. Langdon, *The Cripple Creek Strike* (Denver, 1904), 3; Lipsey, *Lives of John James Hagerman,* 169, 186, 210; and Wyman, *Hard Rock Epic,* 80, 170–71, 212–20.

35. Interview with Governor Waite, Hagerman Committee, 2 June 1894, in Smith, *Rocky Mountain West,* 179; and Organization Statement and Articles of Association, Colorado Mining Association, 12 June 1896, Smith Papers.

36. *Labor Statistics, 1895,* 21; Wyman, *Hard Rock Epic,* 171–72; and Smith, *Rocky Mountain West,* 180–81.

37. The WFM remained strong only in its hometown of Butte. George G. Suggs, Jr., *Colorado's War on Militant Unionism: James H. Peabody and the Western Federation of Miners* (Detroit: Wayne State University Press, 1972), 84–145 passim; Smith, *Rocky Mountain West,* 182–86; and Wyman, *Hard Rock Epic,* 172, 218–22.

38. *Eleventh Biennial Report of the State Coal Mine Inspector, 1903–1904* (Denver: Smith-Brooks Printing Co., 1905), 5; Scamehorn, *Mill and Mine,* 45–46, 52, 56; and Athearn, *Coloradans,* 196–97.

BIBLIOGRAPHY

Manuscripts and Government Documents

Colorado Historical Society
Baca Irrigating Ditch Company Records
William Abraham Bell Papers
George Bent Letters
Bessemer Town Collection
Bill-Jim Mining Company Collection
Mark L. Blunt Collection
John J. Burns Papers
Luke Cahill Manuscript
John F. Campion Collection
Walter Scott Cheesman Papers
Colorado Cattleman's Association Minutes
Colorado Central Railroad Company Collection
Colorado Fuel & Iron Company Collection
Colorado Land and Immigration Company Records
Colorado Midland Railroad Company Collection
Denver Pacific Railway & Telegraph Company Collection
Denver, Texas & Fort Worth Railroad Collection
James Villa Dexter Papers
James Rood Doolittle Papers
Governor John Evans Private Papers
First National Bank of Denver Records
Fort Lyon, Colorado Papers
Edward N. Garbutt Collection
William Gilpin Papers

Grand Junction Fruit Growers' Association Collection

Frank Hall Collection

Edwin Harrison Collection

Henry James Hawley Diary

Nathaniel Peter Hill Collection

Reminiscences of George Hodgson

William A. Hover Collection

J. S. Hoy Collection

David M. Hyman Collection

William S. Jackson Papers

John Lathrop Jerome Papers

Kansas Pacific Railway Company Collection

George Washington Kassler Collection

Stuart Lindley Collection

Samuel Mallory Collection

Manitou & Pike's Peak Railway Collection

Manitou Mineral Springs Foundation Collection

Manitou Mineral Water Company Collection

Matador Land & Cattle Company, Ltd. (Dundee, Scotland) Records

Mechanics' Mining and Trading Company Records

August R. Meyer Collection

David H. Moffat Collection

John Kernan Mullen Collection

Edward Nicholson Collection

William Jackson Palmer Papers

Henry Miller Porter Papers

Prairie Cattle Company Collection

Rossiter Worthington Raymond Collection

Realtors Collection

Frank S. Reardon Papers

Albert Eugene Reynolds Paper

Fred S. Rockwell Collection

Charles Ruter Collection

T. A. Schomburg Collection

Peter G. Scott Collection

Silver Reduction Works (Georgetown) Collection

Thomas Skerritt Papers

Smuggler Consolidated Mining Company (Leadville) Records

Samuel F. Tappan Collection

Senator Henry Moore Teller Papers

Union Colony of Colorado Collection

Robert F. Weitbrec Collection

Jerome B. Wheeler Collection

Daniel W. Working Papers

E. Dunbar Wright Collection

Edward W. Wynkoop Collection

Colorado State Archives

Agricultural Possibilities of Eastern Colorado: Wonderful Opportunities for the Homeseeker or Investor; Lands in Yuma and Washington Counties, Colorado. [Denver: Colorado Board of Immigration, 1909].

Agricultural Statistics of the State of Colorado, Secretary of the State Board of Agriculture.

A Look Back: A Sixty-Five-Year History of the Colorado Game and Fish Department: 1961 Annual Report of the Colorado Game and Fish Department. Denver, 1962.

Forestry in Colorado (First Annual Report of the State Forest Commissioner). Denver: Collier and Cleaveland, [1885].

General Laws and Joint Resolutions, Memorials and Private Acts. Territory of Colorado, 1861–1876.

John Evans Letterbook, Executive Papers, 1861–1870.

Mined Land Reclamation Division, Annual Report for 1988. Denver: Department of Natural Resources, Mined Land Reclamation Division, [1989].

The Natural Resources and Industrial Development and Condition of Colorado. Denver: State Bureau of Immigration and Statistics, 1889.

Proceedings of the Constitutional Convention of Colorado, 1875 and 1876. Denver, 1906.

"Official Information: Colorado," A Statement of Facts Prepared and Published by Authority of the Territorial Board of Immigration. Denver: Rocky Mountain News Steam Printing House, 1872.

The Story of Colorado. Denver: State Board of Immigration, Farming, Mining and Manufacturing Series, [1918].

Reports of the Colorado State Horticultural and Forestry Association

Reports of the Bureau of Labor Statistics of the State of Colorado

Reports of the Fish Commissioner of the State of Colorado

Reports of the Fish Commissioner and Game Warden of State of Colorado

Report of the Forest Commissioner of the State of Colorado

Reports of the Secretary of State of Colorado

Reports of the State Board of Agriculture

Reports of the State Board of Horticulture

Reports of the State Bureau of Mines, Colorado

Reports of the State Forest, Game and Fish Commissioner

Reports of the State Inspector of Coal Mines

Denver Public Library

Arkansas Valley Land and Cattle Company Papers

Michael Beshoar Records

Bobtail Gold Mining Company Records

George S. Bowen Papers

William Henry Brewer Papers

William Newton Byers Papers

Chicago-Colorado Colony Charter and Minutes

Denver Board of Trade Records

Denver Chamber of Commerce, Annual Reports

Denver Chamber of Commerce Records

Harry Faulkner Diary, 1859

Letter from George, Greeley

Greeley Farmer's Club Minutes

Gregory Diggings, 1859

John Hartzell Collection

B. K. Howard Papers

Hubert Mining Company Records

Kountze Family Collection

Harry Lake Notes

Margaret McBride, Notes and Reminiscences

Nathan Cook Meeker Papers

David H. Moffat Papers

Quartz Hill Mining and Tunneling Company Records

Alfred Rockwell Papers

Lewis C. Rockwell Papers

Rocky Mountain National Bank (Central City) Records

Eben Smith Papers

Dennis Sullivan Letters

Henry Moore Teller Letters

Seth Terry Papers

Union Colony Papers

Edward Oliver Wolcott Papers

Dunham Wright, Reminiscences

U.S. Government Reports

Hayden, F. V. *Annual Report to the United States Geographical and Geological Survey of the Territories Embracing Colorado, Being a Report of Progress of the Expedition for the Year 1873.* Washington, D.C.: Government Printing Office, 1874.

Hayden, F. V. *Annual Report to the United States Geographical and Geological Survey.* Washington, D.C.: Government Printing Office, 1876.

Kappler, Charles J., ed. *Indian Affairs Laws and Treaties.* Volume 2. Washington, D.C.: Government Printing Office, 1904.

Powell, John Wesley. *Report on the Lands of the Arid Regions of the United States, with a More Detailed Account of the Lands of Utah.* Washington, D.C.: Government Printing Office, 1879.

Report on Labor Disturbances in the State of Colorado from 1880 to 1904 Inclusive. Washington, D.C.: Government Printing Office, 1905.

Trees Native to the Forests of Colorado and Wyoming. Washington, D.C.: Department of Agriculture, 1908.

Trees Native to the Forests of Colorado and Wyoming. U.S. Department of Agriculture, Forest Service, Rocky Mountain Region, rev. 1945.

U.S. Army Corps of Engineers. *Report of the Exploring Expedition from Santa Fe, New Mexico to the Junction of the Grand and Green Rivers of the Great Colorado of the West, in 1859.* Washington, D.C.: Government Printing Office, 1876.

U.S. Department of the Interior, Bureau of the Census. *Eighth Census of the United States, 1860 Population.* Washington, D.C.: Government Printing Office, 1864.

U.S. Department of the Interior, Bureau of the Census. *Ninth Census of the United States, 1870 Population.* Washington, D.C.: Government Printing Office, 1873.

U.S. Department of the Interior, Bureau of the Census. *Tenth Census of the United States, 1880 Population and Social Statistics.* Washington, D.C.: Government Printing Office, 1880.

Primary Documents

About Colorado Farming; Agriculture by Irrigation in Colorado. Denver: Colorado Land and Loan Co., 1884.

Alamosa Land and Canal Company Brochure.

Aspen, Pitkin County, Colorado: Her Mines and Mineral Resources. Aspen, Colo.: The Aspen Daily Ledger, 1892.

Bald Mountain Mining Company of Leadville Prospectus.

Baskin, O. L. *History of the City of Denver, Arapahoe County and Colorado.* Chicago: O. L. Baskin and Co., 1880.

Bell, William. *New Tracks in North America: A Journal of Travel and Adventures Whilst Engaged in the Survey of a Southern Railroad to the Pacific Ocean, 1867–1868.* 2 Vols. London: Chapman and Hall, 1869.

Beshoar, Michael. *All About Trinidad and Las Animas County, Colorado.* Denver: Times-Steam Printing House and Blank Book Manufactory, 1882.

Bliss, Edward. *A Brief History of the New Gold Regions of Colorado Territory.* Denver, 1864.

Bowles, Samuel. *Across the Continent: A Summer's Journey to the Rocky Mountains, the Mormons, and the Pacific States.* Springfield, Mass.: Samuel Bowles, 1865.

———. *The Switzerland of America.* Springfield, Mass.: Samuel Bowles, 1869.

Boyd, David. *A History: Greeley and the Union Colony of Colorado.* Greeley, Colo.: Greeley Tribune Co., 1890.

The Broadmoor, Colorado Springs, Colorado: European Luxury in the Rockies. Colorado Springs: Colorado Springs Gazette Printing Co., 1896.

Brockett, L. P. *Our Western Empire: Or the New West beyond the Mississippi.* Philadelphia: Bradley, Garretson and Co., 1851.

Buckman, George. *Colorado Springs, Colorado at the Foot of Pike's Peak, Its Manifold Attractions as a Health Resort, a Pleasure Resort, A Scenic Center and a Residence City, Together with a Collection of Medical Facts Concerning Colorado Springs.* Colorado Springs: Gazette Printing Co., 1892.

Bulletin on Fruit Growing in Colorado. Denver: Chamber of Commerce and Board of Trade, [1908].

Burnley, James. *Two Sides of the Atlantic*. London: Simpkin, Marshall, 1880.

Byers, William N. *National Land Company Circular*. Denver, May 1871.

Caldwell, Charles. *Thoughts on the Original Unity of the Human Race*. Cincinnati: J. A. and U. P. James, 1852.

Cattle Canning. Denver: Chamber of Commerce and Board of Trade, 1884.

Chicago-Colorado Colony. Chicago: Republican Printing and Engraving Company, [1871].

Coffin, Morse H. *The Battle of Sand Creek*. Waco, Tex.: Wm. Morrison, 1965.

Colorado as an Agricultural State, the Progress of Irrigation. Denver: The Local Committee of Arrangements for the National Irrigation Congress, 1894.

The Colorado, Glenwood Springs, Colorado: In the Heart of the Rocky Mountains. [N.p.: 1893].

Colorado Mortgage and Investment Company. *Farmlands in Colorado*. Denver: Rocky Mountain News Printing Co., 1879.

Colorado Resources and Industries. Denver: Colorado Midland Railroad Company, 1906.

Constitution of Colorado Springs Mining Stock Association.

Crested Butte, Gunnison County, Colorado: The Great Coal, Coke and Ore Centre of the Gunnison County, Depot for the Only Anthracite Coal West of Pennsylvania. Pueblo(?): Denver and Rio Grande Railroad, 1881.

Crofutt, George A. *Crofutt's Grip-Sack Guide of Colorado*. Omaha: Overland Publishing Co.; Denver: Alvord and Co., 1881.

Davis, Richard Harding. *The West from a Car Window*. New York: Harper and Brothers, 1892.

Denison, Charles. *The Influence of the Climate of Colorado on the Nervous System*. Denver: Richards, 1874.

————. *Rocky Mountain Health Resorts, An Analytical Study of High Altitudes in Relation to the Arrest of Chronic Pulmonary Disease*. Boston: Houghton Mifflin, 1881.

Denver & Rio Grande Railway. Philadelphia, 1870.

The Denver and Rio Grande Railway of Colorado and New Mexico. London, 1871.

Denver & Rio Grande Railway Brochures.

Denver Chamber of Commerce and Board of Trade Articles of Incorporation and By-Laws. Denver: News Printing Company, 1884.

Eggleston, Thomas. *The Boston and Colorado Smelting Works*. Philadelphia: Sherman and Co., 1877.

Farmland in Colorado. Denver: Rocky Mountain News Printing Co., 1879.

A Few Words about Colorado Springs and its New Hotel, the Antlers. Chicago: R. R. Donnelly and Sons, Printers, [1883].

First Annual Report of the Union Colony of Colorado, including a History of the Town of Greeley, from its Date of Settlement to the Present Time. New York: George W. Southwick, 1871.

First Annual Report to the Stockholders of the Denver & Rio Grande Railroad. Denver, 1872.

Fiske, S. A. "Colorado for Invalids." *Popular Science Monthly* 25 (July 1884): 310–14.

Fossett, Frank. *Colorado: Its Gold and Silver Mines, Farms and Stock Ranges, and Health Resorts.* New York: C. G. Crawford, 1879.

Fur, Fin and Feather. Denver: Colorado Midland Railroad Company, 1897.

Gilpin, William. *The Central Gold Region: The Grain, Pastoral and Gold Region of North America.* 1859. Reprint, St. Louis: E. K. Woodward, 1860.

———. *The Cosmopolitan Railway: Compacting and Fusing Together All the World's Continents.* San Francisco: The History Company, 1890.

Glenwood Springs, Colorado: A Health and Pleasure Resort. Glenwood Springs: Glenwood Hot Springs Co., [1891].

The Gold Fields of Colorado. Denver: Denver & Rio Grande Railway, 1896.

Gordon, S. Anna. *Camping in Colorado.* New York: W. B. Smith and Co., 1879.

Grand Junction Chamber of Commerce. *The Valley of the Grand, the Place for You.* Denver: Smith-Brooks Press, [1906].

The Great San Luis Valley, Colorado: Sunshine, Irrigation, Independence. Issued by the Alamosa Land and Canal Company, Alamosa, Colorado. Denver: C. F. Hoeckel, Printer, 1892.

Greatorex, Eliza. *Summer Etchings in Colorado.* New York: G. P. Putnam's Sons, 1873.

Greeley, Horace. *An Overland Journey: From New York to San Francisco in the Summer of 1859.* New York: C. M. Saxon, Barker, 1860.

Hall, Frank. *The Early Seekers for Gold in Colorado: The Exploration of "The Louisiana Purchase." Pamphlet of Historical Information for the Prospector.* 1860. Reprint, Denver: Mineral Department of the State Board of Land Commissioners, 1934.

———. *The History of Colorado.* 4 Vols. Chicago: Blakely Printing Co., 1889–1995.

Hayes, A. A., Jr. *New Colorado and the Santa Fe Trail.* London: C. Kegan Paul and Co., 1881.

The Health Resorts of Colorado Springs and Manitou. Colorado Springs: Gazette Publishing Co., [1883].

Health, Wealth and Recreation: Idaho Springs, Colorado. Issued by the Chamber of Commerce of Idaho Springs. Denver: Smith-Brooks Printing Co., [1902].

The Heart of the Continent. Chicago: Rand McNally and Co., 1892.

Historical and Descriptive Review of Colorado's Enterprising Cities: Their Leading Business Houses and Progressive Men. Denver: Jno. Lethem, 1893.

History of the Arkansas Valley, Colorado. Chicago: O. L. Baskin and Co., 1881.

Hollister, Ovando J. *Colorado Volunteers in New Mexico.* 1863. Reprint, Chicago: Lakeside Press, 1962.

———. *The Mines of Colorado.* Springfield, Mass.: S. Bowles, 1867.

Hooper, S. K. *The Fertile Lands of Colorado.* Denver: Denver & Rio Grande Railroad, 1899.

Howbert, Irving. *The Indians of the Pike's Peak Region.* New York: Knickerbocker Press, 1914.

———. *Memories of a Lifetime in the Pike's Peak Region.* New York and London: G. P. Putnam's Sons, 1925.

Hyde, George E. *Life of George Bent, Written from his Letters.* Edited by Savoie Lottinville. Norman: University of Oklahoma Press, 1968.

Idaho Springs, Colorado. Idaho Springs: Chamber of Commerce, [1902].

Iddings, Lewis. "Life in the Altitudes: The Colorado Health Plateau." *Scribner's* 19 (1896): 143–47.

Immigrant's Guide to the Great San Luis Park. Denver: Republican Publishing Co., 1884.

Ingersoll, Ernest. *Knocking Round the Rockies.* New York: Harper and Brothers, 1883.

In Summer, Fall or Winter, Go Visit the Great Rocky Mountain Resorts of Colorado Via the Kansas Pacific Railway. Chicago: Rand McNally and Co., 1875.

Jackson, Helen Hunt. *Bits of Travel at Home.* Cambridge, Mass.: Roberts Brothers, 1878.

———. *A Century of Dishonor: A Sketch of the United States Government's Dealings with Some of the Indian Tribes.* New York: Harpers, 1881.

———. *Ramona.* 1884. Reprint, Boston: Little, Brown and Co., 1903.

"Jerome B. Wheeler and Pitkin County." *Frank Leslie's Illustrated Newspaper* 68 (22 February 1890): 68.

Langdon, Emma F. *The Cripple Creek Strike.* Denver: Great Western Publishing Co., 1904.

Larimer, William Henry Harrison. *Reminiscences of General William Larimer and His Son William H. H. Larimer.* Lancaster, Pa.: New Era Printing, 1918.

Leadville: A Silver Setting in a Sea of Silver. Leadville, Colo.: John Nowland and Company, 1890.

Legislative, Historical and Biographical Compendium of Colorado. Denver: C. F. Coleman, 1887.

Lomax, E. L. *Colorado: Resources of the State, Population, Industries, Opportunities, Climate, Etc.* Omaha: Union Pacific Railroad Company, 1906.

Majors, Alexander. *Seventy Years on the Frontier.* Chicago and New York: Rand, McNally and Co., 1893.

Marcy, Col. R. B. *Thirty Years of Army Life on the Border.* New York: Harper and Bros., 1866.

McCloud, Richard. *Durango as It Is.* Durango, Colo.: Durango Board of Trade, 1892.

"Memorial of H. M. Teller Remonstrating Against the Admission of Colorado as a State into the Union," 40th Congress, 20 February 1868. Washington, D.C.: Government Printing Office, 1868.

Mills, Enos A. *Wild Life on the Rockies.* 1909. Reprint, Lincoln and London: University of Nebraska Press, 1988.

Mills, Enos, A., and W. G. M. Stone. *Forests and Exotic Trees of Colorado.* Denver: Colorado State Forestry Association, 1905.

Mills, Jared Warner. *Mills' Constitutional Annotations.* Chicago: E. B. Myers and Co., 1890.

Moore, Charles J. *Leadville, Up-to-Date Literature concerning the "Greatest Mining Camp on Earth."* Leadville, Colo.: Press of the Herald Democrat, [1895].

Morton, Samuel George. *Crania Americana or, a Comparative View of the Skulls of Various Aboriginal Nations of North and South America. To Which is Prefixed an Essay on the Varieties of the Human Species.* Philadelphia: J. Dobson, London, Simpkin, Marshall, 1839.

Nesmith, J. W. *The Interests of Colorado in the Iron and Steel Manufacture.* Denver: Press of C. J. Kelly, 1890.

The Official Manual of the Cripple Creek District. Colorado Springs: Fred Hills, 1902.

Our New Saratoga: Colorado Springs and La Font. Denver, 1871.

Pabor, William E. *Colorado as an Agricultural State.* New York: Orange Judd Company, 1889.

Pike's Peak by Rail. Manitou: Manitou and Pike's Peak Railway, 1893.

Porter, Henry M. *Autobiography of Henry M. Porter.* Denver: World Press, 1932.

———. *Pencilings of an Early Pioneer.* Denver: World Press, 1929.

Prospectus, Articles of Incorporation and By-Laws of the Cache La Poudre Irrigating Company. Greeley, Colo.: Greeley Tribune Book and Job Printing, 1878.

The Pueblo Colony of Southern Colorado. Lancaster, Pa.: Enquirer Printing and Publishing Co., 1879.

Pueblo, Colorado: Its Resources and Developments. Pueblo: The Daily Chieftain, [1891].

Resources and Attractions of Colorado for the Home Seeker, Capitalist, and Tourist. Chicago: Rand, McNally and Co., 1899.

Resources of Colorado. Issued by Board of Trade of Denver City, Colorado. Brooklyn, N.Y.: The Union Steam Presses, 1868.

Richardson, Albert D. *Beyond the Mississippi: From the Great River to the Great Ocean.* Hartford, Conn.: Times Press, 1867.

Roberts, Edward. *Colorado Springs and Manitou.* Colorado Springs: Gazette Publishing Co., 1883.

Rolker, Charles. "Report on the Property of The Colorado Coal & Iron Co." New York: Jno. C. Rankin, Jr., 1884.

Russling, James. *Across America: Or the Great West and the Pacific Coast.* New York: Sheldon, 1874.

Sebastian, John. *Under the Turquoise Sky in Colorado.* Chicago: Rock Island-Frisco Lines, 1907.

Silver Plume Mines and Scenery. Silver Plume, Colo.: Board of Mines and Trade, [1903].

Sketch of the Pueblos and Pueblo County, Colorado. Pueblo: Board of Trade, Chieftain Steam Print, 1883.

Smiley, Jerome. *History of Denver.* Denver: Sun Publishing, 1901.

Solly, Samuel Edwin. *Colorado for Invalids.* Colorado Springs: Gazette Pub. Co., 1880.

———. *Manitou, Colorado, U.S.A., its Mineral Waters and Climate.* St. Louis: Jno. McKittrick & Co., 1875.

Statistical History of Clear Creek County from 1859–1881. Georgetown, Colo.: Miners Printing Co., [1882].

Strahorn, Robert E. *Gunnison and San Juan.* Omaha: The New West Publishing Co., 1881.

———. *To the Rockies and Beyond, or a Summer on the Union Pacific Railroad and Branches, Sauntering in the Popular Health, Pleasure and Hunting Resorts of Nebraska, Dakota, Wyoming, Colorado, New Mexico, Utah, and Idaho.* Omaha: Omaha Republican Press, 1881.

Summer in Colorado. Denver: Richards and Co., 1874.

Sunny Colorado: The Healthful Winter Resort. Burlington Route, 1905.

There is Gold in Colorado and Plenty of It: How and Where to Find It, Being a Compilation of the Latest Information Concerning the Gold Resources of Colorado, including the history of the revival of the old gold camps and the discoveries of many new ones. Denver: Rocky Mountain News, [1894].

Tice, John H. *Over the Plains and on the Mountains.* St. Louis: Industrial Age Printing Co., 1872.

Townsend, R. B. *A Tenderfoot in Colorado.* London: Chapman and Hall, 1873.

Townshend, Samuel Nugent. *Colorado: Its Agriculture, Stockfeeding, Scenery and Shooting.* London: The Field Office, 1879.

The Ute War: A History of the White River Massacre and the Privations and Hardships of the Captive White Women among the Hostiles on Grand River. Denver: Denver Tribune Printing Co., 1879.

Villa La Font: The Fountain Colony. Denver, 1871.

Villard, Henry. *The Past and Present of the Pike's Peak Gold Regions.* St. Louis: Sutherland and McEvoy, 1860.

Wallihan, Samuel S. and T. O. Bigney, eds. *Rocky Mountain Directory and Colorado Gazetteer for 1871.* Denver: S. S. Wallihan and Co., 1870.

Warren, Henry Lee Jacques. *Cripple Creek and Colorado Springs; A Review and Panorama of an Unique Gold Field, with Geologic Features and Achievements of Five Eventful Years, Including Outlines of Numerous Companies.* Colorado Springs: Warren and Stride, 1896.

Wharton, Junius. *History of the City of Denver from Its Earliest Times.* Denver: Byers and Dailey, 1866.

When in Colorado. Denver: C. J. Kelly Printer and Bookbinder, 1894.

Legal Cases

Coffin v. Left Hand Ditch Co. (1882), 6 Colo. 443.

In Re Casual Deficiency (1895), 21 Colo. 403.

In Re Morgan (1899), 58 Pacific 1071.

Siedler v. Seeley (1896), 8 Colo. App. 499.

Tameling v. U.S. Freehold & Emigration Co. (1874), 93 U.S. 644.

U.S. v. Maxwell Land Grant Company (1887), 121 U.S. 325.

Wheeler v. Northern Colorado Irrigation Co. (1887), 10 Colo. 582.

Wyatt v. Larimer & Weld Irrigation Co. (1893), 18 Colo. 298.

Yunker v. Nichols (1872), 1 Colo. 551.

Newspapers

Colorado Chieftain (later, *Pueblo Daily Chieftain*), 1871–1900.

Colorado Springs Gazette (Gazette-Telegraph), 1871–1946.

Daily Mining Journal (Black Hawk, Colo.), 1864–1867.

Denver Daily Commonwealth and Republican, 1864.

Denver Republican, 1901.

Denver Times, 1865.

Denver Tribune, 1867–1877.

Engineering and Mining Journal, 1877–1891.

Greeley Tribune, 1874.

Miner's Register (Central City, Colo.),1862–1868.

Rocky Mountain News (Denver), 1859–1901.

Western Mountaineer (Denver), 1860.

Secondary Sources

Books

Abbott, Carl. *Colorado: A History of the Centennial State.* Boulder: Colorado Associated University Press, 1976.

Alberts, Donald E. *The Battle of Glorieta.* College Station: Texas A&M University Press, 1998.

Alexander, Thomas G., and James B. Allen. *Mormons and Gentiles: A History of Salt Lake City.* Boulder, Colo.: Pruett Publishing Co., 1984.

Anderson, George L. *General William J. Palmer: A Decade of Colorado Railroad Building, 1870–1880.* Colorado Springs: Colorado College, 1936.

Athearn, Robert G. *The Coloradans.* Albuquerque: University of New Mexico Press, 1976.

———. *Rebel of the Rockies: A History of the Denver and Rio Grande Western Railroad.* New Haven and London: Yale University Press, 1962.

Atherton, Lewis. *The Cattle Kings.* Bloomington: Indiana University Press, 1961.

Barth, Gunther. *Instant Cities: Urbanization and the Rise of San Francisco and Denver.* New York: Oxford University Press, 1965.

Bates, Barbara. *Bargaining for Life: A Social History of Tuberculosis, 1876–1938.* Philadelphia: University of Pennsylvania Press, 1992.

Bender, Thomas. *Toward an Urban Vision: Ideas and Institutions in Nineteenth-Century America.* Lexington: University Press of Kentucky, 1975.

Berk, Gerald. *Alternative Tracks: The Constitution of the American Industrial Order, 1865–1917.* Baltimore: Johns Hopkins University Press, 1994.

Berkhofer, Robert F., Jr. *The White Man's Indian: Images of the American Indian from Columbus to the Present.* New York: Alfred A. Knopf, 1978.

Berthrong, Donald J. *The Southern Cheyenne.* Norman: University of Oklahoma, 1963.

Bieder, Robert E. *Contemplating Others: Cultural Contacts in Red and White America: An Annotated Bibliography on the North American Indian.* Berlin:

John F. Kennedy-Institut für Nordamerikastudien, Freie Universität Berlin, 1990.

―――――. *Science Encounters the Indian, 1820–1880: The Early Years of American Ethnology.* Norman: University of Oklahoma Press, 1986.

Bogue, Allan G., and Margaret Beattie Bogue, eds. *The Jeffersonian Dream: Studies in the History of American Land Policy and Development.* Albuquerque: University of New Mexico Press, 1996.

Brayer, Herbert O. *William Blackmore.* Vols. 1 and 2. Denver: Bradford-Robinson, 1949.

Brechin, Gray. *Imperial San Francisco: Urban Power, Earthly Ruin.* Berkeley: University of California Press, 1999.

Briggs, Charles L., and John R. Van Ness, eds. *Land, Water, and Culture: New Perspectives on Hispanic Land Grants.* Albuquerque: University of New Mexico Press, 1987.

Brown, Dona. *Inventing New England: Regional Tourism in the Nineteenth Century.* Washington, D.C.: Smithsonian Institution Press, 1995.

Brundage, David. *The Making of Western Labor Radicalism: Denver's Organized Workers, 1878–1905.* Urbana and Chicago: University of Illinois Press, 1994.

Camby, Henry S., ed. *The Works of Thoreau.* Boston: Houghton Mifflin, 1937.

Cochrane, Willard Wesley. *The Development of American Agriculture: A Historical Analysis.* 2d ed. Minneapolis: University of Minnesota Press, 1993.

Coel, Margaret. *Chief Left Hand: Southern Arapaho.* Norman: University of Oklahoma Press, 1981.

Courtwright, David T. *Violent Land: Single Men and Social Disorder from the Frontier to the Inner City.* Cambridge: Harvard University Press, 1996.

Craig, Reginald. *The Fighting Parson, the Biography of Colonel John M. Chivington.* Los Angeles: Westernlore Press, 1959.

Cronon, William. *Nature's Metropolis: Chicago and the Great West.* New York: W. W. Norton and Company, 1991.

Cronon, William, ed. *Uncommon Ground: Toward Reinventing Nature.* New York: W. W. Norton and Co., 1995.

Cronon, William, George Miles, and Jay Gitlin, eds. *Under an Open Sky: Rethinking America's Western Past.* New York and London: W. W. Norton and Co., 1992.

Dale, Edward Everett. *The Range Cattle Industry.* Norman: University of Oklahoma Press, 1930.

Davis, John H. *The Guggenheims: An American Epic.* New York: William Morrow and Company, 1978.

Deutsch, Sarah. *No Separate Refuge: Culture, Class, and Gender on an Anglo-Hispanic Frontier in the American Southwest, 1880–1940.* New York: Oxford University Press, 1987.

Dorsett, Lyle W. *The Queen City: A History of Denver.* Boulder, Colo.: Pruett Publishing Company, 1977.

Dunbar, Robert G. *Forging New Rights in Western Waters.* Lincoln and London: University of Nebraska Press, 1983.

Dunn, William R. *"I Stand by Sand Creek."* Fort Collins, Colo.: Old Army Press, 1985.

Ebright, Malcolm. *Land Grants and Lawsuits in Northern New Mexico.* Albuquerque: University of New Mexico Press, 1994.

Ellis, Elmer. *Henry Moore Teller, Defender of the West.* Caldwell, Idaho: The Caxton Printers, 1941.

Emmons, David M. *Garden in the Grasslands.* Lincoln: University of Nebraska Press, 1971.

Fell, James E., Jr. *Ores to Metals: The Rocky Mountain Smelting Industry.* Lincoln: University of Nebraska Press, 1979.

Fifer, J. Valerie. *American Progress: The Growth of the Transport, Tourist, and Information Industries in the Nineteenth Century West seen through The Life and Times of George A. Crofutt, Pioneer and Publicist of the Transcontinental Age.* Chester, Conn.: Globe Pequot Press, 1988.

Fite, Gilbert C. *The Farmers' Frontier, 1865–1900.* New York: Holt, Rinehart and Winston, 1966.

Fleharty, Eugene. *Wild Animals and Settlers on the Great Plains.* Norman: University of Oklahoma Press, 1995.

Foster, Mark S. *Henry M. Porter: Rocky Mountain Empire Builder.* Niwot, Colo.: University Press of Colorado, 1991.

Frankenberg, Ruth. *White Women, Race Matters: The Social Construction of Whiteness.* Minneapolis: University of Minnesota Press, 1993.

Friedman, Lawrence M. *A History of American Law.* 2d ed. New York: Simon and Schuster, 1985.

Gates, Paul W. *History of Public Land Law Development.* Washington, D.C.: U.S. Government Printing Office, 1968.

Ghost Towns of Colorado. American Guide Series. New York: Hastings House, 1947. Compiled by Workers of the Writers' Program of the Work Projects Administration in the State of Colorado.

Goff, Richard, and Robert H. McCaffree. *A Century in the Saddle.* Denver: Colorado Cattleman's Centennial Commission, 1967.

Green, Nicholas. *The Spectacle of Nature.* Manchester: Manchester University Press, 1990.

Gressley, Gene M. *Bankers and Cattlemen.* New York: Alfred A. Knopf, 1966.

Griswold, Donald L., and Jean Harvey Griswold. *The Carbonate Camp Called Leadville.* Denver: Denver University Press, 1951.

Grossman, James R., ed. *The Frontier in American Culture.* Berkeley: University of California Press, 1994.

Guice, John D. W. *The Rocky Mountain Bench: The Territorial Supreme Courts of Colorado, Montana, and Wyoming, 1861–1890.* New Haven: Yale University Press, 1972.

Hafen, LeRoy R., ed. *Pike Peak's Gold Rush Guidebooks of 1859.* Vols. 9 and 10. Glendale, Calif.: Arthur H. Clark Company, 1941–1942.

Hafen, LeRoy R., and Ann W. Hafen, eds. *Reports from Colorado: The Wildman Letters, 1859–1865.* Glendale, Calif.: Arthur H. Clark Company, 1961.

Hamer, David. *New Towns in the New World: Images and Perceptions of the Nineteenth-Century Urban Frontier.* New York: Columbia University Press, 1990.

Hareven, Tamara K., ed. *Anonymous Explorations in Nineteenth-Century Social History.* Englewood Cliffs, N.J.: Prentice-Hall, 1971.

Hogan, Richard. *Class and Community in Frontier Colorado.* Lawrence: University Press of Kansas, 1990.

Hoig, Stan. *The Sand Creek Massacre.* Norman: University of Oklahoma Press, 1961.

Horsman, Reginald. *Race and Manifest Destiny: The Origins of American Racial Anglo-Saxism.* Cambridge: Harvard University Press, 1981.

Horwitz, Morton J. *The Transformation of American Law, 1780–1860.* Cambridge: Harvard University Press, 1977.

Hoyt, Edwin P., Jr. *The Guggenheims and the American Dream.* New York: Funk and Wagnalls, [1967].

Huber, Thomas. *Colorado: The Place of Nature, the Nature of Place.* Niwot: University Press of Colorado, 1993.

Hughes, Donald J. *American Indians in Colorado.* Boulder, Colo.: Pruett Publishing Co., 1977.

Hundley, Norris, Jr. *Water and the West: The Colorado River Compact and the Politics of Water in the American West.* Berkeley and Los Angeles: University of California Press, 1966.

———. *The Great Thirst: Californians and Water, 1770s–1990s.* Berkeley: University of California Press, 1992.

Hurst, James Willard. *Law and the Conditions of Freedom in the Nineteenth-Century United States.* Madison: University of Wisconsin Press, 1956.

———. *Law and Economic Growth: The Legal History of the Lumber Industry in Wisconsin, 1836–1915.* Cambridge, Mass.: Harvard University Press, 1964.

Hyde, Anne Farrar. *An American Vision: Far Western Landscape and National Culture, 1820–1920.* New York and London: New York University Press, 1990.

Irwin, William. *The New Niagara: Tourism, Technology, and the Landscape of Niagara Falls, 1776–1917.* University Park: Pennsylvania State University Press, 1996.

Jackson, Donald, ed. *The Journals of Zebulon Montgomery Pike, with Letters and Related Documents.* Norman: University of Oklahoma Press, 1966.

Jones, Oakah L. *Los Paisanos: Spanish Settlers on the Northern Frontier of New Spain.* Norman: University of Oklahoma Press, 1979.

Josephy, Alvin M., Jr. *The Civil War in the American West.* New York: Alfred A. Knopf, 1991.

Kasson, John F. *Rudeness and Civility: Manners in Nineteenth-Century Urban America.* New York: Hill and Wang, 1990.

Kelsey, Harry E., Jr. *Frontier Capitalist: The Life of John Evans.* Denver: Pruett Publishing Co., 1969.

Klein, Maury. *The Life and Legend of Jay Gould.* Baltimore: Johns Hopkins University, 1986.

Klyza, Christopher McGrory. *Who Controls Public Lands? Mining, Forestry, and Grazing Policies, 1870–1990.* Chapel Hill: University of North Carolina Press, 1996.

Knobloch, Frieda. *The Culture of Wilderness: Agriculture as Colonization in the American West.* Chapel Hill: University of North Carolina Press, 1996.

Kulikoff, Allan. *The Agrarian Origins of American Capitalism.* Charlottesville and London: University Press of Virginia, 1992.

Lamar, Howard Roberts. *The Far Southwest, 1846–1912: A Territorial History.* 1966. Reprint, New York: W. W. Norton and Co., 1970.

Larsen, Lawrence H., and Barbara J. Cottrell. *The Gate City: A History of Omaha.* Boulder, Colo.: Pruett Publishing Co., 1982.

Lears, T. J. Jackson. *No Place of Grace: Antimodernism and the Transformation of American Culture, 1880–1920.* New York: Pantheon Books, 1981.

Lecompte, Janet. *Pueblo, Hardscrabble, Greenhorn: The Upper Arkansas, 1832–1856.* Norman: University of Oklahoma Press, 1978.

Leonard, Stephen J., and Thomas J. Noel. *Denver: Mining Camp to Metropolis.* Niwot: University Press of Colorado, 1990.

Limerick, Patricia Nelson, Clyde A. Milner II, and Charles E. Rankin, eds. *Trails toward a New Western History.* Lawrence: University Press of Kansas, 1991.

Lipsey, John. *The Lives of James John Hagerman: Builder of the Colorado Midland Railway.* Denver: Golden Bell Press, 1968.

MacCannell, Dean. *The Tourist: A New Theory of the Leisure Class.* New York: Schocken Books, 1976.

Mahoney, Timothy R. *River Towns in the Great West: The Structure of Provincial Urbanization in the American Midwest, 1820–1870.* Cambridge: Cambridge University Press, 1990.

Marsh, Charles S. *People of the Shining Mountain.* Boulder, Colo.: Pruett Publishing Co., 1982.

Marsh, George Perkins. *Man and Nature: or, Physical Geography as Modified by Human Action.* Edited by David Lowenthal. Cambridge, Mass.: Belknap Press of Harvard University Press, 1965.

Marshall, James. *Santa Fe: The Railroad That Built an Empire.* New York: Random House, 1945.

Mathes, Valerie Sherer. *Helen Hunt Jackson and Her Indian Reform Legacy.* Austin: University of Texas Press, 1990.

May, Dean L. *Three Frontiers: Family, Land and Society in the American West, 1850–1900.* New York: Cambridge University Press, 1994.

McEvoy, Arthur F. *The Fisherman's Problem: Ecology and Law in the California Fisheries, 1850–1950.* Cambridge: Cambridge University Press, 1986.

Mehls, Steven F. *The Valley of Opportunity: A History of West-Central Colorado.* Denver: Bureau of Land Management, 1982.

Meinig, D. W. *The Interpretation of Ordinary Landscapes.* New York: Oxford University Press, 1979.

Melville, Elinor G. K. *A Plague of Sheep: Environmental Consequences of the Conquest of Mexico.* Cambridge: Cambridge University Press, 1994.

Milner, Clyde A., II, Carol O'Connor, and Martha A. Sandweiss, eds. *The Oxford History of the American West.* New York: Oxford University Press, 1994.

Mitchell, Robert D. and Paul A. Groves, eds. *North America: The Historical Geography of a Changing Continent.* Totowa, N.J.: Rowman and Littlefield, 1987.

Moffat, Riley. *Population History of Western U.S. Cities and Towns, 1850–1990.* Lanham, Md., and London: Scarecrow Press, 1996.

Mohl, Raymond, ed. *Searching for the Sunbelt: Historical Perspectives on a Region.* Knoxville: University of Tennessee Press, 1990.

Monkkonen, Eric. *America Becomes Urban: The Development of U.S. Cities and Towns, 1780–1980.* Berkeley: University of California Press, 1988.

Mumey, Nolie. *History of the Early Settlements of Denver (1599–1860).* Glendale, Calif.: Arthur H. Clark Company, 1942.

Nobles, Gregory H. *American Frontiers: Cultural Encounters and Continental Conquest.* New York: Hill and Wang, 1977.

Noel, Thomas J. *The City and the Saloon: Denver, 1858–1916.* Lincoln and London: University of Nebraska Press, 1982.

Norris, Jane E., and Lee G. Norris. *Written in Water: The Life of Benjamin Harrison Eaton.* Athens: University of Ohio Press, 1990.

Nostrand, Richard L. *The Hispano Homeland*. Norman: University of Oklahoma Press, 1992.

Novak, William J. *The People's Welfare: Law and Regulation in Nineteenth-Century America*. Chapel Hill and London: University of North Carolina Press, 1996.

Opie, John. *The Law of the Land: Two Hundred Years of American Farmland Policy*. Lincoln: University of Nebraska Press, 1987.

Ott, Katherine. *Fevered Lives: Tuberculosis in American Culture since 1870*. Cambridge, Mass.: Harvard University Press, 1997.

Paul, Rodman. *The Far West and the Great Plains in Transition, 1859–1900*. New York: Harper and Row, 1988.

———. *Mining Frontiers of the Far West*. New York: Holt, Rinehart and Winston, 1963.

———, ed. *A Victorian Gentlewoman in the Far West: Reminiscences of Mary Hallock Foote*. San Marino, Calif.: Huntington Library, 1972.

Peake, Ora Brooks. *The Colorado Range Cattle Industry*. Glendale, Calif.: Arthur H. Clark Company, 1937.

Pearce, W. M. *The Matador Land and Cattle Company*. Norman: University of Oklahoma, 1964.

Pearson, Jim Berry. *The Maxwell Land Grant*. Norman: University of Oklahoma Press, 1961.

Peterson, Merrill. *Thomas Jefferson and the New Nation, A Biography*. New York: Oxford University Press, 1970.

Pisani, Donald J. *To Reclaim a Divided West: Water, Law, and Public Policy, 1848–1902*. Albuquerque: University of New Mexico Press, 1992.

———. *Water, Land, and Law in the West: The Limits of Public Policy, 1850–1920*. Lawrence: University Press of Kansas, 1996.

Pomeroy, Earl. *In Search of the Golden West: The Tourist in Western America*. New York: Alfred A. Knopf, 1957.

———. *The Pacific Slope: A History of California, Oregon, Washington, Idaho, Utah, and Nevada*. New York: Alfred A. Knopf, 1966.

Prucha, Francis Paul. *American Indian Treaties: The History of a Political Anomaly*. Berkeley: University of California Press, 1994.

Pulcipher, Robert S. *First of Denver . . . A History*. Denver: Robert S. Pulcipher and the First National Bank of Denver, 1971.

Pyne, Stephen. *How the Canyon Became Grand: A Short History*. New York: Penguin Books, 1998.

Reps, John W. *Cities of the American West*. Princeton, N.J.: Princeton University Press, 1974.

———. *The Making of Urban America: A History of City Planning in the United States*. Princeton, N.J.: Princeton University Press, 1965.

Robbins, William G. *Colony and Empire: The Capitalist Transformation of the American West.* Lawrence: University Press of Kansas, 1994.

Rohrbough, Malcolm. *Aspen: The History of a Silver-Mining Town, 1879–1893.* New York: Oxford University Press, 1986.

Rothman, Sheila M. *Living in the Shadow of Death: Tuberculosis and the Social Experience of Illness in America.* New York: BasicBooks, 1994.

Saxton, Alexander. *The Rise and Fall of the White Republic: Class Politics and Mass Culture in Nineteenth-Century America.* London and New York: Verso, 1990.

Scamehorn, H. Lee. *Albert Eugene Reynolds: Colorado's Mining King.* Norman and Lincoln: University of Oklahoma Press, 1995.

———. *Mill and Mine: The CF&I in the Twentieth Century.* Lincoln and London: University of Nebraska Press, 1992.

———. *Pioneer Steelmaker of the West: The Colorado Fuel and Iron Company, 1872–1903.* Boulder, Colo.: Pruett Publishing Company, 1974.

Scott, Bob. *Blood at Sand Creek: The Massacre Revisited.* Caldwell, Idaho: The Caxton Printers, 1994.

Sears, John F. *Sacred Places: American Tourist Attractions in the Nineteenth Century.* New York: Oxford University Press, 1989.

Sherow, James Earl. *Watering the Valley: Development along the High Plains Arkansas River, 1870–1950.* Lawrence: University Press of Kansas, 1990.

Simmons, Virginia McConnell. *The Upper Arkansas: A Mountain River Valley.* Boulder, Colo.: Pruett Press, 1990.

Smedley, Audrey. *Race in North America: Origin and Evolution of a Worldview.* Boulder: University of Colorado Press, 1993.

Smith, Duane A. *Horace Tabor: His Life and the Legend.* Boulder: Colorado Associated University Press, 1973.

———. *Mining America: The Industry and the Environment, 1800–1980.* Lawrence: University Press of Kansas, 1987.

———. *Rocky Mountain Boom Town: A History of Durango, Colorado.* Boulder, Colo.: Pruett Publishing Co., 1980.

———. *Rocky Mountain Mining Camps: The Urban Frontier.* Bloomington: Indiana University Press, 1967.

———. *Rocky Mountain West: Colorado, Wyoming, and Montana, 1859–1915.* Albuquerque: University of New Mexico Press, 1992.

———. *Silver Saga: The Story of Caribou, Colorado.* Boulder, Colo.: Pruett Publishing, 1974.

———. *When Coal Was King: A History of Crested Butte, Colorado, 1880–1952.* Golden: Colorado School of Mines Press, 1984.

Smith, Henry Nash. *Virgin Land: The American West as Symbol and Myth.* 1950. Reprint, Cambridge, Mass.: Harvard University Press, 1970.

Spence, Clark C. *British Investments and the American Mining Frontier, 1860–1901.* Ithaca, N.Y.: Cornell University Press, 1958.

———. *Mining Engineers and the American West: The Boot-Lace Brigade, 1849–1933.* New Haven, Conn.: Yale University Press, 1970.

Spence, Mark. *Dispossessing the Wilderness: Indian Removal and the Making of the National Parks.* New York: Oxford University Press, 1979.

Sprague, Marshall. *Money Mountain: The Story of Cripple Creek Gold.* 1953. Reprint, Lincoln and London: University of Nebraska Press, 1979.

———. *Newport in the Rockies: The Life and Good Times of Colorado Springs.* 1961. Reprint, Chicago: Sage Books, 1971.

Stegmaier, Mark J., and David H. Miller, eds. *James F. Milligan: His Journal of Fremont's Fifth Expedition, 1853–1854; His Adventurous Life on Land and Sea.* Glendale, Calif.: Arthur H. Clark Co., 1988.

Steinberg, Theodore. *Slide Mountain: Or, the Folly of Owning Nature.* Berkeley and Los Angeles: University of California Press, 1995.

Steinel, Alvin T. *History of Agriculture in Colorado.* Fort Collins, Colo.: State Agricultural College, 1926.

Suggs, George G., Jr. *Colorado's War on Militant Unionism: James H. Peabody and the Western Federation of Miners.* Detroit: Wayne State University Press, 1972.

Svaldi, David. *Sand Creek and the Rhetoric of Extermination.* Latham, Md.: University Press of America, 1989.

Sweezy, Carl. *The Arapaho Way.* Edited by Althea Bass. New York: Clarkson N. Potter, 1966.

Taylor, Morris F. *O. P. McMains and the Maxwell Land Grant Conflict.* Tucson: University of Arizona Press, 1979.

Thwaites, Reuben G., ed. *Early Western Travels, 1748–1846.* Vol. 15. New York: AMS Press, 1966.

Trachtenberg, Alan. *The Incorporation of America: Culture and Society in the Gilded Age.* New York: Hill and Wang, 1982.

Trenholm, Virginia Cole. *The Arapaho, Our People.* Norman: University of Oklahoma Press, 1970.

Ubbelohde, Carl, Maxine Benson, and Duane A. Smith. *A Colorado History.* 6th ed. Boulder, Colo.: Pruett Publishing Co., 1988.

———. *A Colorado Reader.* Boulder, Colo.: Pruett Publishing Company, 1962.

Underwood, Kathleen. *Town Building on the Colorado Frontier.* Albuquerque: University of New Mexico Press, 1987.

Van Ness, John R., and Christine M. Van Ness, eds. *Spanish and Mexican Land Grants in New Mexico and Colorado.* Manhattan, Kans.: Sunflower University Press, 1980.

Voynick, Stephen M. *Leadville: A Miner's Epic.* Missoula, Montana: Mountain Press, 1984.

Wade, Richard. *The Urban Frontier: The Rise of Western Cities, 1790–1830.* 1959. Reprint, *The Urban Frontier: Pioneer Life in Early Pittsburgh, Cincinnati, Lexington, Louisville, and St. Louis.* Chicago: University of Chicago Press, Phoenix Books, 1964.

Ware, Vron. *Beyond the Pale: White Women, Racism and History.* London: Verso, 1992.

Webb, Walter Prescott. *The Great Plains.* Boston: Ginn and Co., 1931.

West, Elliott. *The Contested Plains: Indians, Goldseekers, and the Rush to Colorado.* Lawrence: University Press of Kansas, 1998.

————. *Growing Up with the Country: Childhood on the Far Western Frontier.* Albuquerque: University of New Mexico Press, 1989.

————. *The Saloon on the Rocky Mountain Mining Frontier.* Lincoln and London: University of Nebraska Press, 1979.

————. *The Way to the West: Essays on the Central Plains.* Albuquerque: University of New Mexico Press, 1995.

White, G. Edward. *The Eastern Establishment and the Western Experience: The West of Frederic Remington, Theodore Roosevelt, and Owen Wister.* New Haven, Conn.: Yale University Press, 1968.

White, Richard. *"It's Your Misfortune and None of My Own": A New History of the American West.* Norman and London: University of Oklahoma Press, 1991.

————. *The Organic Machine: The Remaking of the Columbia River.* New York: Hill and Wang, 1995.

Whittaker, Milo L. *Pathbreakers and Pioneers of the Pueblo Region.* Philadelphia: Milo L. Whittaker, 1917.

Wiebe, Robert H. *The Search for Order, 1877–1920.* New York: Hill and Wang, 1967.

Wiley, Peter, and Robert Gottlieb. *Empires in the Sun: The Rise of the New American West.* New York: G. P. Putnam's Sons, 1982.

Willard, James F. *The Union Colony at Greeley, 1869–1871.* Boulder: University of Colorado Press, 1918.

Willard, James F., and Colin B. Goodykoontz, eds. *Experiments in Colorado Colonization, 1869–1872: Selected Company Records Relating to the German Colonization Company and the Chicago-Colorado, St. Louis-Western and Southwestern Colonies.* Boulder: University of Colorado Press, 1926.

Williams, Michael. *Americans and their Forests: A Historical Geography.* New York: Cambridge University Press, 1990.

Wood, Nancy. *When Buffalo Free the Mountains.* Garden City, N.Y.: Doubleday and Co., 1990.

Worster, Donald. *The Dust Bowl: The Southern Plains in the 1930s.* New York: Oxford University Press, 1979.

———. *Rivers of Empire: Water, Aridity and the Growth of the American West*. New York: Pantheon Books, 1985.

———. *An Unsettled Country: Changing Landscapes of the American West*. Albuquerque: University of New Mexico Press, 1994.

———. *Under Western Skies: Nature and History in the American West*. New York and Oxford: Oxford University Press, 1992.

———. *The Wealth of Nature: Environmental History and the Ecological Imagination*. New York: Oxford University Press, 1993.

Wrobel, David M., and Michael C. Steiner, eds. *Many Wests: Place, Culture and Regional Identity*. Lawrence: University Press of Kansas, 1997.

Wyckoff, William. *Creating Colorado: the Making of a Western Landscape, 1860–1940*. New Haven, Conn.: Yale University Press, 1999.

Wyckoff, William, and Larry M. Dilsaver, eds. *The Mountainous West: Explorations in Historical Geography*. Lincoln and London: University of Nebraska Press, 1995.

Wyman, Mark. *Hard Rock Epic: Western Miners and the Industrial Revolution, 1860–1910*. Berkeley and Los Angeles: University of California Press, 1979.

Young, Otis. *Western Mining*. Norman: University of Oklahoma Press, 1970.

Articles

Abbott, Carl. "Frontiers and Sections: Cities and Regions in American Growth." *American Quarterly* 37 (1985): 395–410.

Bakken, Gordon. "The Influence of the West on the Development of Law." *Journal of the West* 24 (January 1985): 66–72.

Behrens, Jo Lea Wetherilt. "'The Utes Must Go'—with Dignity: Alfred B. Meachams's Role on Colorado's Ute Commission, 1880–1881." *Essays and Monographs in Colorado History* 14 (1994): 37–71.

Boyd, David. "Greeley's Irrigation Methods." *Irrigation Age* (January 1, 1892): 348–59.

Buege, Douglas J. "The Ecologically Noble Savage Revisited." *Environmental Ethics* 18 (spring 1996): 71–88.

Burkey, Elmer R. "The Georgetown-Leadville Stage." *Colorado Magazine* 14 (September 1937): 177–87.

Cronon, William. "The Trouble with Wilderness or, Getting Back to the Wrong Nature." *Environmental History* 1 (January 1996): 7–28.

———. "The Uses of Environmental History." *Environmental History Review* 17 (fall 1993): 1–22.

Denevan, William M. "The Pristine Myth: The Landscape of the Americas in 1492." *Annals of the Association of American Geographers* 82 (1992): 369–85.

Dunaway, Wilma. "The Incorporation of Mountain Ecosystems into the Capitalist World-System." *Review: Fernand Braudel Center* 19 (fall 1996): 355–81.

Dunbar, Robert G. "The Adaptability of Water Law to the Aridity of the West." *Journal of the West* 24 (January 1985): 57–65.

Falck, Depue, E. R. Greenslet, and R. E. Morgan. "Land Classification of the Central Great Plains: Parts 4 and 5, Eastern Colorado." *United States Department of the Interior Geological Survey.* Washington, D.C.: Government Printing Office, 1931.

Flores, Dan L. "Bison Ecology and Bison Diplomacy: The Southern Plains from 1800 to 1850." *Journal of American History* 78 (September 1991): 465–85.

————. "Zion in Eden: Phases of the Environmental History of Utah." *Environmental Review* 7 (1983): 325–44.

Gardiner, Harvey N. "Finding New Mines within Old Mines at Leadville, Colorado." *Journal of the West* 31 (October 1992): 71–79.

Gates, Paul W. "An Overview of American Land Policy." *Agricultural History* 50 (January 1976): 213–29.

Hafen, Thomas K. "City of Saints, City of Sinners: The Development of Salt Lake City as a Tourist Attraction, 1869–1900." *Western Historical Quarterly* 28 (autumn 1997): 345–77.

Hamilton, Richard. "The Hotel Marketing Phenomenon: Souvenirs, Mementos, Advertising, and Promotional Materials." *Historical New Hampshire* 50 (spring/summer 1995): 95–108.

Hart, Richard H. and James A. Hart. "Rangelands of the Great Plains before European Settlement." *Rangelands* 19 (February 1997): 4–11.

Isenberg, Andrew. "The Return of the Bison: Nostalgia, Profit, and Preservation." *Environmental History* 2 (April 1997): 179–96.

————. "Toward a Policy of Destruction: Buffaloes, Law, and the Market, 1803–1883." *Great Plains Quarterly* 12 (fall 1992): 227–41.

Jacoby, Karl. "Class and Environmental History: Lessons from the 'War in the Adirondacks.'" *Environmental History* 2 (July 1997): 324–42.

Kepfield, Sam S. "Great Plains Legal Culture and Irrigation Development: The Minitare (Mutual) Irrigation Company, 1887–1896." *Environmental History Review* 19 (winter 1995): 49–66.

Kirby, Jack Temple. "Rural Culture in the American Middle West: Jefferson to Jane Smiley." *Agricultural History* 70 (fall 1996): 583–89.

Lindauer, Ivo E. "A Comparison of the Plant Communities of the South Platte and Arkansas River Drainages in Eastern Colorado." *Southwestern Naturalist* 28 (August 1983): 249–58.

Littlefield, Douglas R. "Water Rights during the California Gold Rush: Conflicts over Economic Points of View." *Western Historical Quarterly* 14 (October 1983): 415–34.

Londoner, Wolfe. "Western Experiences and Colorado Mining Camps." *Colorado Magazine* 6 (March 1929): 65–72.

Mahoney, Timothy R. "Down in Davenport: A Regional Perspective on Antebellum Town Economic Development." *Annals of Iowa* 50 (summer 1990): 451–73.

———. "Urban History in a Regional Context: River Towns on the Upper Mississippi, 1840–1860." *Journal of American History* 72 (September 1985): 318–39.

McMechan, Edgar C. "The Founding of Cripple Creek." *Colorado Magazine* 12 (January 1935): 13–35.

Mehls, Steven F. "Success on the Mining Frontier: David H. Moffat and Eben Smith—A Case Study." *Essays and Monographs in Colorado History* 1 (1981): 91–105.

Meinig, D. W. "American Wests: Preface to a Geographical Interpretation." *Annals of the Association of American Geographers* 62 (1972): 159–84.

Meyer, David R. "A Dynamic Model of the Interpretation of Frontier Urban Places into the United States System of Cities." *Economic Geography* 56 (September 1980): 120–40.

Moehring, Eugene P. "The Civil War and Town Founding in the Intermountain West." *Western Historical Quarterly* 28 (autumn 1997): 317–42.

———. "The Comstock Urban Network." *Pacific Historical Review* 66 (August 1997): 337–62.

Morrison, A. M. "An Excursion to Alamosa in 1878." *Colorado Magazine* 19 (January 1942): 27–39.

Neel, Susan Rhoades. "Tourism and the American West: New Departures." *Pacific Historical Review* 65 (November 1996): 517–24.

Pisani, Donald J. "Enterprise and Equity: A Critique of Western Water law in the Nineteenth Century." *Western Historical Quarterly* 18 (January 1987): 15–37.

———. "Promotion and Regulation: Constitutionalism and the American Economy." *Journal of American History* 74 (December 1987): 740–68.

Prentice, C. A. "Captain Silas S. Soule, A Pioneer Martyr." *Colorado Magazine* 12 (November 1935): 224–28.

Pritchard, Sandra F. "The Agricultural Landscape of Summit County, Colorado." *Pennsylvania Geographer* 13 (spring/summer 1995): 3–22.

Redford, Kent. "The Ecologically Noble Savage." *Cultural Survival Quarterly* 15 (winter 1991): 46–48.

Robbins, William G. "The 'Plundered Province' Thesis and the Recent Historiography of the American West." *Pacific Historical Review* 55 (November 1986): 577–97.

———. "Western History: A Dialectic on the Modern Conditions." *Western Historical Quarterly* 20 (November 1989): 429–49.

Schweikart, Larry. "Frontier Banking in Colorado: A New Perspective on Public Confidence and Regulation, 1862–1907." *Essays and Monographs in Colorado History* 8 (1988): 15–33.

Shaffer, Marguerite S. "'See America First': Re-Envisioning Nation and Region through Western Tourism." *Pacific Historical Review* 65 (November 1996): 559–81.

Sherow, James E. "Utopia, Reality, and Irrigation: The Plight of the Fort Lyon Canal Company in the Arkansas River Valley." *Western Historical Quarterly* 20 (May 1989): 163–84.

————. "Watering the Plains: An Early History of Denver's High Line Canal." *Colorado Heritage* 4 (1988): 3–13.

Shoemaker, Nancy. "How Indians Got to Be Red." *American Historical Review* 102 (June 1997): 625–44.

Somers, Margaret R. "Rights, Relationality, and Membership: Rethinking the Making and Meaning of Citizenship." *Law and Social Inquiry* 19 (winter 1994): 63–112.

Stelter, Gilbert. "The City and Westward Expansion: A Western Case Study." *Western Historical Quarterly* 4 (April 1973): 187–202.

Taylor, Alan. "Unnatural Inequalities: Social and Environmental Histories." *Environmental History* 1 (October 1996): 6–19.

Turner, Frederick Jackson. "The Significance of the Frontier in American History." *Annual Report of the American Historical Association for the Year 1893* (1894): 199–227.

Westermeier, Clifford. "The Legal Status of the Colorado Cattleman, 1867–1887." *Colorado Magazine* 25 (July 1948): 132–40.

Wyckoff, William. "Incorporation as a Factor in the Formation of an Urban System." *Geographical Review* 77 (1987): 279–92.

————. "Revising the Meyer Model: Denver and the National Urban System, 1859–1879." Urban Geography 9 (1988): 1–18.

Young, Bradley J. "Silver, Discontent, and Conspiracy: The Ideology of the Western Republican Revolt of 1890–1891." *Pacific Historical Review* 64 (May 1995): 243–65.

Zimmerman, Tom. "Paradise Promoted: Boosterism and the Los Angeles Chamber of Commerce." *California History* 64 (winter 1985): 22–31.

Dissertations

Barnett, Paul Sibley. "Colorado Domestic Business Corporations, 1859–1900." Ph.D. diss., University of Illinois, Urbana, 1966.

Edwards, Susan Jane. "Nature as Healer: Denver, Colorado's Social and Built Landscapes of Health, 1880–1930." Ph.D. diss., University of Colorado, 1994.

Stradling, David. "Civilized Air: Coal, Smoke, and Environmentalism in America, 1880–1920." Ph.D. diss., University of Wisconsin, Madison, 1996.

INDEX